# THREE TRU

*a memoir*

# Other books by Graham E. Fuller

*A World Without Islam*
*Little Brown, August 2010*

*The New Turkish Republic: Turkey's Pivotal Role in the Middle East*
*US Institute of Peace, 2008*

*The Future of Political Islam*
*Palgrave, May 2003*

*The Arab Shi'a: The Forgotten Muslims (with Rend Francke)*
*St. Martin's, 1999*

*Turkey's Kurdish Question (with Henri Barkey)*
*Rowman and Littlefield, 1997*

*A Sense of Siege:*
*The Geopolitics of Islam and the West (with Ian Lesser)*
*Westview, 1994*

*The New Foreign Policy of Turkey:*
*From the Balkans to Western China (with Ian Lesser)*
*Westview, 1993*

*The Democracy Trap: Perils of the Post-Cold War World*
*Dutton, 1992*

*The Center of the Universe: The Geopolitics of Iran*
*Westview, 1991*

*How to Learn a Foreign Language*
*Storm King Press, 1987*

# THREE TRUTHS AND A LIE

## *a memoir*

Graham E. Fuller

www.GrahamEFuller.com

ISBN: 1479274313
ISBN-13: 978-1479274314
Library of Congress Control Number: 2012916863

CreateSpace Independent Publishing Platform
North Charleston, South Carolina

Author photograph by Ana Santos
Designed & produced by Margreet Dietz

*This book is dedicated first to my immediate family who experienced this tangled journey with me: my wife Prue, and my daughters Samantha and Melissa.*

*And to my son-in-law Jim—and to our grandchildren who will only know Luke from this account: Mercedes, Reeve and Cian.*

*And to Luke's cousins—Dylan, Elijah, Laura, Grayson, Laurel, and Erin— who shared time with Luke as contemporaries.*

*And to my siblings and their spouses David and Graham, Meredith and Jim, Faith and Marita—all of whom knew Luke and were involved in or touched by these events in one way or another.*

*And to Luke's many friends over the years.*

*Life can only be understood backwards, but it must be lived forwards.*

Søren Kierkegaard

# PROLOGUE

I knew he was dead the moment I laid eyes on him. The glazed eyes, devoid of life, still visible through a narrow aperture. The abnormal, angular position of the body on the mattress. The open mouth not quite in a grimace. The twisted sheets around him.

I instinctively reached out to touch his neck, to search for a feeble pulse of life. In my pounding heart I knew it was to no avail, but still I reached out. The first touch said it all, even before locating the carotid. His skin was cold, long and irrevocably cold, belying the bright sun streaming in through the window on this crisp autumn morning.

My son was dead, OD'ed on crack, age twenty-one.

*      *      *

This is the story of Luke, our adopted son from Korea, who entered our lives at age one and who came to lose his life's way.

This is also my story, his adoptive father. It's about my struggle—wise, misguided, passionate, foolish, dedicated, naive, ultimately unsuccessful—within the family to save him. And having failed to save him, to understand what his life—and death—has meant for my own life.

It is also the story of a search: Who was Luke? What did he represent? He passed like a comet into the atmosphere of our lives and out of it again in a twenty-year erratic trajectory. Here was a generous but frustratingly opaque spirit whose genuine warmth and humor was but one face of a darkening and declining ability to cope. What do I make of his life—and its impact on mine.

# CHAPTER ONE

# CONCEPTION

## 16 February 1975 - JFK Airport, New York

We bundle up against the blustery night wind blowing in off the ocean. It's a maze of parking lots here at JFK, the silver light poles swaying in the wind in counterpoint to the penetrating beacons of moving lights rising and falling with the roar of the aircraft. The sharp smell of jet fuel invades the nostrils. We make our way to the international arrivals terminal—my wife Prue, our young daughters Samantha and Melissa, and myself. We're finally here, the long drive up the turnpike from Washington DC now behind us. I glance at my watch; it's coming up eight pm.

"When will the plane get here?" Samantha asks.

"Soon, let's look and see what the arrivals board says," I reply.

"He better be on the plane," Melissa yawns, "after all this drive."

"I hope so," I say, "they said they were putting him on this flight."

"It better not crash," she sagely adds.

My parents are also with us, and we spot my sister Meredith and her three-year-old adopted Korean daughter already inside the terminal; they've driven down from Cape Cod. It's like a family get-together, congregating at a hospital for a birth. It *is* a birth; we're here to meet a 707 that in a few short hours should yield up our new son, arriving from Seoul, South Korea. They told us he's now one year old. But he is very much in a process of being reborn—out of the tubes of a jetway into an utterly new world about which he knows nothing. Left far behind is his former existence in Korea, about which we know virtually nothing. Two distinct, distant, unbridgeable worlds.

And now the blinking arrivals board promises a touchdown in about an hour. "I can handle one more hour of wait," Prue says, "considering that my pregnancy with Luke has actually lasted eighteen months."

It has been a long haul: from our initial decision eighteen months ago to adopt an orphan from Korea we've had to jump through multiple bureaucratic hoops to make it happen.

Truth be told, I'm still a little surprised myself that here we are, about to receive this adopted being as the third child in our family. How did I get here? It hadn't seemed in the cards. I don't know about other young men, but fatherhood didn't come naturally to me at first. I had always expected to have children, sure, but that was down some theoretical road. I'd had early anxieties about facing the reality of being a father— the likely revolution in my life, the sudden and demanding centrality of a new being in my existence, the emotional demands I wasn't sure I was ready for, the sneaking sense that I wasn't mature enough, the end of independence when Prue and I could just jump into our VW Beetle and take off for the weekend—in selfish freedom. No, Prue had said, you shouldn't be anxious, we'll still be able to do a lot together, you'll see, we just need to manage it right.

Nor had the children come early. We'd spent three of our first four years of married life in Turkey. "How many children do you have?"—the predictable question Turks put to us as we traveled around the countryside. "What, no children? How long have you been married? You're waiting? For what?" Procreation *is* the purpose of marriage in the Turkish countryside. In village eyes it positively smacks of the salacious that marital sexuality should have any other priority. After four years even my mother had begun to pose "tactful" questions about whether we were encountering any potential problems in planning a family.

"The time has come," Prue informed me after we got back to Washington She was right; we'd had four years of carefree adult life running around overseas. Now we were back home in the US for a year. And then she was pregnant with Samantha. Conceived in America, yes, but Samantha was to see the first light of day in Lebanon. After Turkey I had been assigned to language school in Beirut, to study Arabic. I'm a CIA officer. And Melissa was to follow twelve months later, also born in Beirut.

And now here we all are, some seven years later, waiting for our third child, at an airport. Samantha and Melissa are excited to finally meet their new brother, but still touched with worries about what his new presence may portend. "He may cry a lot," Samantha offers, "or he may take our toys." Indeed. They had been too hopped up to sleep in the car on the way up to New York. Now they run around the airport in excitement, each armed with a toy of their own choice to present to Luke on arrival—generic fuzzy creatures.

Northwest Airlines flight 53 flashes up on the board, just in from Seoul. It's after ten pm. Samantha and Melissa jump up and down, eyes peeled for a Korean child to be carried out. Many more minutes and yes! There we spot them; several Korean women emerging from Immigration, approaching a small assembled group of us, each carrying a child wrapped in a colorful Korean blanket with a name tag looking for a family. The new arrivals have all had their diapers recently changed and been put into a clean Korean national

3

outfit to ensure the initial moments of the relationship start off on as unsullied a footing as possible.

"Mr. and Mrs. Fuller?"

We show our papers.

"Here is Pak Byung Bae for you!"

They smilingly hold out a bundle to Prue who gratefully and emotionally receives it. Luke has at last arrived. And what do you see, Luke? A huge building, noise, lights, you're thirteen hours behind your time zone. People who look different, have different eyes, big noses, make incomprehensible sounds you've never heard before. You're being delivered over to the arms of a total stranger and passed around to various admirers, surrounded by a stream of meaningless and unfamiliar sounds.

He is a study in seriousness, neither crying, nor smiling, looking intently around, wary, uncertain. Does he sense he's been down this road before, when suddenly everything in life changes around him?

As Prue takes him into her arms, we all crowd around looking. His appearance is sharply Korean, his lidded Asian eyes very prominent, along with his long nose and long earlobes. I take him out of Prue's arms and into my own. It's not quite like that riveting moment of seeing Samantha for the first time when she was born—that stunning biological awareness of holding one's first born, a piece of myself in a joint creation. Nonetheless, as I hold Luke, I feel like something new and quite different has entered my life, not just a child but a piece of Asia, a place that has always gripped my imagination and soul. And this is a tiny new soul whose destiny has been vouchsafed to us out of Asia. A further enrichment of our family life. I feel a spiritual attachment.

Samantha and Melissa each want to hold him, they call his name, a meaningless sound he doesn't respond to. They hand him their offerings of toys, but there is too much else going on for a stuffed animal to grab his attention. "Never mind," I say to their disappointment, "he'll be more interested later on when things calm down."

On the way home Samantha and Melissa sleep in the back seat, while Luke is in Prue's arms in the front, deadly quiet on his four-hour ride. What might he be contemplating? No tears, no babbling. Just wary watchfulness.

It's after three am, and Pamuk, our white Samoyed, greets us at the door, sniffing the new bundle. Prue takes Luke for his first diaper change and reports back a few minutes later that he is indeed a boy. Still no crying. Prue has put up a crib in the room with the girls because she figures he's used to the shared spaces of the orphanage. But it's Seoul time and Luke is not ready to sleep, and for the next hour or so throws his newly acquired toys out of his bed onto the floor and keeps the girls up, early violation of their space. So Prue brings him out and lies down alongside of him on the floor in the living room for the night, a vital touch of human contact and warmth amidst the sea of change. Asia and the orphanage are far away.

Luke does not cry until morning, and it is not prolonged. We feed him his milk in a bottle, but also the plain rice to which he is accustomed. He eats the rice with his fingers, careful to pick up every single grain on his little chair-table with studied seriousness. Rice is not always forthcoming, better cherish it and eat it while you can. But his concentrated focus upon every last individual grain of rice diminishes within the week; the supply appears reliable in this new place. He's learning to waste some now.

And an emotional breakthrough: after a few days he begins to smile at us. We call him regularly by his name and keep the language very simple. The girls are fascinated by the experience, enjoy holding him and are enshrined in photos with him for posterity. They have also read up on Korea; they have three books about the country including *Tales of a Korean Grandmother*, Korean folk tales. Meanwhile Luke learns not to shrink from Pamuk who licks his face while scavenging for stray grains of rice on Luke's low chair-table. We try not to leave Luke alone much for the first week. There he is, perched on his backpack on Prue's back or mine as we go about daily chores inside and out, helping speed up the bonding process. I'm at work during the day, but one evening we even take him in his backpack to a party with friends, an object of attention, surprise, interest, perhaps not total approbation in every case, but it's mostly to avoid leaving Luke alone—and maybe a little show-off. Within a few weeks Luke is walking, he's thirteen months after all. But how do we gauge his birthday? Like nearly everything else vital to him, his legal birthday, too, was arbitrarily assigned by a doctor at the orphanage as 6 February 1974—like telling age from a horse's teeth. We further confuse the case by deciding that his "real" birthday for family celebration will henceforth be 16 February, the date of his arrival into our family. Close enough. But years onward, Luke is never comfortable with this casual flexibility surrounding his actual date of birth. He's even less comfortable with our arbitrary reassignment of what was already an arbitrary date. "It's my birthday, after all," he will say. I wonder if we should have let him choose it, as his own? Luke will try to cling on to at least the few semi-facts in his bureaucratically reconstructed life.

\*    \*    \*

Over the next weeks and months, Luke seems to adapt to life with us fairly rapidly. In a month or two the English starts to come: a few words about his wants, "ice" for "rice" and "mick" for "milk" and soon picking up on the power-word "no." In his initial long silences, he has surely grasped that Korean words don't work. He is not a crier. He smiles readily. He is stubborn, always wanting to do things on his own, especially feeding himself. He eats a lot, and we've been letting him eat as much as he wants to reassure him that he is in good hands. But now he starts getting plump. His passport photo from that time seems to say it all: the lean Byungbae of the early orphanage photo has now given way to a somewhat overweight Luke in his new passport photo: he looks like a poster child for a baby Chinese Happy Buddha. We cut back to more disciplined-sized food portions and he slims down again, for good. Strangely, it's still a bit hard for us to fully absorb that he's now simply another family member in these first months, just a normal new baby. We experience a slight element of surprise when outsiders refer to him as "your son." Yes, of course he is our son now, come to think of it, no longer our adoption project.

*         *         *

Because it *had* been a long adoption project. Adoption agencies don't make things easy for you. On my sister's recommendation we had gone through Holt, an experienced international adoption agency with expertise in Korea. Holt does not shrink from examining our credentials, lifestyle, and rationale in an early questionnaire. They put it on the line from the get-go: do you really want to do this?

*International adoption is not for every family, just as adoption isn't for everyone. Many adoptive parents are excellent parents to a child of their own race, but are not necessarily cut out to be good parents to a child of another race or background.*

Well, we reply, we do think we know what we're getting into. Prue is English, I'm American, we've already lived in four different countries around the world, we're familiar, comfortable and interested in different cultures and languages. So a Korean child does not pose any particular problem to us. But the questionnaire persists:

*What are your ideas about race? What characteristics do you think Oriental or Korean people have? Do you expect your child to have these characteristics? The children become Americanized; therefore try to visualize that cute little baby growing into a child—a teenager—an adult—a parent. Try to think about grandchildren.*

We don't have any preset ideas or expectations about race, we say. Our adopted child will grow up under the same conditions as our own biological children. We have no problem with being a multiracial family. Grandchildren from an ethnic mixture are fine too; isn't this increasingly a pattern of the American future?

*How do you feel about getting lots of public attention, stares, etc.?*

We're already used to public attention as foreigners with blond-haired kids around the Middle East so we're not worried about public curiosity. Then:

*How do you raise an Oriental child in a white family? Do you raise him to have the same identity as you or your other children? Do you help him develop his own identity as a Korean person? Should he have a Korean name? What relationship will his name have to his sense of "Who am I"? Imagine a child you know and love being sent to China to be adopted. How would you want him raised?*

Well, we explain to Holt, we expect to raise an adopted child as a total family member, an American, with no special consideration within the family. We would preserve part of his Korean name, we say, and we would bring him up with a family appreciation of his Korean culture heritage as well as American.

But these Holt people still push the issue:

*How can you learn to know what it's like being non-white and growing up in a white society? You don't know this from your own experience, so you will have to find out how to teach or educate yourself to become sensitive to your child's world. Discrimination or pressure on Oriental people is more subtle than against black people, therefore less obvious to a white person, and will require more sensitivity to subtleties.*

Yes, we know there may be some subtle forms of discrimination. We will be sensitive to it (but in the event not enough—Luke would open our eyes to these subtler forms of discrimination, even unconscious.) And, we tell Holt, we will be prepared to back our child one hundred percent. Furthermore, we will probably be living in communities in America that are international and ethnically mixed.

*Your family will now be interracial for <u>generations</u>. Adoption of a mixed-race child is not just a question of an appealing little baby. How do you feel about interracial marriage?*

Holt has obviously been there. We feel very comfortable with this, we reply. Yes, we believe a multiracial family structure will enrich our family life and give us all new perspectives. And so we had proceeded with the adoption.

7

\*               \*               \*

Luke's life will soon undergo yet another major change, a new phase. I have just been assigned to the American Embassy in Kabul, Afghanistan, our fifth overseas posting. This is a strange and distant country, but such moves are no longer unusual for us; in fact we actually asked to go (in the happier years before endless war broke out there.) We are comfortable that we can take Afghanistan in stride. I feel very confident. We are scheduled to leave in June, a few months away. We quickly need to get an adoption lawyer to expedite the court process in formalizing the adoption so that we can get Luke American citizenship and a US passport. Our social worker who facilitates the process warns us that the judge has strong religious beliefs and is likely to seriously inquire about our religious views as a vital part of the proper upbringing of a child. We think about what we are going to say. And, indeed, the judge does ask. "Your Honor, we were both raised in religious homes; we are not regular church goers, but we have definite belief in the importance of spiritual values and the need to impart them to our children."

We try to present a picture of a family ideally suited for adopting a child. The girls are briefly coached into suitably adoring sisters—although under questioning Samantha lets the judge know that their brother steals their toys. The judge fortunately does not seem to view this as an insuperable bar to adoption. But Samantha seems to have premonitions.

Ten days later the formal letter arrives!

*Enclosed is the Final Decree granted in your adoption of LUKE BYUNGBAE. On April 25 1975 the incidents of the parent-child relationship were established, including all rights of inheritance and family succession. Very truly yours …*

I'm struck by the terms: *issues of inheritance, family succession?* Right out of a Victorian novel, not what I associate with a newly arrived infant. To top it off, at age one Luke is now swiftly issued his American citizenship, and his own United States of America passport—the black diplomatic version no less. On the inside page the passport officially requests he be granted "full diplomatic immunity" while in Afghanistan. Kind of a get-out-of-jail-free card for a toddler. At the time it was amusing to contemplate. Years later perhaps Luke could very much use just such a card.

\*               \*               \*

Our full family is now legal. We're good to go, and we begin the exciting process of packing up our household once again for a move overseas. Samantha and Melissa select their most beloved possessions for a small trunk to go by quick air freight to Afghanistan; the rest will come more slowly by boat. Luke can only sense that the house is being turned upside down, but with little understanding of what it means for him. Asia awaits our newly-multicultural family.

# CHAPTER TWO

# DISCOVERING LUKE

Asia was Luke's past. But here, five months after his arrival in the US, it's now his future again as well. This isn't exactly the Americanization process the Holt adoption agency had envisaged for him. Still, these are innocent days, full of hope and aspiration. As we take Luke into the bosom of our family all possibilities are open.

We had always felt that growing up overseas could only be an enriching experience. Luke's sisters had already lived in Saudi Arabia and Yemen as small children, with no ill effects, and many positive ones. That experience touched, shaped and challenged all of our identities and outlooks—mine included. But what would it mean for a little kid with no other life experience and with a whole lot more complex set of identity issues. *Who am I? And who are these people I'm with?*

In our Asian sojourn of mutual discovery, what are the signals that offer some clue about who he is? What are the events that help make him what he is? It is only with hindsight that I can identify a few signposts in small revelations, possible markers with deeper significance.

## *July 1975 - Seoul, Korea*

We stop off in Korea on the way to Afghanistan, flying via the Pacific. Of course we'd never have stopped here it if wasn't for Luke. We feel a special interest in seeing the place, to get even a brief feel for his homeland that has entered our lives in a personal way. Our daughters have read stories about Korea, about childhood there and its traditional ways. "Can we see some of the real Korean dresses that are in our Korean book?" Samantha asks. So on the second day, after getting some hot spicy noodles for lunch at a street stall out front, we head into Lotte, a big Korean department store where we look for the section that sells traditional Korean clothing.

The girls run excitedly into the children's section where they are surrounded by child-size mannequins dressed in traditional outfits. The young saleswoman is amused—and pleased—that these Western girls are interested in Korean dresses. She opens boxes and brings out various colorful robes. Samantha's and Melissa's eyes light up as they see the bright colors emerging from the box. "Look at us," they call out, posing in front of the mirror,

10

showing off the ballooning bright red silk skirts with gold bodices and rainbow-colored sleeves; the brilliant colors circle the arm in rings down the sleeve in a riot of shades. "Aren't they great?" Prue says. "You can choose the one you like." She kneels to help them open more boxes. They struggle over the hard choice; their trophies are wrapped up and put into eager hands. These robes become part of their proud collection of outfits from other countries we have lived in.

For Luke, of course, this *is* his heritage; we get him the special traditional Korean outfit for little boys, simpler but with a pale pink silk long-sleeved shirt, and baggy pink pants tied around the waist—OK, pink here is clearly the color for small boys. On top of that is a distinctive full-length boy's long blue vest decorated with gold-imprinted Confucian designs and the same rainbow-colored sleeves. A pair of rubber shoes—like slippers, painted ornate colors with different Korean designs, similar to the ones he wore when he arrived at JFK—round out the outfit. I wonder if he ever would have been put into a traditional formal outfit like this if he had stayed in Korea with the people who abandoned him?

It's hot and muggy in Seoul. We take the bus out of town to a re-creation of a traditional Korean village, complete with daily village life, traditional activities, preparation of foods, re-enactment of a village wedding, music and folk dancing. Samantha and Melissa, from reading the classic *Tales of a Korean Grandmother* know their way around the artifacts—huge kimchee jars and tofu paddles, wooden and swinging rope toys—better than Prue or I do. We feel the heat and humidity of a hot Korean summer afternoon, but soon a huge cloudburst takes place, bringing some relief. As we sit on the veranda of a Korean rural wooden dwelling looking out over the wooded countryside and hills, Luke and Benji—the two-year-old son of friends who are with us—take off their clothes and dance around in the warm rain. I am in East Asia for the first time, I feel it, yield to it, feel a kinship.

But next day I get an early and sobering reminder that I am not of here, and that we are a "cross-cultural family." We visit a Korean nature garden in Seoul. Luke gets tired and starts to resist. He won't walk any more. OK, we'll rest a few minutes. Here, take your bottle of milk. No! The bottle is hurled down into the dirt. OK, I'll carry you on my shoulders. No! Come on Luke, it's only a short way and then we'll be back at the bus stop. No! What do you want then? Silence. Well, if you won't say, then we'll just have to leave you here. He starts to yell, won't be distracted by a candy. I take him by the hand to walk along, he refuses to budge, throws himself down on the ground in a tantrum, kicks violently when picked up, falls back down on the ground screaming. We then pretend to walk on and leave him behind—a tactic I later decide probably isn't very wise with an abandoned kid—all to no effect. Persuasion fails and I lose my patience. I yell at him and swat him on the bottom to get him going. Screams only get louder. Then I look around in dismay: bystanders have stopped in the middle of the park and are intently watching us. What do they perceive? Some Westerner beating up on a Korean kid. Some shake their heads, a few even wag their finger at me in disapprobation. I feel exposed, vulnerable, my cultural moorings have torn loose. I realize I am not one of them; nor do they see Luke as one of us. I am creating a small cross-cultural incident.

I pick up a screaming Luke and we hasten away from the disapproving eyes back to the anonymity of our hotel.

And I wonder: has hearing the sounds of Korean around him again, five months after his arrival in the States, kicked off further rounds of identity confusion in his mind?

### *August 1975 - Kabul, Afghanistan*

We fly high over the snowcapped Hindu Kush that signal our arrival in Afghanistan. Kabul will be our home for the next three years: a brown brick city, cool at an altitude of over five-thousand feet, the smell of kebabs grilling on the street, endless little glasses of strong dark honey-colored tea consumed at every social encounter, donkey carts, turbaned tribal figures along the streets. The start of Afghanistan's descent into hell is still a few years off: the communist military coup, the subsequent Soviet invasion, the anti-Soviet jihad, years of civil war followed by Taliban rule and then Osama Bin Laden all yet to come. Right now life here is relatively calm and beguiling. But I know we've gotten to the other end of the cultural world when Samantha and Melissa find special local Afghan dolls to add to their doll collection. Eat your heart out, Barbie, you've been displaced by an Afghan version complete with black burka over her head and body—outdoor wear, removable so that when she is at home she can wear her traditional Afghan long shirt and baggy pants and take off her veil. And all this is *pre*-Taliban days.

This world is remote from America: no TV, no movies, no malls. The girls have books, friends, hobbies, travel around the Afghan countryside with us for picnics and explorations on weekends. Luke is still too little to be seriously touched by the Afghan environment, at least consciously.

No, we don't do much football or baseball here. Luke and the girls are instead socialized into *buzkashi* as a spectator sport—a wild, violent game, the essence of Central Asian horsemanship where riders grapple and whip each other at full gallop for possession of a calf carcass, earlier beheaded, gutted and filled with sand. Once a rider has snatched up the heavy calf he must race off to a goal post far off avoiding the other riders who try to grab it or whip the rider, sometimes inadvertently plunging into the ranks of the spectators in the heat of strife, spreading pandemonium—the closest we get to taking the kids to a football game back home.

Whatever his age, Luke is still soaking up impressions, images, faces, smells around him, the food, the variety of languages, the look of city streets and people on the sidewalks in Afghanistan. Over the next three years these make up the major, formative impressions of his life. To me it's exotic, but to him it's the *only* world he knows outside the house. I watch him quietly observing his surroundings, watchful, stolid, independent, taking it all in, taking *us* in.

I think back to the Holt Adoption Guidance Pamphlet:

*Pre-school years: The people your adopted child now loves the most will look different from him. It will be natural for him to want to resemble those he loves, or else understand why he is different, and to learn that that difference is not a bad thing.*

And there is Luke, now spending a lot of time looking into the mirror, fascinated with his appearance. One day I walk down a main street in Kabul; he's three now and riding on my shoulders. We pass a camera store. In the shop window is a big poster for Fuji film, featuring the beaming face of a Japanese kid. Out of the blue I ask, "Luke, who is that kid?" "That's me," he replies.

The amount of time adolescents spend in front of the mirror is legendary; it's a time of measuring your own looks against the expectations of yourself and others. But in Luke's case he's clearly exploring facial differences between himself and *everybody* else around him. *Why do I look so different?* He doesn't even need mirrors for introspection, the outside world serves as one. Random people on the street, unrestrained by political correctness, query us right in front of him. "How come that boy looks different than you?" "Where is he from, he doesn't look like you."

One time we all go on a vacation trip to nearby India. In one of those typical three am arrivals at Delhi airport we go up bleary-eyed to a money changer to buy rupees. He looks at me and the rest of us, scrutinizes Luke, then back at me. Head wagging, he addresses me in sing-song intonation, "And will you permit me to enquire sir, as to the exact nature of the relationship between yourself and that child?"

"Yes, he's my son," I say.

"Oh … Adopted I presume?"

"Yes."

"Oh … How sweet."

It starts to sound familiar.

"Luke, you're adopted." He hears it all the time from us, before he even fully understands what it means. So far it may not mean much more than "I have come to live with a different family." But the deeper meaning of adoption and its implications for him come later—the social, biological, genetic, emotional, sexual, psychological. They will emerge, deepen and take on shifting character in his psyche over the years. *Who am I? Who will I be? What made me what I am?*

We wouldn't have wanted to conceal anything from Luke anyway. We'd read about American white children being adopted into other white families in earlier generations where the adoption was to be kept a total family secret forever, only to be blurted out years later by some unsuspecting or insensitive distant cousin—with devastating psychological consequences upon the adoptee, even as adults. That kind of revelation is instantly shattering—nothing in you has really changed, of course, but suddenly everything has changed.

I know from experience. There was a moment in my own life when I was around twenty-four, visiting a busybody distant great aunt in southern Virginia to introduce Prue to her. Over dinner she casually referred at one point to "your mother's first marriage."

"What," I cried, "What 'first marriage?'"

"Oh dear, you didn't know? Your mother had an unfortunate brief first marriage—for about eight months. It was only later on that she married your father."

At that moment I felt a bolt of electricity course through my body—not that a divorce was so terrible—but *maybe my father isn't my real father.* My world shattered in a second; could I be facing a new reality about my origins? But the thought vanished just as quickly: no, I thought, no, that can't be true, I know I look exactly like him, he is my real father. The emotional tsunami receded and I recovered my equilibrium. Of course it was foolish that our parents had never told us of this—it should have been no big deal—but my father's ego apparently had led him to "protect" us from it. My mother's first brief marriage had had no offspring. But for me it had been a firsthand small taste of how questions of paternity can matter viscerally—maybe more so at twenty-four than four, but the biology still gets to you eventually.

I detect in Luke small signs of secretiveness; he's thinking about things but he doesn't want to talk about it. We encourage him all the time to ask questions on the whole adoption thing but he almost never broaches it. *No questions. That's OK, it's cool.* I sense he does not like to share intimate concerns.

Years later we run across a book called *On Being Adopted.* We learn that while some adoptees don't spend much time thinking about it, many other adoptees *never stop* thinking about the fact they're adopted—it becomes a central fact of their existence. Periodic visits with his adopted Korean cousin Laura may help reinforce and normalize the concept of adoption for Luke. In later years we'll sometimes spot a family somewhere with a clearly adopted kid of a different race in tow and I will point it out to Luke, hoping to reassure him of its fairly commonplace character. But he seems annoyed; *why are you pointing these differences out to me? So what?*

With time, though, Luke eventually does bring up a few of the predictable questions that the Holt Adoption Agency had alerted us to early on. "Who is my real mother, and where is she? Why did she give me away?"

We go into the song and dance.

"Well, we don't know what happened to your mother, but she probably wasn't able to take care of you, maybe she got sick and died. But she loved you and you were left in a police box so as to be safe and found and sent to an orphanage."

"OK, but why did *you* adopt me?"

"Well, there were lots of reasons, Luke. We adopted you because we wanted to have a third child, we had a special interest in Asia, and we knew about your cousin Laura from Korea, we wanted to have a boy in the family, you were an orphan and we believe that all children should be able to grow up with parents. We wanted you, you're part of the family, and we love you just as much as Samantha and Melissa."

Too many messages to absorb here all at once? I wonder just how much he wants to know.

That's about his mother. But strangely, Luke never inquires about his father, until once, many years later as a teenager. And of course there is absolutely zilch to tell him. He knows fathers exist of course—there's me, and all his friends have fathers, they're all around. But that he has a direct *biological and genetic* relationship with a Korean male somewhere—that won't really register with him yet. It's only with sexual awareness that its full significance will dawn on him.

It's not only that he doesn't look like us. He looks more like many Afghans than we do. One time we're off on a camping trip to Bamyan in Central Afghanistan. Our photo shows Luke sitting on his potty in the morning outside a yurt we're staying in; the sun strikes the massive Buddha figures carved into the cliff face across the valley, images the Taliban some twenty-five years later would unforgivably destroy. I think of Buddhist culture reaching out to touch me, one of the emotional links I feel to Asia; here in Central Asia Buddhas now stare out across the valley at Luke, like Buddhas back in Korea. And then family photos of us on picnics by streams in these beautiful barren mountains, when curious Afghans often wander over to talk with us. Luke is always a special hit with Afghans. He looks more like *them*.

A few years later in Hong Kong, shortly after we arrive there, we needlessly crowd his identity again when it comes to nursery school. Now he's four, still too young to go to the American school with his sisters. Prue and I—naively, romantically cross-cultural when Luke needs stolidity—think it might be good if Luke could go to a local Chinese play school and learn some Chinese. So Prue starts to take him down the hill every morning to a local Anglo-Chinese nursery school. It's evident pretty soon that Luke hates the place. The "Anglo" part of the school ends up being mainly Luke, everyone else is local Chinese and nearly everything is conducted in Cantonese. Luke, of course, doesn't understand a word, but to the teachers who don't know him he looks like he should belong there. Every morning now before Prue takes him there's a scene, tears; it's clear this was a really dumb idea. We decide to jettison this overloaded identity basket. What are *we* doing, playing cultural dollies with him?

Luke's identity instead needs grounding—but then, grounding in what, except the family? Everything else out there is shifting. For that matter, am I grounded in all these swirling foreign cultures that I seem to thrive in, for whatever reason? That's why I'm good at my job I guess, an ability to relate to all these foreign cultures and languages and peoples and operate among them—even though I grew up entirely in the US myself, including life on a Vermont farm over my formative years. As my cultural empathy to diverse foreign cultures and languages pile up in my head over the years, where do I belong? And of course Luke gets taken for Chinese around the city and in school, on more occasions than we always hear about. When he's eight, near the end of our stay in Hong Kong we go to a big movie theater in Central to see *Star Wars*. The theater is crowded. A Chinese couple comes in and sits down next to Luke. Entirely unsolicited, Luke turns to the man and says, "Don't try to talk Chinese to me because I'm not Chinese and I don't understand it."

*Don't judge me by my face, I'm not who any of you think I am.*

16

\*　　　　　　　\*　　　　　　　\*

I'm trying to read Luke's signals. One thing we note early on is a fierce sense of self-reliance. From age two he regularly demands, whenever we try to help him with anything, to do it "by self." On a trip to a mountain village we take a local bus up to the top; the bus driver obligingly lifts Luke down the stairs to the ground just as he was seeking to negotiate them for himself. Luke flies into a fit of fury, screams in rage—"No, by self!"—a tantrum on the ground for ten long minutes. Anger isn't usually his thing, it's more silent or passive resistance. But as "do it by self" becomes the rule of the day for him, I wonder, is this survival of the fittest among the orphan pack? An acquired fear of any unnecessary dependence upon potentially unreliable people? This message comes over me hard: I'm determined now never to let him feel I'm not reliable—even though this will lead into uncharted waters for me later on.

On various trips he's always running off from us, even at age three and four, and disappearing in temple compounds or hotel corridors, seemingly unconcerned about getting lost. "Yes," my sister Faith, a psychologist, tells me years later when I recount this propensity in Luke, "sounds like what they sometimes call 'attachment disorder,' when an adopted child may lack the full range of appropriate emotional bonds to his family and is inclined to run off from his parents without a lot of anxiety."

Well, maybe … Or is he just a slightly reckless boy? I observe he's often accident-prone. While physically capable and bold, he's the one that falls off the top of the jungle gym and breaks his wrist, falls off a big rock into a stream, falls from a wall and breaks an arm, dislocates an arm when I swing him around one time.

He's outgoing but also seems to keep his own counsel most of the time. He doesn't volunteer much. "How did you like the raft ride, Luke?" "It was OK." "Were you afraid you might fall off into the water?" "No." "What did you like the best?" "It was all OK." Hard to get a lot of reaction out of him sometimes, and that can bug me. I like to hear reactions, get feedback, but he deprives me, makes me work harder at it—maybe makes me even a bigger pain in the ass to him. He can seem content with the way things are, but I'm the one who feels deprived that I'm not getting through.

\*　　　　　　　\*　　　　　　　\*

And then, near the end of our three-year stay in Afghanistan, a violent civics lesson: a pro-communist military coup takes place in Kabul in 1978, heralded by pitched tank battles in the streets, bombing and strafing runs just outside our house. As the CIA Station Chief I remain in the embassy all day and all night, along with a few colleagues, to keep up real-time reporting to Washington and maintaining contact with our sources. But in any case I'm trapped in the embassy for two days, the streets are closed down, and tanks are firing right outside the building, jet fighters screaming overhead on strafing missions against the Afghan Presidential Palace a few blocks away. Armed troops impose a tight curfew, I can't get out, phones are down; I'm worried sick about Prue and the kids who are so close to the military action. Prue puts up blankets over some of the windows at home against flying glass and they all huddle beneath tables or the stairs as the aerial and street battles and strafing of the presidential palace progress nearby; a shell falls through the roof of our neighbor's house—mercifully empty at the time.

Some windows in our house are shattered. It's terrifying with huge ground-shaking explosions, the metallic pop of tank fire in the street outside our wall. Living overseas in the these parts you quickly lose your innocence about big bangs: we no longer think it's truck backfire. We think gunshot, bomb. Late the next afternoon in Kabul the shooting and air strikes have died away; I can get home at last, and along with Afghans we circumspectly ease our way out into the street to view the ruins of the presidential palace a few blocks off and all the other battle damage. The president of the country was captured along with his family and summarily shot. "But why did they have to kill the president's family?" Samantha asks. Welcome to Third World politics. Melissa will go on eventually to write her PhD dissertation on political violence in Indian and Mexican politics.

Luke is too small to remember much of this except the shattering bangs and explosions, but he hears about it forever after as part of family lore. Who knows, maybe the violence in Kabul floats to the surface of consciousness when he plays Nintendo games at an older age, making the game just a little more real. Or life just a little less certain and secure. Our family inevitably bonds under these hardships … crises that thankfully spared us any real harm. And Luke will have one more tale to spin of his past life.

Still, I wonder sometimes what trade-offs take place in our children's development. They are unquestionably developing a sense of the harsher circumstances of life latent in developing countries, a greater awareness that politics can have real consequences: life is insecure, people get killed. This experience maybe wasn't what Holt bargained for either in sending Luke off to America, ostensibly to live in security. I debate in my mind how much exposure to reality is good, and where the limits might be. Most of the rest of the world lives in these harsher environments, after all. I still think I favor the exposure to reality, at least so far. And Luke's future personal "reality" will become more corrosive than simply witnessing a live coup d'état. There seems to be something in him that finds danger exciting, a daredevil, impulsive characteristic that maybe passes for fun, excitement. He seems to need it.

### September 1978 - Tehran

On our way back home to Washington from Kabul for a brief consultation I am asked to stop off in Tehran to brief the ambassador and the CIA station chief there about the recent communist coup in Afghanistan and its implications. This was less than a year before the Shah himself was overthrown by the ayatollahs in the Iranian Revolution.

At some point the whole family gets into the car of the station chief to go to his house where we are staying. These are revolutionary times in Tehran, terrorist attacks have occurred against Americans who are the Shah's chief supporters. The car is bulletproof and there is a security alarm and siren that can be activated by either the driver or the passenger in the back. The chief notes to the kids to be careful about the button on the floor in the back. Some half an hour later in the middle of bumper to bumper traffic Luke can no longer resist, pushes the alarm; sirens and whoopings burst out all around, and the embassy is electronically alerted. Marine guards from the embassy are forced to make their way somehow through the traffic to find the car and make sure there has been no security breach.

We see it again here—a kind of compulsion in Luke to test the boundaries without fear of consequences—a readiness to "push buttons." A desire for excitement. In Hong Kong when Luke is five Prue goes off with him on a yacht trip around Hong Kong harbor with his kindergarten class. Luke disappears, Prue is deeply concerned; he finds his way up to the control room and starts pushing buttons on the console. The captain runs in to intervene just in time. Fortunately the yacht does not have a self-destruct-in-thirty-seconds button.

He goes to the American School in Hong Kong with his sisters. He's often a nuisance on the school bus. Prue serves as bus monitor once a week, and finds Luke squirming, unable to sit still, jumping all over the place—even compared to other boys. Chinese mothers bring candy on board when they are monitors to bribe kids into good behavior, but it doesn't keep Luke still. One time he gets kicked off the school bus for a week for not staying in his seat in the moving vehicle. We take him to the school psychologist to check out what seems to us classic hyperactivity, yet he says he finds only "partial signs" of hyperactivity. At the same time Luke has a sunny disposition, a good sense of humor and adds spice to our lives.

19

At school Luke has a poor attention span, gets into mischief. He tends to resist authority—not confrontationally, but by simply opting out, doing his own thing, sneakily disobeying the rules. I've never been a great one for bowing to authority, so I don't worry too much right now about this. But at least I work within the confines of a disciplined profession; for Luke this may be the beginning of a different pattern. Prue tells me I should watch Luke more closely; she often spots these things faster than I do. For me he's mostly being a boy. But I had always been more conscientious as a kid, the oldest of four. Maybe I vicariously relate to the rebelliousness in Luke's behavior and cut him too much slack.

Luke is always game, possesses skills, but he seems to have little follow through. Towards the end of our stay in Hong Kong Prue and I encourage Luke to go jogging with us for a few miles as we often do. One time I talk him into to signing up for a three-kilometer kids' run around Peak Road, overlooking Hong Kong harbor. He's got a runner's build, lanky, wiry. I cajole him around the course a few times on practice runs. When race day comes he does well; he even gets a medal for finishing among the top ten. Luke clearly has running skills. "Luke, that's great, next time I'm sure you can do even better. Let's try in the fall." "Nah, thanks Ba, I don't think so." He has little ambition to use his talents; he soon refuses outright to run with us anymore. I remain on the prowl for other suitable outlets for his talents, to create new interests in him.

### December 1980 - Thailand

We all take a vacation trip to Thailand and travel around the up-country. In a forest we visit some ruins with a lot of monkeys around. Luke leers at a monkey nearby and then starts jumping up and down in front of it, scratching his sides chimpanzee-like, mocking the creature and making monkey noises. Monkey is offended and jumps down onto him, sinks its teeth into his neck by the shoulder. Luke has to be taken to a Thai hospital for stitches, rabies vaccinations. This is not his first run-in with animals—never cruelty, just incitation. We also visit a temple which houses a "holy elephant." Fortunately this time Luke doesn't incite it, nor does the elephant gore him. Instead, for a few bills placed in his trunk, the elephant will gently place his trunk atop his head in a beneficent blessing. We have a photo of the kids getting blessed by the elephant. In later years Luke will use this event as one of many truths in a Three Truths and a Lie game. He's accumulating experiences.

But who is Luke in the eyes of others? We're sometime surprised. Towards the end of the Thai trip we go to a resort on the beach in Pattaya. Luke,

Samantha and Melissa are all playing on the beach, building sandcastles. A beefy Aussie kid comes up and talks to them, then kicks over Luke's sandcastle. "What are you doing playing with this Chink?" he leers. Samantha and Melissa are outraged and rise up to him. "He's our brother, get lost, dork." They are loyal to Luke, always stick up for him despite his periodic aggravations, as any little brother can be with older sisters. But he's definitely *their* brother. They watch out for him. We take his family identity for granted, but obviously many others do not.

Still, the question of dealing with Luke each day begins to draw more of Prue's time and attention within the family; he's a higher maintenance kid than the girls are. And inevitably he is always in a special category because of his adoptive status as well. Hadn't Holt actually forewarned us about this in their adoption guidance booklet? When an adopted kid is taken into a family alongside of biological kids, Holt says:

*1. The adopted child can get too much attention in the family;*

*2. The other children in the family tend to get left out of this attention.*

Prue and I had intellectually grasped this at the outset, but it's another thing to successfully avoid it. Samantha and Melissa sense the added time devoted to managing Luke. They accept some of its logic but complain on occasion and it becomes the basis of greater tensions between them and Luke over time. "Why do we have to do things Luke wants to do on the weekend? We want more time for our own activities." And we do make greater efforts to ensure the time is more balanced between them. But I can see it in myself already: *I am erring on the side of making sure Luke feels he is fully and unconditionally accepted in the family.*

*          *          *

Like all of our kids by now, he knows his way around Chinese restaurant offerings, including Ants Climbing a Tree, Potstickers, Killer Chicken, and Fish-Fragrant Eggplant. From his Chinese friends at the American school he develops a taste for some of the more exotic Chinese street food that turns off the rest of us, such as the gross red squid snack in a cellophane bag, or the rubbery fish balls. He seems to gravitate to Asian food by choice. He's also quietly developing an interest in Asian cooking. I wonder whether fondness for soy sauce becomes genetic over time in Asia. Do I already spot a talent for food developing here?

*          *          *

Luke has always hit it off with adults when there's no authoritarian role involved. One of Luke's favorites is Steve Ching, and his wife Kathy. They're colleagues of mine in the American Consulate and we become fast friends. Steve is ethnic Chinese, intensely Asian-looking, but California-born with a strong sense of irony about his Chinese background and a witty, slightly self-mocking tendency to over-dramatize that Asian background—including extravagant claims on occasion to be descended from Genghis Khan. He's a gourmet as well as gourmand, a Commander in the US Naval Reserve with huge love for navy tradition, yet by nature irreverent, irrepressible, unconventional and loyal.

Steve and Kathy often invite us out on the weekend on their small leased Chinese junk, engine-powered, complete with wizened Muslim Sino-Indonesian captain. Steve is fantastic with Samantha and Melissa to whom he relates tales of Chinese and Asian lore with great gusto. We often anchor off small islands that dot Hong Kong waters and wade ashore with the kids in tow with small buckets and screwdrivers to pry shellfish off the rocks for Steve's sundry seafood dishes for later occasions. Whenever Prue or I might warn Luke not to do something on board the junk, Steve would nudge him saying, "We Asians have to stick together." That line echoed over the years whenever Steve saw Luke, who was much in awe of "Uncle Steve." He will see Steve again towards the end of his life.

One time near the end of our stay in Hong Kong—Luke's about seven—we are returning to port in the setting sun on the Chings' junk in the golden waters of the South China Sea. I go up top to sit high up on the roof of the captain's cabin where I hold Luke on my lap as we watch the marine action around us. Suddenly we hit a big wave, the wake from a huge passing container ship, and the junk pitches unexpectedly sharply to the left. I lose my perch entirely; I have no choice but to hold on to Luke and give a special leap out and into the sea—to avoid falling down on top of the railing down below us. But we've been pitched right into the shipping lane. Luke and I are separated with the plunge. He has his life jacket on of course, but he's terrified; it's scary to be in the water, big boats all around. I grab Luke and he clings onto my neck for dear life in the turgid waters of the China Sea. Steve responds immediately and throws us a life preserver attached to a rope and we're hauled back up quickly into the junk. I had been irresponsible in sitting up so high with Luke in my lap, without rails. And I feel something else too, some sense of strange gratitude—even pride—in his clinging on to me for dear life in the water—physical evidence that he can perceive me as a source of safety to him.

\*　　　　　\*　　　　　\*

We've spent four years in Hong Kong. It's time to leave. Our departure is a milestone: we will never live all together overseas as a family again. Luke at age eight is going "home"—to a country he's never lived in, for his first hands-on genuine Americanization.

But what kind?

## CHAPTER THREE

# THE FIRE WALL OF THE PAST

*1973 – Maryland*

Luke's origins are murky; we are on a journey of discovery from the first day we hear about him, seeking to ascertain the basic facts of his identity and existence. The quest starts one day when Prue goes out to the mailbox and there, among bills and flyers, is a brown envelope with foreign stamps. It's from Holt in Korea! We are about to learn who our adoptive child will be. We have jumped through all the hoops: filled out laborious adoption forms, undergone close scrutiny by Holt regarding our suitability as an adoptive family, and waited many more months for final approval—and then, there it is: the first details of Luke's existence! More information will be rationed out to us in various communications from Holt over the coming months; but it will be thin.

Prue waits till I get home before we open the first letter. With Samantha and Melissa crowding around at the dining room table we slit open the envelope: the first official information about *our* child—his name is Pak Byung Bae. He is eight months old. And there, stapled to the top of a page written in Korean and English, is the first small photo, the face of a child who seems a bit confused, grimacing. "He looks like he's crying," Samantha says. "Yeah," I say, "he does. Maybe he's just nervous about being in a new place." "He has a funny nose," Melissa comments. And indeed, he does, it is longish, slightly flattened, typical of many northern Asians. His eyes in the photo are black, set behind an upper eyelid that comes straight down giving him a strong "oriental" look. It isn't an especially flattering photo, more like a snapshot for an ID, but it's the first real, palpable evidence that our child exists. Holt promises another photo and more information soon.

"But how did the orphanage know what his name was when they found him?" Samantha asks. "I don't think they did know," Prue says, "that's probably just a name they gave him at the orphanage." "But do we have to call him that? I thought we were going to call him Luke." "Yes, we will," I say. And then, the following week, another envelope, this time thicker. We all gather around again together to go through the information.

We decide we will keep part of his Korean name for his middle name: we will call him Luke Byungbae Fuller. And then, for our eager eyes, we get the first, and virtually only, information we will ever get about who this person is. Pak Byung Bae, we read, had been found early one morning in a police traffic box in the southern Korean coastal city of Daegu and had been immediately brought to the White Lily Orphanage. "Why was he left in a police box?" Melissa asks. "Well, I guess the people who left him wanted him to be found by responsible people and taken care of," I speculate. "It looks like the police brought him straight to the orphanage." "Wow, that's lucky the police found him. If he had been left somewhere else they might never have found him and he might have died," says Samantha. She has zeroed in on the heart of the matter.

This piece of information is a kind of comfort—that Luke had been abandoned, yes, but "responsibly." It might also be comforting for Luke to know that in the future. At least, when he begins to inquire about his own origins, the report seems to say "your mother cared enough to make sure you would be properly taken care of." But for us this whole concept is still like something out of a Victorian novel, we've been thrown back in a time warp to a Dickensian world—Luke starting life as a "foundling." Prue notes that the report tersely describes his condition upon being delivered to the White Lily Orphanage as "fair." "I wonder what 'fair' means?" she asks. Is this a translation from a Korean phrase meaning "OK"? Or only *fair* as opposed to *good*, that is, possible signs of mistreatment, starvation, filthy conditions, neglect? Sphinx-like, the White Lily Orphanage does not commit itself.

In later years we were to discover that many of these orphanages routinely offer a "comforting" version of the adoption story suitable to all adoptive parents. No plunging into the dark heart of social reality; no out-of-wedlock story of illegitimacy that might be religiously or socially upsetting to potential adoptive parents; no one forced to grow up as a "bastard," no account of mistreatment, drugs, or longer-term neglect that could represent traumatic information to the adopted child down the road. Apparently the orphanage believes this kind of benign air-brushed account to be a harmless mistruth—indeed an act of kindness, providing a basis for psychological health for the adopted child and the family. And maybe there is a certain wisdom to this, even in our era of insistence on full disclosure. It's like the Big Bang—there is no way you can ever know what happened before the child arrived at the orphanage. And so Holt firmly shuts the information door on any further traumatic speculation on our part. You were simply found and brought to responsible people. That's it. Nobody can ever know anything else.

Come to think of it, what does one want to hear, or believe, about one's origins? Samantha is eight, Melissa seven; they are old enough to grasp a lot about the adoption process. "Why," Samantha asks, "did Luke's mother abandon him?" "I guess we can't ever know," I reply. And we talk about what might have happened.

This is powerful stuff; we are in the realm of myth here. We've all read the childhood fairy tales: the mistreated daughter of a poor woodcutter's family is later revealed to have been a princess at birth, and all is well. Or Moses, the son of a king, is left a foundling in a little boat of reeds on the Nile to be adopted by poor but honest people and to become a prophet to his people. Or a prince is stolen at birth, only to be rediscovered as a young man by the ring he is wearing. Dickens often writes of foundlings. Yes, there is mystery in this term: a stranger suddenly appears in society, the secret of his background unknown, maybe never to be revealed. And suddenly these stories now have relevancy to our own family life, far from the woodcutter in the forest. How could we not speculate about such a huge turning point in Luke's early life? White Lily's simple "origin-story" offered only the bare bones, it cried out for the spinning of various fully-wrought fantasy scenarios about Pak Byung Bae. In fact, as we sit around the dinner table we do construct our own modern-day true-to-life stories—imagined alternative tales—dissecting Luke's potential fairy-tale pasts before he ever gets to hear of it.

Our family favorite: Pak Byung Bae was born into a poor but loving family. "Maybe he was the third child," Melissa speculates, conscious of the impact of pecking orders. "No, maybe the sixth or seventh," Samantha counters. "Yeah, and they would have been really poor and couldn't pay for food." "Maybe they decided they couldn't afford another child in the family," and our speculation escalates. "And so they put him in a police box at night when no one was there watching." "Yeah, and I bet his mother was crying when she left him there," they reflect soberly. "That way they knew the police would quickly take him to an orphanage and go to America." Samantha offers a variation: "Maybe his mother got some terrible disease and died." "Yeah," says Melissa, "or maybe his parents were killed in a car accident and his grandmother couldn't take care of him."

And these stories are all just about tough luck; they are all reassuring of the appropriate moral order—nice people just falling on hard times.

Not quite for discussion with Samantha and Melissa at that age are darker adult versions that Prue and I speculate about:

• Pak Byung Bae was the illegitimate offspring of a young Korean girl of good family and some punk; her family insisted the child of this liaison be given up for adoption to save the family's name and reputation.

• Pak Byung Bae was born out of wedlock to a druggy mother who was barely capable of looking after him; his father a transient wastrel who walked out on them. Social workers found the child left alone for long periods, sick and malnourished, and he was taken away to an orphanage.

• Pak Byung Bae was unwanted, born of a prostitute, left still bloody in a dumpster wrapped up in a newspaper to die, and only the alertness of passerby heard the child's cries and rescued him from near death.

OK, sheer speculation on our part, for sure. But aren't we presaging Luke's own future puzzlements on the matter? Won't he spend vastly more time lying in bed at night contemplating his origins than even we do now, as we take in the scant facts of his less-than-one-year-old life? And, most haunting, is there some story, some detail, some event, even some unknown or unrevealed genetic cast of the dice—one we could never know about—that could fatefully affect Luke's own future?

"I wonder if his mother is even still alive. Do you think she thinks about him now, does she miss him?" Melissa asks. "Maybe she cries about him," Samantha offers. "She may feel bad about what she did." We wonder, did she indeed regret what she did? Would she ever try to cross the ocean in search of her lost son? Or did she feel she did the best thing for him? These were big growing-up questions for our daughters to ponder, they introduced a hint of the real world, lurking instability, elements of fate and uncertainty into their own somewhat protected lives. This is far from their own experience in life, but it has already been the experience of their brother-to-be.

Above all, what will these questions mean for Luke himself? So many unknowable things. How will he choose to explain it to others down the road?

Most of all, what story will he believe in his own heart?

\*         \*         \*

Then, a month or two later, we receive a Child's Progress Report from the orphanage, this time with a nicer photograph of Luke. It is the face of someone we have now begun, awkwardly, to think of as "our son."

A photo, a one-by-three inch black and white snapshot of Pak Byung Bae. He is in a baby seat that is perched upon a straight-backed chair in the middle of a room with cribs visible in the background. He is dressed in a bright white singlet, a "onesy" complete with booties; his slightly dark complexion is highlighted against the white of his outfit; his black hair is short, little tufts of black hair creeping down a broad forehead. His eyes stare intently ahead at the camera, uncertain, a mixture of curiosity and slight apprehension. We note his earlobes are slightly elongated, what my Chinese language teacher will tell me a few years later are "spiritual ears," a sign of spiritual potential in Buddhist tradition. He looks thin. "I don't think they're feeding him enough," Samantha says. One hand clutches the edge of the baby seat for physical reassurance.

On the right side of his lap sits a placard. At first I think it looks like something in Korean letters, but closer examination of the small photo reveals a number, K-5858—his first ID! It strikes me that this number is probably a more important designator in his life right then than Pak Byung Bae—a name quite routinely and arbitrarily assigned to him by orphanage administrators. But how socially empty this orphanage name is! Names matter, they have power, they indicate. In our own society our birth names right from the beginning carry messages about our ethnic origins, family affiliations, and maybe even our initial place in society; but this name signifies nothing of Luke's past, and even less of his future. His number is almost surely more meaningful to the administrators.

Indeed, what's in a name? Or what's in a number? This is luck of the draw I realize—a processing sequence of induction into the orphanage. So there he is, K-5858. Not a bad number, a certain pleasing repetition. But who is K-5857? And K-5859? What are their stories, and where did they go, what became of them, where are they now? K-5858's biological parents produced this child, with a whole set of given genetic characteristics. They supplied the "nature" part. But some good clerk at White Lily had at least as important a shot at playing God as Pak Byung Bae's progenitors did, for that clerk, in probably quite stunningly casual fashion, got to determine the "nurture" part of Luke's future; it was that clerk who rolled Pak Byung Bae's environmental dice in a disturbingly *routine* daily procedure of matching numbers against prospective adoption applicants. Our number came up—it's that simple, Mr. Social Engineer.

And what might have been the casual circumstances under which this massively fateful decision was made, both for Pak Byung Bae and for us? Who knows whether a momentary distraction over a cup of tea, a phone call, "Mr. Song, will you come in here a minute," a dropping of a sheaf of papers on the floor then reshuffled, an arbitrary refiling sequence in the in-box—anything may have cataclysmically, irrevocably and totally changed Pak Byung Bae's future life. Instead, K-5857 or K-5859 might have come to us. Indeed, Prue and I had only two stipulations as applicants: we asked for a boy, and we said we would frankly have trouble coping with mental retardation; physical problems were acceptable.

So, with far less passion than the erotic grapplings that led to the fusion of sperm and egg creating him, a bureaucrat in the White Lily Orphanage routinely assigned Pak Byung Bae to us for life—for his life. The die is cast: his fate is relinquished to a specific set of total strangers half way around the globe.

I ask you, isn't this the stuff of fables? In other cultures they might call it fate, karma, kismet. Indeed, why and how things happen are mysteries. And no, we will not be able to say to Luke much later on in good conscience that we had "chosen you especially." This, my son, was a pure stroke of fate.

But whoever we are, however we will try to bring you up, we have already done one quite significant thing for you. No, it's not that we brought you to a land of plenty. That's cornball, there's something else. Think how circumscribed your options in Korea were the moment you were abandoned and became a foundling. In Korea, as in so many parts of the world, family *is* who you are; it is your identity, your status, your everything. Adoption in Asia is an uncommon thing; people adopt only orphaned relatives, rarely a child of utterly unknown origins. So, with no family ties, backing or status, if you had stayed in Korea you would surely have carried the burden of "no family," the whiff of illegitimacy that condemns you to the lower rungs of the social ladder—a major challenge to overcome in creating a successful life. That may be the single most important thing we helped you escape.

*       *       *

Another Child's Progress Report—this time it includes a comment from his White Lily caretaker: "He responds to his name by turning his head."

To what name, to "Pak Byung Bae?" Come to think of it, this is already your *second* name, for administrative use at White Lily. But what did they call you back in the alley/street/shack/slum/apartment/mansion/penthouse in which you were born—"the kid?" Don't let this early association of sound and self become too ingrained, for this name too will be stripped from you again in another four months in favor of yet a new name, after you arrive in America. Three names, three identities, three futures, all shifting in the first year of life.

From the White Lily report: *Relationship with adults: Deeply attached to his bomo (foster mother), and cries when she leaves but is happy again when she returns. Somewhat shy with strangers.*

This is the second time in eight months that some kind of budding maternal relationships are beginning to take form, this time between you and your *bomo*. But that budding relationship of love and trust will also be uprooted again soon. The *bomo* of the orphanage was not even your first encounter with people. Who had been the one who took care of you when you were born, who nursed you, looked after you, fed you, comforted you? Or neglected you, hit you, starved you, abandoned you? What is the impact of a rapidly shifting series of "mothers" in which Prue will shortly be mother #3? Yes, mother #3 for K-5858.

Little more information is vouchsafed to us; the firewall to the past is impenetrable.

# CHAPTER FOUR

# THE GREAT AMERICAN WEST

## July 1982 - Portland, Oregon

We're disembarking at the international airport in Portland, Oregon after the long flight across the Pacific from Hong Kong. "Long haul, but we're back home, kids!"

"For you this may be home, Baba, but for us it isn't," Samantha reminds me. "Don't forget, I've only lived here once for two years and that was when I was five. So to me this doesn't feel like home." She'll be starting sophomore year in high school where she will rapidly find out how "non-American" she is; she's basically unfamiliar with American suburban teenage interests, TV programs, values, lingo and lifestyle. Her clothes are different until she refashions her wardrobe, and in fact, her classmates will tend to think of her as a foreigner—despite her name and native American English. She'll never quite find it a comfortable adjustment.

It's slightly easier for Melissa starting as a freshman, before real cliques have formed; she catches on quickly about ditching her overseas clothes. "You know, Baba, most of my classmates don't even want to hear about my life overseas," Melissa confides. "Sure, they're polite, but basically they're not interested. So if I want to fit in, I just shut up about that whole part of my life." Samantha concurs. "I feel much closer to the foreign students here in the high school than I do with most of the American kids," she says, even after a year being back. I come to realize how much their identity has already been affected, what it means to "belong," what is "home." Luke may be only eight years old, but who is he now as he enters the school system with an Asian face after four years in Hong Kong?

To celebrate our return, to get in touch with our native land, we had decided to drive from Portland slowly across the Great American West before we head back to the East Coast and my reassignment to CIA headquarters in Washington.

It's the first time for any of us in the American West. The girls have been reading up on their Western lore: the pioneers on the Oregon Trail, books on the famous mountain men John Colter, Jim Bridges, Kit Carson, Indian lore and tribes, Lewis and Clark, Sacajawea, Buffalo Bill, Sitting Bull. They've told

31

Luke stories about many of them, and we've found a few younger books on the topic that we read to Luke as well. We plan for the Rockies, Yellowstone, the Grand Tetons, Glacier Park and the Devil's Tower of *Close Encounters* fame.

We'll go car camping all the way. It'll be a great experience and help make it affordable. We outfit ourselves with a tent, a camp stove, sleeping bags and other basics for the five weeks on the road. The kids are really excited at the prospect. "Can Melissa and I have our own tent?" Samantha asks. Not this time, but we agree, Luke will sleep on the far side of the tent with us so he won't pester them.

And so every few nights we pull into a new campground, usually KOA. Luke and I trudge off to the men's section of the barn-like bathrooms and washing facilities every morning and night. Here we are now rubbing shoulders with Americans from all over the country, sharing the common adventure of camping, planned destinations, swapping experiences, road lore. I feel a keen new interest welling up inside me as I discover my own Americanness out here in the Great American West where I've never been before. Here we're nothing special, we don't need to talk with anybody about Hong Kong or the Middle East, we're all just campers and travelers together. For us this is as exotic a trip as any.

The American West is a revelation. We develop a passion for rodeos and go every chance we get to watch the steer wrestling, roping contests, bucking broncos, bull-riding and clowns. To get into the spirit we get the kids Western hats and boots. Luke looks great in his, with a somewhat Native American appearance, but a few days later, despite my cajoling, he abruptly refuses to join the girls in wearing them. He doesn't want to do cowboy. He may feel he's being turned into a mannequin, dressed up with whatever culture-of-the-moment enthusiasm we have. Maybe another case of identity overload that—in hindsight—I wasn't sensitive to at the time.

In Idaho we finally decide to take the adventure that we'd often talked about: we sign up with a rafting company for a white water trip. It's down the Snake River—even the name evokes disquiet. But it's a beautiful, dry Rocky Mountains day, hot sun, smell of fir in the surrounding forests, fierce, cold, milky river, the roar of the rapids running through it. There are four rafts going out that afternoon—they put our family in the last one, with a guide/helmsman to steer the heavy steel-reinforced rubber boat. We all put on thick life jackets and grip the ropes along the edge of the raft as we push out into the river; the current catches hold, we bounce, buck, feel the spray wash over our faces as waves rush past in a roar. A real rush, a fantastic family adventure as we bob and plunge down the raw American western river.

Just as we're getting used to the pitching and maneuvering, a wall of water suddenly looms up from the right, forcing the heavy raft to rear up, twist to the left … and then, unbelievably, in one heart-stopping moment, the raft flips up and over. In a flash we're hurled into the fast mountain waters. When I come up seconds later in the freezing water I desperately look around, find Prue and Melissa nearby, and we grab onto the ropes along the side of the inverted raft as it plunges on down through the rapids and rocks. But where are Samantha and Luke? I yell for them, look all around, but I can't see them anywhere in the water or around the raft. I'm terrified. Two minutes later Samantha appears in the water next to us. She has Luke in tow. She and Luke had been thrown out the other side of the raft from us; they ended up under the now upside-down raft, in the air space inside the boat. She knew where she was, had held on to Luke until they figured out what was happening and then ducked under and dragged him out to the outside of the raft where we were.

It's a minor miracle that they're alive, and Luke, even with his life jacket on, probably wouldn't have made it without Samantha. I want to strike out for the nearby bank with everybody, but the guide yells to us to hold on tight and keep our feet up to avoid rocks below, that we'll be out of this stretch of the white water in a few minutes. The water is numbingly cold, our hands clenched and frozen on the raft cord. Soon the water slows, calms, flattens out onto a gravel plain, gentle once again. We can climb up on the inverted boat until we reach a beaching place. The other three boats ahead of us, one loaded with a vocal and macho outdoor bunch, had seen us flip and were waiting to help us, grab us if they could. We reach the beach and, with the river's energy slaked for the moment, we are able to pull the raft up onto the shore. We're trembling with cold and with emotion, but we all exchange smiles and hug each other over our incredible experience and survival.

A bus eventually comes to pick us up, give us hot soup. To my considerable anger our guide disappears without a word, he can't face us. The manager of the outfit has come to meet us, profuse with apologies, says it's the first time this has happened in seven years of rafting trips. But they seem mostly worried about whether we'll sue. No, we won't sue, we're alive and safe and that's the main thing. Chalk it up to a lucky misadventure. We get a free T-shirt out of it.

But nobody in the family proposes any more white water rafting after that, and Luke is the first to put on his life jacket every day thereafter whenever we go in a boat or canoe. In the merciful absence of a family tragedy the raft spill on the Snake has become a bonding experience, a memorable part of a family lore in the turgid waters of our early new American life.

*     *     *

I am enthralled by Glacier Park in Montana and its soaring snow mountains, an environment close to my soul. I even find myself buying a big belt buckle that proclaims "Montana is what America was." Is this some kind of reactionary slogan? Or a dim awareness of intensifying national loss of something important? That's what I read into it, but when I get back East I can hardly find a friend who has ever been to Montana; they look at the belt buckle, shake their heads and wonder about me.

In the museum at Glacier Park in Montana I notice a Plains Indian in partial native regalia looking at the exhibits at the end of the hall. We've been reading stories about them. Excited and pleased at the cultural opportunity, I bring Luke over and discreetly draw his attention to him at the other side of the room. Luke looks annoyed with me and pointedly walks away—*what in hell are you doing, pointing out people who look different*, he seems to say.

We've had a lot of enforced togetherness—long distances in the car each day, sleeping bags arrayed in a row in the tent at night, and meals around the campfire or in the tent if it's raining. It's hard to get away from each other and spats often break out as the three kids share the back seat hours on end. We often have to bring Luke up to the front with us to let the girls have some peace. I find Luke often skipping out when it's time to share chores, work together, put up the tent, fetch firewood, water, get the camp set up, wash dishes, unpack and pack up again. Samantha and Melissa notice this and complain that Luke is always getting away with stuff. I agree and tell Luke to shape up.

One night I'm really pissed. It's been a long day, we couldn't get into several campgrounds and now it's dark and it's raining. We struggle to set up the tent, but where is Luke? Not around, as usual, probably playing video games in the reception area. We're all wet and tired. Water is flowing into the tent. Prue has trouble cooking in the rain and has to put the camp stove part way under the front flap. After the meal I tell Luke he's got to do all the dishes since he skipped out on fixing the tent or getting firewood. "Why should I," he retorts, "I did it yesterday." "Because everybody in the family has to do their share. You're no better than anybody else." "I did it yesterday, I'm sick of this trip and always having to do chores." He walks out of the tent. I see red, grab him and drag him back into the tent. "Luke, I'm ordering you to come here and finish your chores." He refuses again, rolls his eyes and gives me a sullen look. I lose it. I chase after Luke around the tent, he knocks the water bucket all over the tent floor; I catch up to him, and in a momentary spasm of fury I slug him, willfully, hard. Blood gushes out of his nose. He cowers back behind the tent pole, terrified at this new side of his father. Samantha and Melissa are appalled and shrink back. *My God, what have I done? Where did it come from, this flash of violence towards one of my own children? What is happening to me?* Prue and the kids stand there, shocked. Overwhelmed, stunned, I grab Luke up to comfort him, apologizing, rocking him in my arms, in our little world of a tent out under the foreign western sky, far from anyplace we know as home. I have discovered a latent vein of violence lying just beneath the surface in myself that has almost never come out before. What does Luke make of this? And the rest of the family? What do I make of myself?

*      *      *

We finally pull into our home in Maryland, car loaded with assorted Western loot -books, cowboy hats, arrowheads, T-shirts from the Montana Buffalo Reserve, Ogallala Indian Reservation, Devil's Tower, Black Hills, the lot. It's been a remarkable trek, an immersion course in Americana.

Luke, too, has absorbed a set of uncommon impressions and experiences over his nearly nine years of life overseas, grist for a personality in the making. He seems to be slowly processing it, weaving this body of diverse experience into a persona that he will increasingly reveal to others as exotic, mysterious, worldly, inscrutable, life lived on the edge. It enables him to flash a peacock-tail of mixed self-images that will distract from some of the less tidy realities of his life. This is a Luke we will hear about from others in the years to come as well. Luke as amateur image-builder, Luke as international traveler, Luke as one cool dude, Luke as poseur, Luke as free spirit, Luke as risk taker.

# CHAPTER FIVE

# AMERICANIZATION

*September 1982 - Rockville, Maryland*

Luke's now in third grade, in a school in America for the first time. He's still young enough to adapt to it readily. He quickly develops a new facet of his personality—the wheeler-dealer entrepreneur. He buys packages of bubblegum, takes them to school where he sells individual pieces to his friends for a profit. Another time he takes a penknife to school to sell—where did he get it? He's caught with it, it's confiscated and he's sent back home. There's no doubt he's interested in knives—so are many boys. To our great relief we observe that Luke is not a fighter. He's not even confrontational, he never gets into physical fights, he doesn't threaten people. But he has an eye for working the angles.

Prue has learned not to give Luke a penny more than he needs for his lunch money, after no change ever comes home. But other disturbing characteristics emerge. By sixth grade he's figured out check books; when Prue gives him a check to take to school for an activity he learns to change the "Pay to the Order of" line and put in his own name. It's crude, but amazingly he gets away with it a few times, in quite small amounts until we discover it. We now have to be careful with giving him checks to pay for things. Just where is the banking system that doesn't catch these crude forgeries?

One day Prue finds a stash of mail under his bed, lots of letters from neighbors' mail boxes. Just what are you doing Luke? No explanation. Almost none seem opened. We take the letters back out under cover of darkness and put them back in the neighbors' boxes. Luke, do you know that tampering with the federal mail, other people's mail is a felony? Do you know what a felony is? He will learn. And he's now aware that mailboxes often contain paper valuables like checks, but that particular mail box incident doesn't recur—so far as we know.

Luke clearly likes to plunge in, improvise, experiment, push buttons, see what happens. For Christmas Samantha gives him an electronics kit with lots of wires, electronic parts, transistors, to wire electricity through various devices and to run others. There is a gradual step-by-step booklet to increase the sophistication of each newly created gadget. Luke ignores the instruction book and simply jumps in, wiring things to other things just to see what will happen. This is alien to Samantha who likes to master the material, step by step, in tune with learning technique. Luke wants the excitement, the novelty; once it gets routinized or takes more sustained input he seems to lose interest.

*   *   *

Dogs. Now that we're back in the States we want to reintroduce one back into our life. Prue has keen interest and feel for dogs. So we acquire a new shepherd-lab mix, Malik, a loving but timid soul, great with kids. Dog number one. Samantha is now no longer at home with us, she's gone off to college at Macalester in St. Paul. Melissa, still at home, has volunteered for a program that entails adopting a puppy for one-year's home socialization before sending it off for training as a future seeing-eye dog. We accept a black lab puppy, Donovan, a klutzy creature, endearing but slow to learn, indiscriminate in bestowing his sloppy affections. Melissa's task is to prepare him for his future life as a seeing-eye dog, walk him along busy sidewalks and streets, urban situations, into stores, malls, up escalators, prepare him for eventual serious training. Dog number two.

"Why can't I have a dog of my own?" Luke asks, now ten years old. A third dog? This is crazy, I think. Prue disagrees, she says she thinks it's an important experience for Luke to learn to develop a sense of responsibility and learn to bond with an animal of his own. In for a penny, in for a pound. So we all go off to the local pound. As we pass down between the cages, a small brown and white dog eagerly, engagingly, desperately leaps up and down on the sides of his cage begging for attention. Luke goes for him—a feisty medium-size, one-year old mutt, half terrier, half Basenji, with perked ears. He is a survivor, a dog who had been abandoned. Maybe this strengthens the connection between them in Luke's eyes, who knows? Luke names him Barney.

But Luke doesn't immediately and fully bond with Barney. As with so many other things, Luke seems to lose interest after early enthusiasms. He spends only limited time with Barney after a week, resists having to take him on walks, feed him, or play much with him. "Luke, I'm putting you on notice," Prue says, "you asked for a dog of your own. If you don't start taking more interest in taking care of Barney, we'll take him back to the pound." And she signs Luke up for ten sessions in a dog-obedience class—great for bonding as Luke learns to put Barney through his paces, in the midst of a pack of other dogs—little, big, black, brown, white, red, shy, aggressive, obedient, stubborn. The process takes, Luke grows more engaged, and Barney starts sleeping on Luke's bed from then on.

On a whim, I "upgrade" Barney's name to Barnaby, a name carrying playful connotations for me from an early childhood comic strip and I use it regularly with him. Some other family members occasionally slip into it themselves. Luke, however, remains steadfastly loyal to his chosen name and Barney answers to both. I'm often given to inventing personal variations of lots of place names. But now, as I look back, I think I subtly undermined Luke's right of giving the name he wanted to his dog; perhaps an unconscious act of imposing my own will. The power of naming is potent. I don't know if Luke ever actually resented my use of "Barnaby" and he never commented on it. Whatever his name, Barney will be around through thick and thin—to the last moment of Luke's life.

One benefit of having a son of course is to get to live vicariously all the things I didn't get to do as a boy myself. Model cars are one. Luke maintains a steady interest in remote control cars: I'm happy to support anything that's serious, long-term and constructive. So we find ourselves at various back lots and abandoned fields around Maryland on weekends with Luke, watching these little vehicles spurt and fart around long dirt tracks, sounding like a plague of locusts, the air heavy with the sweet smell of exhaust from their reddish fuel. Males of every age, all still boys, field vehicles that run the gamut from Luke's more modest vehicle to larger beasts lumbering down the tracks, the Humvees of model car racing. But these wretched vehicles all require constant tweaking, adjusting, tampering, regulating, consultations and endless new parts to keep them in working order. It seems like I'm off to the car shop with Luke every week, explaining problems, encouraged to upgrade to fancier new parts and accessories. I'm not mechanic enough to share all the hands-on tinkering, and I can't really talk the car talk, but Luke keeps the old man at a face-saving distance in the background while he talks shop.

Luke has also developed an interest now in martial arts from kung fu films. He likes us to sit with him to watch the *Kung Fu* series on television with David Carradine—corny, shlock Zen, but fun. Luke amuses us with his imitation of the old Chinese sage giving Buddha-flavored advice to Grasshopper, the boy novice, Zen monk-to-be. It inspires him to want to take tae kwon do lessons. I'm delighted at his interest at last in something related to his own cultural background. We scout out a local *dojang* nearby.

In our photo we see Luke, age eleven, intensely Asian in his tae kwon do uniform, dark complexion against the white jacket, white baggy pants and colored sash. Here is my photogenic Asian son, unselfconscious in his full native combat regalia. Am I an Asian wannabe? Or is Luke discovering his traditions? We're hoping this is something that might bring mental and physical discipline into his life. Bruce Lee as mentor.

And Luke does well at tae kwon do: in the course of two years he's worked his way up to the threshold of juvenile black belt. We now spend a lot of time in the car on weekends accommodating everybody: horse tournaments and dressage for Samantha, Melissa and Prue, dog shows for Melissa and Prue, and periodic weekend trips to tae kwon do tournaments where Luke is competing.

Luke lacks the killer instinct—and I'm relieved at that; he's still somewhat young but his style is good. Apart from the flying kicks and fists, we watch as he learns to break boards with the classic "hiyaa!," using fist from above, or the running-flying kick straight out to the side that shatters the board held by his teammates. Then at a larger tournament months later we sit up in the stands along with many other parents as the junior warriors in their white robes and bare feet file in and bow to the master who is seated under a Korean flag. This time Luke is matched up against a much older boy in a tournament. The sparring commences and Luke seems to hold his own, until, in one heart-stopping moment, the older boy knocks Luke to the floor with a sharp kick to the head. Luke lies unconscious for what seems like an eternity—maybe one minute. We rush down and take him off to an emergency clinic; the doctor calls it a concussion and he must be kept awake but the concussion seems to have no lasting effects. But from this point on Luke's enthusiasm for tae kwon do begins to wane and he no longer wants to go to tournaments. Understandable, after taking the hit. It's also part of a pattern: Luke develops some serious skills and then abandons them.

Through Luke we also get to know the main body of Bruce Lee films, especially his masterpiece, *Enter the Dragon*. Lee has a powerful charismatic presence and Luke himself bears a passing resemblance to Bruce Lee—or so many people tell him, which warms his heart. It is tagged onto his self-persona.

He also develops an interest in martial arts weapons outside of the *dojang*; they seem to come with the turf. Bruce Lee employs these weapons with dramatic flourish and devastating ends in his films. Luke inveigles me into taking him to some martial arts stores. "I don't think we should be encouraging Luke to be interested in weapons at all," Prue says. But I'm fascinated myself, "We can keep it under control," I assure her.

I do feel ambivalent about the strange blend of messages in these martial arts places though. You walk in and feel like you're entering a cultural shrine dedicated to the traditions of upright, virtuous Zen-like discipline, the austere Asian warrior way of life with its cultural artifacts: swords, helmets, masks, bamboo staves, stories of the Way of the Japanese Warrior. I love that. On the other hand, these places also exude the darker impulses of a latent underworld: switchblades, sheath knives, brass knuckles, billy clubs, and a disturbing propensity towards cult interest in World War II German army memorabilia, and even the cult of the Nazi. That's a long way from the Asian Way of the Warrior and I don't want to go there.

Luke wants to get some stars—three-, four-, or five-pointed razor-sharp steel star-shapes thrown with lethal effect in martial arts films. Even though they can be used with a cork dartboard for practice, they're too potentially dangerous so we nix that. Luke would like a switchblade too—sorry.

But I do let Luke get some *numchucks*, two wooden handles attached with about three feet of light chain, kind of like short jump ropes, that are used for demonstration and potentially as a serious weapon. Just watch the spectacle as Bruce Lee spins them around up over his head and around his body at high speed, whooshing through the air in a breathtaking pyrotechnics of deadly proficiency. Luke is not a fighter, so we're not really worried they'll be used violently. But—foolishly, typically—Luke takes them to school one day and of course they're instantly confiscated. Luke, you're an idiot to do that, didn't you know what would happen? Glum silence. Goodbye *numchucks*.

Next thing on the agenda: Prue wants to introduce Luke to horseback riding, a much healthier pursuit. She has long been a good rider, and Samantha and Melissa both took a lot of riding lessons in Hong Kong. Me, I don't really do horses. But back in Maryland we go with the girls to numerous competitions where they've won prizes in jumping and dressage competitions. Samantha has gotten a blue ribbon for her age at local competitions on several occasions. So Luke now starts his riding lessons too. He does well in them, although he pays little attention to the finer points, and is more inclined to want to gallop around. His teacher actually tries to put a little fear of God into him by giving him a fast horse, hard to control—and Luke loves it. But after a year or so, when he's just beginning to gain some skills, Luke loses interest, says he doesn't want to go anymore. We tell him to finish the course—at least even this much skill will stand him in good stead later. It seems to be a constant quest for the excitement of the new. Same thing in music as he quickly picks up the trumpet in music classes in school, shows talent, only to abandon it later.

*         *         *

One day in the fall I'm up on the roof of the house, losing the annual struggle with oak leaves in the gutters; like a pot of gold at the end of a rainbow, I find a six-pack of beer sitting up there, tactfully out of sight from the ground. I haven't seen Luke up there, have never smelled beer on him—how long this has been going on? "Luke, what's the deal with this beer business?" I ask that evening. "Beer?" he asks blandly. "Up on the roof." "Oh, Eric took some from his dad and didn't want him to find it so we put it up there." "Well, I don't want it up there, and I don't want you drinking beer. You're too young. Get rid of it." This isn't good, he's only twelve. But then, didn't I once try beer with friends when I was twelve on the farm—although I hated it? But I didn't have a six-pack up on my roof either. Is Luke a purveyor to friends as well?

Luke's now thirteen. One day he and his friends—fairly normal kids from what we can see—get involved in a paintball shootout, running around the neighborhood, but the venue then shifts to a local multi-story parking structure, ideal for sneak attacks on enemies hiding behind a sea of cars. A number of cars get splattered; some of the drivers see the shootout and call the police. The boys all get picked up. The police charge them with "destruction of property." A letter from the Rockville Maryland Juvenile Services Administration informs us they are examining whether grounds exist for formal prosecution. That's really worrying. But then we get a letter:

*28 Dec 1987; Juvenile Services Administration, Adjustment Notification: I have reviewed the facts concerning the offense referred to above (Destruction of property) and have decided not to authorize Juvenile Court action. The Juvenile was issued a reprimand and warned against future involvement in delinquent activities. First offense, respondent willing to pay 1/3 of outstanding restitution; parents took appropriate action; court services do not appear necessary in this matter.*

We know some of the other parents; we all agree it was irresponsible action, but we do not believe this involved deliberate vandalism or wanton destruction. It was boys being boys being stupid. We parents all pay a sum to contribute to the cleaning of the cars. Charges are dropped. We ground Luke for a period, take away some privileges. This is Luke's first formal run-in with the Law. But he now has a mini-start on a police record. He hangs his head in silence after the incident, seeming regret. But increasingly we spot a pattern here. Luke does have *genuine regret* after all these events end poorly. But it's never that what he did was inherently wrong, or that he showed bad judgment. What he regrets is having caused *us* some pain, that he has upset *us*, especially Prue. He doesn't seem to perceive any apparent direct relationship between his decisions (or non-decisions) and the pain or damage he has caused. It's like he's some bystander, pained at the outcome of unfortunate

41

but inevitable events played out on a stage before him. He just doesn't seem to associate action with consequence. No clear grasp of right and wrong as abstract concepts, they're just events with good or bad outcomes.

*     *     *

Big changes are now afoot for me. At age fifty and after twenty-five years of federal service, including a stint heading up long-range strategic estimates at CIA's National Intelligence Council, I have decided to retire from the Agency and accept an invitation to join the RAND corporation in Santa Monica, a large private non-profit think tank. I've always wanted to go west, live in California; it will be a welcome change from my long years in the East Coast. We'll move out to Santa Monica as soon as Luke's school year is up in six months. I'm really psyched up for the move, the change of life, a new world.

California, land of surfers and babes, should be an infinitely exciting prospect to a now fourteen-year-old boy. But Luke is nervous about moving, leaving his friends. He's always been less adaptive to new situations than his sisters. His behavior begins to show some strain, some slippage.

Other more serious tensions are arising at home. Samantha is back from college with us for a while on a summer internship in Washington. She has many issues with Luke, especially that he takes her stuff without asking. She doesn't approve of his lackadaisical sense of values. Luke is also acting out somewhat on the eve of pulling up stakes after six years in Maryland.

My sister Faith, who has done a lot of training in Buddhism, describes Samantha as a "warrior," a classic archetype in Buddhist and Jungian terms, also embodied nicely in *Star Trek*'s Worf. The warrior embraces a passionate commitment to upholding honor, tradition, values, respect, trust, dignity, strength. Samantha is serious, feisty, determined, an activist, self-starter, strong and loyal, with its inevitable flip side of the coin—some inflexibility, certain rigidities in moral thinking. And, in typical eldest child syndrome, she has come to feel that Luke does not honor the family sufficiently, that his behavior too easily slips off into an amorality of weakness and dishonor. She feels he's taking advantage of the family and is thoughtless and irresponsible. It bugs her to watch his easy-come easy-go way of life. And she probably resents that a male child is classically the bearer of the line in traditional thinking—a line of honor to which she—and not Luke—has been far more seriously dedicated.

It's true, Luke's sense of morality is elusive; he shows instinctively decent instincts towards other people, rather kind-hearted, generous, but amoral often seems the closer description. He often acts in impulsive ways that hurt other people, even if it's not his intention. And the pattern seems to be growing. It just doesn't seem to occur to him that it's plain wrong to do certain things, regardless of outcome. How do you fix this except by constant reminding, and demonstrating consequences? Samantha feels that we—especially me—are giving Luke too much leeway. A lot of these problems with him are classic teenager-management stuff. But Prue and I are the ones on the daily frontlines. I feel like Mao Zedong in a guerrilla war: we have to make the tactical decisions of when to hold the line, when to retreat, when to press forward. It can't be all-hard-line all-the-time as Samantha seems to feel.

Samantha has always been the more tomboyish of our two girls and, as first-born, very much aspiring for her father's eye. She and I share a huge number of interests—books, music, politics, world events, foreign culture, classic movies, other intellectual interests, hiking, her sports skills, her intellectual curiosity about the world—lots of stuff, a lot of laughs. We're instinctively close, sharing a wavelength on a lot. We've done many things together in the seven years before Luke ever arrived on the scene, and after. But she perhaps feels that Luke, by virtue of little else than accidental maleness and a problem profile, somehow displaced her in this role of her father's son. She's right that Luke has absorbed a disproportionate amount of our attention since his arrival. He *is* different: he's the only boy, he's adopted, he's more trouble-prone, he takes more time and supervision. I search out those few boy things that I can share with him and I love that, but there are not that many of them—nothing approaching the range of things I share with Samantha and Melissa.

I feel torn. Because of Luke's elusiveness, opaqueness, I struggle twice as hard to communicate, to get through, to arrange special activities that we can do that will help me to reach him, to create more meaningful bonds between us. I don't have to do that with Samantha and Melissa, those bonds are there, and I feel great pride in them. Admittedly, I know I feel more daunted by the mysteries of teenage girls. Many years too late I wish, for example, that I could have celebrated their coming of age with their first menstruation, but I felt embarrassed, awkward with the issue when informed about it by Prue and I said nothing to them.

So Luke offends Samantha in his total lack of those very warrior—or manly—qualities: he is often devious, indirect, does not greatly respect property of others, and his values are uncertain, unclear. He is even-tempered, happy-go-lucky, rarely gets angry. But if you happen to trespass upon one of Luke's few personal preserves of sense of dignity—hard to find, but there are some—there is a certain sense of "face," a red line. But this is not a warrior's dignity; Luke is not into "the warrior" tradition. It's about being *dissed*.

43

Luke's attitude towards personal possessions is also puzzling. He sees no real boundaries, not even for himself. He will simply borrow someone else's property, not *steal* it, just take it for whatever purpose he has in mind. Nor is his own property sacrosanct. He is quick to give away things of his own to others, doesn't particularly mind when people take his things. He's not acquisitive or a hoarder, he's not possessive. Boundaries are vague, property is vaguely communal when needed. He seems oblivious to imagining how other people might feel. And his sisters, in the first instance, get pissed off about it.

Trouble especially seems to happen with Luke when I'm away. Is it *because* I'm away that things happen? Prue is no pushover in discipline herself, but maybe the temporary absence of a male authority figure gives Luke greater license—or maybe he resents my absence, who knows.

Weeks before Prue, Luke and I move out to LA in June, Samantha comes back from college and will take a summer job in Washington. I go off on a trip for a few days to RAND in Santa Monica. When I arrive back at Dulles airport around 9pm I head for the baggage pick-up where Prue routinely meets me. I give her a hug—and see she is agitated, upset.

"We've just had a bad scene at home between Samantha and Luke, I thought somebody was going to get killed," she reports, shaken. "You know how Samantha has been really critical of Luke? This time he took her credit card and charged up some CDs. I was in the kitchen getting dinner ready when Samantha came charging up the stairs—she'd just found out about it. I told Samantha that Luke's action was unacceptable and that we would deal with it later when you got home and we could all talk it over and take some action. But Samantha was really angry and chewed Luke out in rough terms, called him trash and a thief. I told Samantha that was enough and she then left angrily to go back downstairs to her room … I don't know, Luke just went wild this time. He rushed to the top of the stairs and shouted back down at her. You know that bronze Chinese horse statue that sits on the railing at the top of the stairs? Well, he picked that up and threatened to throw it down on top of her."

"My God," I say, "I've never seen him do anything like that." I snatch my bag off the luggage carousel and we head quickly out to the parking lot.

"So what happened then?"

"Well, Samantha then came charging back up the stairs and grabbed Luke around the neck, some kind of a choke-hold. I rushed over to break it up, to force Samantha to let go. I guess they were back into the kitchen by this point, scuffling. Luke was backed up against the counter. As he broke Samantha's hold, he reached around and grabbed a large kitchen knife off the counter and brandished it at Samantha to keep her distance. Samantha then really flew into a rage."

"What about Melissa, what was she doing in all of this?"

"Melissa got really scared at all the shouting and violence and retreated from the kitchen to her room. And the dogs were all barking furiously." Prue's voice trembles. "At that point I grabbed Luke's arm to get him to drop the knife. I don't think he really wanted to use it, but he was looking crazy, sort of threatening. I don't know … I think he was just standing his ground. I ordered him to drop the knife before something terrible happened. He and Samantha just glared at each other, and he finally threw the knife down onto the floor and stormed out of the house … I don't know … running out into the woods, somewhere out back. I went out after him and called for him but he didn't answer. I didn't know where he was exactly. I knew I was going to have to leave in a few minutes for the airport to pick you up, but I really wondered whether I should even leave the house at all. I was afraid that they might start up something again while I was gone."

"My God, that's really bad … At least thank God no one got hurt. And this had to happen with you while I was away. Or do you think it was because I was away?"

"No … probably not. But it's harder to control the situation when I'm alone. Let's just get home."

Half an hour later as our car swings into the driveway the headlights probe searchingly into the darkness beyond, deeper into the woods of the parkland behind the house. Is Luke still out there somewhere? My stomach is churning, I'm fearful at what we might find when we arrive. I have no idea how to defuse this.

Samantha's in the kitchen, thank God alone, when we walk in the door. I greet her and hug her, but she is stiff with anger.

"What's all this about," I say.

"It's *your* son, Luke. I'm tired of having my stuff taken. He's a little thief." Her voice is trembling.

"OK, Samantha, I've heard about it … and I agree, what he's done is serious. And you have every right to have your stuff protected. But we just can't let this descend into violence and knives. Somebody could get really hurt."

I pick up the corkscrew that's on the table and twist the handle around the spiral, trying to focus my thoughts on what to do next.

"I've warned him before about taking my stuff. Now he's taken my credit card and tried to use it to buy CDs."

"But how did this lead to the whole knife fight?"

"I told him what I thought of him, and his lying ways. He threatened to throw that Chinese horse on top of me and I came up and grabbed him. He can't get away with that kind of threat with me. He has no sense of right or wrong."

She looks me hard right in the eyes, burning in her own sense of indignation and violation.

"But, Samantha, I'm appalled that this led to what could have been a terrible fight, somebody could have gotten killed. You're a lot older. I agree we've got to do something about Luke, but I look to you to keep things from getting out of hand."

"OK, then tell your son"—she spits the word out—"to straighten himself out and respect other people's property."

"I promise you we'll work on this. But you're just here for a few weeks before we pack up, Luke is upset about the move. For God's sake let's try to keep the lid on things. I'll make up any loss on your credit card if there is one."

"Just keep him out of my way and there won't be any trouble."

Luke isn't in the house. God knows where he's gone. I grab a flashlight and go out back into the dark woods and shine it all around, calling his name. Finally he emerges from behind some trees about fifty yards from the house. I greet him and hug him, but he's shaken, sullen, non-communicative, crying.

"Luke, what in hell happened tonight?"

"Nothing … Samantha just freaked out and attacked me."

"And why did she freak out?"

"I dunno, I took her credit card, just to buy some CDs. I was going to pay her back."

"Luke, dammit, you know that she really gets pissed off when you take her stuff, and I don't blame her. That's stealing. From your own family. That's just not acceptable."

Luke is silent.

"And what happened tonight is even worse than the stealing. One or both of you could have gotten badly hurt over this knife business. Even killed, for chrissake."

"I wasn't going to use the knife, I just wanted her to stay away from me. She was choking me."

"Look, I agree that's no good. But violence like this—it's intolerable. And you started this whole thing. Now I want you to go back into the house and apologize to Samantha for stealing her credit card. You owe it to her."

46

"OK, but she can't talk to me the way she did. And I didn't use the card in the end."

"Yeah, but only because the store called up to verify the card, she says. And of course they did, stupid—that's not your name on it. But you did try to use it … Now, I don't know what Samantha said to you, but she was really pissed and I don't blame her."

He is silent.

"Look, Luke, we're leaving for California in a few weeks. I know you're nervous about leaving your friends and moving and all, but I expect you to control yourself and stay the hell out of trouble for the rest of the time we're here. And for God's sake, leave Samantha and her stuff alone."

Luke comes back into the house and I call Samantha into the kitchen.

Luke looks down at the floor. "I'm sorry I took your credit card, Samantha," he says in a low voice.

Samantha looks right at him, staring hard for some moments. "Just stay away from my stuff, Luke!"

They each go off to their own rooms. This is the first time that there has been this kind of physical violence within the family. Mercifully it ended without any terrible consequence. It feels like some dark psychological wounds are surfacing and I'm not really sure what they all are. Or that I know how to heal them.

*      *      *

Luke has a good friend from Tilden Middle School, John. We've gotten to know John somewhat. He and Luke have been together since elementary school and are very close, and both get into occasional minor scrapes together. John is a bright kid, a little wild, but seems basically decent and I like him. Moreover, he's adopted too, giving him a special bond with Luke. He complains about his parents being too tough on him. The shit hits the fan one night around eleven when John—about thirteen—shows up, bangs on the door. We let him in.

"Can I stay the night with you guys?" he asks. "What's going on, John?" "I've just had a big fight with my dad and he's grounded me for no reason, he's just pissed off at me. I just can't take it anymore. I walked out." We've heard from him before about the strict Catholic regimen he lives under. John has a sister, the biological daughter of his parents, with whom he doesn't get along too well either. "John, you've at least got to let your parents know where you are. I'd be happy to speak to him if it would help." So John calls up and tells his father he's at Luke's. Phone over to me. His dad is understandably irate, he asks what I'm doing getting involved in this, and wants John to come home now. "Conrad, I will recommend to John that he go home tonight, but I can't expel him from our house. Knowing from our own blowups with Luke … you know, sometimes it's just better to give things a little breathing space. We'd be happy to have John stay here tonight and calm down and we'll make sure he goes back in the morning."

Grumblings, but the issue is over for the night. I talk with John about all this. It sounds like his parents are decent enough, but a bit up-tight, there are many tensions in the family. His father shows up the next morning, first time I've ever met the guy. He's angry but controlled. He thanks me gruffly for housing John. We talk a little about some of these shared problems; our commonality of concern. Our shared sense of frustrated compasslessness in the adolescent wilderness melts the ice.

There are other neighbors. Luke has had a series of run-ins with the next-door neighbors, the Gardiners. They're a young yuppie couple, very much control freaks. Before they've been in their new house very long, they've agitated the neighbors to get the slightly batty elderly widow down the street committed under the recognizance of her family; she'd been wandering up to the Gardiners' house some nights and peered in the window. She's harmless, a nuisance on occasion, sometimes given to chasing kids up the street, but the Gardiners are sticklers in seeking full application of local ordinances—with which they are acquainted chapter and verse, for them a kind of zoning Sharia. And the telephone number of the local police always springs readily to hand with them. They also come over regularly to see us on numerous petty issues of exact property lines and tree issues and who is responsible for what.

When Luke is twelve he asks if he can have a bb gun. In one of my many moments of reliving my own boyhood, I naively think, "What the hell, I had a bb gun at that age, it's what boys do as they come of age." But then of course I lived on a farm in Vermont at the time and, anyway, that was in the old-fashioned days. I buy Luke a bb gun and am determined to teach him about using such devices responsibly. He is under firm instructions not to take it off the property; basically I keep possession of it, and it is only to be used in my presence. John comes over one time and we line up some tin cans below our deck leading down towards the woods; any miss goes straight into the ground in our line of sight. We do some target practice. Late that day the Gardiners inform us that we are not allowed to fire any bb gun from the back of our house, in any direction. I argue about it, pointing out I'm in full control. They fall into default mode, threatening to call the police. I'm unsure of my legal ground, so I back off. A day later the police show up at our doorstep.

"We have a complaint from a next-door neighbor that you have been shooting a bb gun on your premises. That is not legal. We're going to have to confiscate it." The neighbors claim Luke and John have fired it up into the air and one bb landed on their driveway. If true, there is no doubt that he has crossed a line. So I surrender the gun. But I'm angry, especially that the Gardiners lacked the civility to come over and discuss it with us instead of reverting to the law. Bad blood springs up; I feel hounded and humiliated when I've tried to accommodate Luke's enthusiasms under a controlled situation. They are out watching us like a hawk. It's all moot, we're moving to California in a month or two. But, it turns out, we still won't be done with the Gardiners yet either.

Meanwhile, to help ease Luke's anxieties about the move, I take him with me the next time I fly out to California for consultations at RAND. We stay at the Holiday Inn overlooking the Pacific along Ocean Avenue next door to RAND in Santa Monica. Luke is excited by the setting. "Man, I've counted more Jags than I've ever seen in my life before," he marvels. We take the forty-five-minute drive up the coast and over the Santa Monica range inland to Thousand Oaks. That's where we've bought a house some months earlier when Prue and I came out on our own. For us easterners, luxury of luxuries, the house has a swimming pool in the back, pretty commonplace out here in California. Luke is thrilled, sees which room he will have, and later we have a nice time walking along the beach back in Santa Monica. He drives his remote control car around the big beach parking lot. He shows the first real excitement about the move.

*          *          *

As I retire from the Agency, the whole family—kids dressed up—goes together to CIA Headquarters for the ceremony where I'm to get a medal. They meet the Director and we have a photo snapped of all of us with him. Samantha and Melissa are old enough now to know what all of this is about, so before we go I tell them for the first time what I've been doing for a living all those years overseas when I was officially a State Department officer. But for Luke CIA is only some parody seen on a television show. He takes it all in with disbelief. Later the experience becomes part of his own CV—he talks about famous people he has met, "including the Director of CIA." Our photo shows Luke and the rest of the family with the Director for a handshake and then standing at the doors by the entrance to the building with the CIA seal visible.

## May 1988 - Turkey

In May I have to go to Turkey to do some research for a RAND project, and I want to take Prue along; she hasn't been back to this country that she loves since we lived there in the mid-1960s. We decide to take Luke along as well; his school has only two months to go, we don't want to leave him with anybody at home, especially before the move, and the educational experience will be great. The school gives permission for him to go if he keeps a log and does some research on the country before he goes, and writes a report when he gets back. I solemnly promise to work with him hands-on on the research and report. "How come Luke gets a reward for being bad?" Melissa asks. I try to explain it's not for being bad, it's to prevent trouble. I would like to have taken her, but it's at senior exam time, she knows she couldn't go anyway.

Turkey is always a delight for us: Istanbul with its fantastic oriental skyline of Ottoman mosques, its throbbing waterways, bustling Grand Bazaar, creative arts, and great food. Luke is at first unsure; he hasn't been overseas since he was eight. To his surprise, several times as we walk in back street neighborhoods in Istanbul, young Turkish boys run up to Luke and shout "Bruce Lee, Bruce Lee!" I guess they don't see many young Asians in the flesh. At first Luke is embarrassed, but the third time around he playfully strikes a tae kwon do pose, and wows them. He is their hero. He's pleased with himself and his street image, and the ice breaks. I translate their questions to Luke and he basks in the new experience. We also get out into the countryside, visit a number of Greek and Roman ruins, including a huge hippodrome—"awesome!"

In our photo Luke, fourteen, is sitting in a night club in Istanbul mesmerized by the belly dancer who is doing her thing right in front of him at the table. Portrait of young adolescence torn between simultaneous lust and abashment; how could we take him to Turkey, drag him around all the mosques and Greek ruins without having an oriental night, seeing a real belly dancer? When he gets back home he does write a good report for the school, minus belly dancer. He's enthusiastic about the experience, decides he loves Turkish food. Luke always loves travel; it's one of the few avenues into his heart and psyche. I take it where I can get it.

## July 1988 - The Trek West

It's time to pack the wagons and go west—Prue, Luke and me—and I'm filled with anticipation. Even Luke seems psyched up. Prue and I are never bored with the drive across the country—we've done it several times over the years, savoring the shifting Americana as we go. We had bought a small pop-up tent trailer a year or so earlier, a cube on wheels that cranks up into a full room with pullout beds, a gas stove, and water pumped up from a tank. No toilet. We also tie our LL Bean fiberglass canoe on top of the pop-up, ready for all eventualities—total American vacation image. After we clear Chicago, the exhilaration of being on the open road really kicks in; the landscape and character of the countryside begins to change. My heart starts to beat as soon as I see the signposts, Route WEST! We stay at campgrounds again with all the local encounters. Luke quickly strikes up conversations and relationships with people everywhere. He knows how to schmooze, and people like him.

Not that Luke is all that fascinated by the shifting of the scenery during the day. He sleeps a lot in the car, or listens to his Walkman—his parents' enthusiasms washing harmlessly over him. But he's pretty good company on the road, as nearly always. He's happy doing his share of setting up camp this time. Our enthusiasm crests as we finally spy the Colorado Rockies shimmering white across the plains in the distance—symbols beckoning a new way of life.

### July 1988 - Yellowstone

Luke likes fishing, whereas my own boyhood on a farm in Vermont pretty well cured me of it. But I get back into it now with Luke for a fishing buddy. We buy Luke his Old Pal, a fishing box with sundry hooks, weights, flies. We get rods and reels for both of us, shamelessly exposing our ignorance to the clerk at the sports shop, and we stop off to try our luck at trout in various mountain streams. We can cook our fish for dinner in our pop-up … when we catch one. Prue enjoys paddling us around in the canoe from spot to spot as we search for the ever elusive spot where fish are biting. Luke usually has more luck than I do.

A moment of incredible foolishness comes at Yellowstone Lake, 7,700 feet high, one of the biggest lakes in the world at that altitude. It's reputedly filled with big, hungry, red-fleshed cutthroat trout. We lug our canoe down to water's edge and paddle out some distance from the shore. The day is beautiful, but the water is really freezing to the touch; there are signs all around that swimming is not recommended for that reason. As Prue paddles us around, we catch two reasonably-sized trout and secure them, trailing behind us in the water. Finally Luke snags a big one, must be over twenty inches; it is thrashing around and may fall off the hook. Adrenalin flowing, I grab for the net and lean over to retrieve Luke's prize. But I lose my balance, and in a split second all three of us are pitched into the freezing lake, about a hundred yards from shore. We'd stupidly left our life-jackets in the pop-up, but it's the immediate cold that is the danger. We know there's no way we can climb back into the overturned canoe, so we agree to abandon it and head off for shore as fast as we can, dressed, but ditching our shoes. I've never had much tolerance for cold water and I feel numbed, but Prue and Luke say they are OK. We're all good swimmers, we stick together, hauling along a floatable oar, finally make it in, shaking with cold, back to the wooded shoreline. We're lucky. We strip off our clothes and wring them out. It's a long walk back around the lake through the woods, especially barefoot, to where our car is parked. I'm grateful, I realize what a close call it could have been if we had been much farther out.

We head for the Ranger's office later to find out how we can get someone to retrieve our canoe. The ranger is pissed: "Are you the crazy folks that were out in that canoe? Someone reported a capsized canoe out there and we went out looking all around, figuring maybe someone had drowned. We hauled it in, it's sitting down at the lakeside. You folks have a world of fines coming."

Indeed, recovery of capsized boat; failure to wear life preservers; a fish over the size limits on our hook; and our week's fishing license had expired the day before. Much soberer and several hundred dollars poorer we return chastened to our trailer. At least they let us keep the fish. Prue says she figures our trouts run about a hundred dollars a pound by the time you figure in rods, reels, licenses, and now fines. "Man, how could you be so dumb standing up in that canoe, Ba," Luke shakes his head in wonder. Yeah, the old man really screwed up. What was I reaching for? Maybe it was a moment of eagerly sought father-son shared success—turned into father-son fiasco. But Luke and I still exchange a sly smile of mutual connivance over the incident. No more hundred-dollar trout on the trip.

A few more weeks on the road in Idaho, Washington, and Oregon, over the border into California, and we finally arrive in Thousand Oaks; we open the door to our new house, spread out our sleeping bags on the floor of the empty living room, under our own roof at last. The moving van is due in the next day. West Coast life is beginning. For me it's a total change of professional life. I've left government, and am now at a think tank. Working as a CIA officer I'd spent most of my life trying to ensure that nobody ever heard of me, avoiding attention or publicity. Now, out in the big world, I need to reverse course a hundred-and-eighty degrees. I need to establish my public reputation fast as a Middle East specialist, starting from scratch at age fifty. I will need to do a lot of writing and publishing—papers, articles, studies, books, op-ed articles in newspapers, get invited to as many conferences and international meetings as I can on Middle Eastern issues in order to meet people, network, establish a reputation if I'm going to survive. And it's going to take a good bit of traveling—which may have some downsides at home.

We've put a continent behind us, we're new settlers. The trip across the country was a great bonding experience. And Luke is now enrolled for his freshman year of high school in Thousand Oaks. New venue, clean slate.

# CHAPTER SIX

# SCHOOL SMORGASBORD: TOUCHY-FEELY

I love coming West. The old setting of soft East Coast woods and settled tradition gradually gives way to a freer, wilder, drier climate of high mountains and unexplored horizons. And California presents new dangers, more potential temptations, mires and snares for the unwary— even to Luke's dog Barney. Barney's feistiness finds challenge in the scrub underbrush of the chaparral in the dry hills all around. There are coyotes in there; Barney sniffs them out and chases them despite his small size. Rattlers lurk in the dry *arroyos* too.

A dog can mean a lot to a teenager in times of uncertainty and Barney and Luke grow closer. By bloodline, a Basenji-terrier cross, Barney is not a water dog by any stretch of the imagination, but he has great trust in Luke. In California he plunges into the risks of our pool with Luke.

Photos show Luke, now fourteen years of age, clutching Barney in his arms, leaping off the diving board into the water below where Barney then surfaces and swims to the edge. Barney sitting on Luke's belly-board, floating around in the pool, occasionally inundated by the wave of Luke cannonballing in from nearby, riled up into a frenzy of excitement, barking furiously. He appreciates Luke unconditionally, he passes no judgment.

Barney guards Luke in his bedroom at night. For Luke, night extends seamlessly well into the next day. Sleep is his reliable escape from the world. But his drift towards full day-night reversal this summer is not healthy either. When we tire of Luke's gentrified schedule, as the hours of sleep drag on past noon many days we'll often go in and rile him out of bed. We'll pull the covers off him as he struggles to stay cuddled up in them. But Barney is driven into furies of savage barking as we violate his master's privacy. Half game, half instinct—who knows what lies in Barney's mind from his own first year and a half of life before *he* got abandoned—he seizes part of the blanket in his teeth, growling furiously, shaking his head violently back and forth in a struggle for control over the blanket. Luke, struggling to protect his cocoon from the intruding world, protests at the invasion, the rude opening of the shutters, the offensive reality of probing sunlight streaming in as if upon a vampire's coffin, the noise and confusion, come on, guys, leave me alone, Barney, be quiet, let me sleep, go get 'em Barney. Barney thrives on the ritual each time it happens until Luke finally stumbles out of bed and into the shower. Unspoken communication between Luke and Barney is at a high level. Barney will guard Luke to the very end.

But Maryland still has some unfinished business for us. A month after we settle into Thousand Oaks I get a call at around eleven pm. Incredibly it is the Gardiners, our officious neighbors back in Maryland—it must be past two in the morning for them. "Just where in hell is Luke?" they peremptorily demand. I bristle at their tone. "Luke is in his room, right here, right now, doing his homework." "He's not in Maryland?" "No, he's been here with us in California, ever since we arrived a month ago." "Well, Luke, or someone associated with Luke, has just thrown a brick through our big plate glass window in the back. It has a note on it, saying 'present from Luke'." "Look, I have no idea about any of this but Luke is right here, in the next room, three-thousand miles away from you. This is ridiculous. You should leave us alone." They fume, hang up.

I go into Luke's room and report the conversation. "What's the deal, Luke?" He spreads a big grin, "That's John, he did that. John hates the Gardiners, too. He did it for me."

I turn hypocrite with Luke. I tell him that he should leave the bloody Gardiners alone, that they are rattlesnakes and he doesn't want to get bitten. But in talking to Luke I'm slightly bothered by my own immature secret delight; under normal circumstances I'd reproach Luke more seriously, but I can't. The Gardiners had trespassed their way deep into my heart and emotions, throwing up legalities as I struggled with my troubles; their style of approach offended my principles and touched off primitive emotions in me as I tried to work with this kid. I take juvenile pleasure at their long-distance come-uppance, however petty—even illegal and wrong.

### September 1988 - Thousand Oaks High School

It's fall, school. We are going to turn a new leaf, aren't we Luke. Yup. We drive him to Thousand Oaks High for his first day as a freshman. It has a good reputation. It's a pleasant place, set off in a small canyon surrounded by shedding eucalyptus trees and dry chaparral scrub, almost a rural setting even though not far from the humming freeway, a whole new scene—a fresh slate, anonymity, new cast of characters.

But even distance has its limits. Within a month some of Luke's old habits have managed to make it across the country not far behind him. We start getting notes from teachers about Luke missing classes, missing homework. We start having to go in for special consultations with his teachers on how to tackle the problem. Within a month or two the issues mount: he is caught smoking on the school grounds and receives a temporary suspension. His teachers complain about his mediocre grades. They threaten to put him into "slower track" classes. I ask them to hold off; we will try to work with Luke.

One evening he goes up on the roof of a friend's house nearby. In some crazy-ass stupidity they end up throwing eggs at passing cars—including a police car. They are apprehended and taken in to the police station. We get the call and have to go down and pick him up. This is a visit that comes to take on greater familiarity over time. It's not only a stupid prank by Luke, but this time it's serious bad judgment. I tell him so, but does such a self-evident fact need to be pointed out? At the hearing Luke is put on probation and assigned a week's worth of community work.

A few weeks later he ups the ante: we get another call. "Mr. Fuller? This is the security office at Sears. Your son Luke and a friend have been detained here in a shop-lifting charge. Can you come down to our office where he is being held?"

Shit. Prue and I pull into Sears, find the dingy security office on the ground floor in the back. There is Luke and his friend scrunched down into their chairs, legs stuck out, avoiding our eyes, staring vacantly at the floor. "Your son tried to steal a cordless phone from the store," the security officer states. "We spotted them on our security monitors and followed them out into the parking lot where we accosted them." I express our dismay. Noting that we are talking to Sears and not the police, I ask, "Is there any way that we can settle this outside of the law?" "Mr. Fuller, you realize that we're not talking a prank here, this is petty larceny." But we reach an informal settlement: since he is only fourteen and has no record of theft, Luke will be banned from entering Sears indefinitely and they will work it out so that he will have to perform twenty hours of community service. Luke, you have been really stupid here. You're lucky that Sears didn't press charges. Don't you realize what you're doing? You've crossed a legal boundary here; any next time will be a lot tougher. Luke nods. "We were just being stupid," he says. The right words, but is anything registering?

With the latest of a dreary succession of parents' conferences at the local high school, a moment of clarity snaps into place in my mind. Luke is not making any progress at Thousand Oaks High School. Indeed, he seems to be drifting into a loser syndrome within the school system. He has now been put into the slower stream, in with the stragglers and losers, a downer in itself, plus we find out he's skipping school a lot.

And now, one evening, Luke crosses another boundary: I smell pot on him. I accuse him of it, he halfheartedly denies it, but with no real determination to deceive us. This whole public school scene is becoming an exercise in futility.

### January 1989 - Ojai, California

OK, we decide, maybe a private school, more tailored to Luke, might be a better venue. The cost is worrisome since we already have the burden of both girls away in college now. Samantha will be graduating only in the following year. Nonetheless we feel compelled to start looking into private boarding schools in the area. One attracts my attention, located in Ojai. Ojai is a special place, a charming little village set in the middle of high dry hills about twelve miles from the Pacific coast well north of LA. Surrounded by a verdant valley of farms, walnut and fruit trees, it's an arty town built in Spanish revival style replete with galleries and artisan shops all around, at one time a little pearl set off far from freeway culture. It was the scene of an old Hollywood film of an unidentified paradise named Shangri-La.

Happy Valley. The school's name puts me off a bit, kind of new agey, perhaps a touch saccharine. But we've got nothing against new age if they run a serious school, and who knows, maybe Luke can respond to that more than to the cookie-cutter public school system. I move fast and Luke expresses interest in a change. The next day we drive with Luke over the desert-like back hills of California, always bleakly beautiful, on the one-hour-and-twenty-minute drive to Ojai. The school is located several miles out of town, in a rural setting among walnut groves, well back from the road. We turn into a small stucco portal and take the winding driveway up to numerous small low-set white buildings set on top of a knoll. It's an understated presence with no frills, the very antithesis of an eastern prep-school of stony gothic permanency and elite gravitas—where my father taught—and that I hated.

The admissions director, casually dressed in blue jeans, explains to us the school's particular emphasis on creative expression. The brochure notes that "the school provides a small, safe and intimate community where students are able to explore and express both their intellectual and creative abilities through challenging academic classes, music, studio art, theater and photography." It's all very hands-on with less than a hundred students, great teacher-to-student ratio. A large yurt in the middle of the grounds immediately attracts my attention; it's where school assemblies are held, everyone sitting around on the floor in a semi-circle. They adopt certain features of Native American tradition in their school assembly, sessions of silence, meditation, even the passing of talking sticks to whoever wants to speak. Kids walk around in a great variety of individual styles, no apparent adolescent tyranny of dress that once was the bane of my high school years.

The place grabs me right away. Eastern prep was never my scene, but at least it was free due to my father's teaching position. But here I really identify with the "alternative" nature of the place. I would have loved to go there myself, with its emphasis on community, a sense of mystical ceremony even if not a religious school, a place to grow, to be an unabashed, unapologetic individualist in an unstructured setting. To be yourself, free of group pressure. Blue sky. This is it. I can see Luke prospering here.

Or am I really imagining myself prospering here?

How about it, Luke? It's cool. Luke seems willing to go along with almost all our various plans for him. And while it is a harsh bite into our budget, we are determined to move ahead. This is the right place. I yank him out of high school with ill-concealed delight the very next day and can't get him off fast enough to begin a new life at Happy Valley. We explain to Happy Valley School that he has had motivational problems and some minor disciplinary problems, but we think Luke will respond to this kind of hands-on community. The school is sympathetic, but warns Luke that there is a strict no-smoking policy—that's cigarettes, not to mention illegal substances.

I quickly feel vindicated. The first few weeks right away show satisfying signs. Luke comes home on the weekends, looking pleased with himself. He's talking much more with us now about all that goes on, often expressing interesting new ideas, passing along little vignettes that he thinks we will like. He brings home a friend every so often, and they seem well above average in caliber. His classes have about five or six kids in them so he can work closely with his instructors. We meet with the teachers who all say they like Luke; he gets along with other kids well, is laid back and has interesting things to contribute in class from his background. Hey, our weekends have become fun with Luke, he's more responsive, we don't have to play the parental heavy all the time. I feel great; I think maybe we've found the right formula.

And then comes one of those rare insights into Luke that only an outsider, an instructor, can afford us during a consultation session. At one of the school's weekly assemblies someone came in as part of an outside speaker program to make the case against abortion. (Earlier on they'd had a discussion of the case for abortion.) The speaker argued that, rather than abort the child and take a human life, let the child be born and put up for adoption, to lead a normal life. "You know what," the instructor told us, "Luke usually doesn't speak up much at these sessions, but at this point he stood up and said to the speaker, 'You don't know what you're talking about. I'm adopted and I do know what it's about. I love my parents and they are good to me. But you don't know what it's like never to know who your parents are or where you come from. It's not like everything is normal.' And then Luke broke into a few sobs, totally stunning the other kids who always saw Luke as one cool customer. One of the girls came over and hugged him."

Luke never told us about this event, probably never would have. In fact, he's almost never sought to have an open and searching talk about being adopted. *We*'ve raised the subject with him now and then, trying to make him feel comfortable with it. It's always "no problem, it's cool." Now we are privileged to see another side of the story. Does it hurt him to discuss it? Or is he trying not to hurt *us* by not discussing his thoughts on the subject? We notice another thing too. Unlike our own biological daughters (or probably most kids) who at some point in anger or frustration may have yelled, "I hate you and I wish I had never been born," or "I wish I had lived in another family," Luke at his most angry has never once uttered those words. My sister Meredith's words, from a letter to us written before we had even adopted Luke, come back to us here:

*Yes, identity crisis sometimes may be more poignant for adopted kids, especially in adolescence. On the other hand, from what I've seen, the majority of these children seem to have a very clear idea of exactly what they have lost and what they have gained. The bold dramatic contrast of being orphaned—and then adopted— is pretty hard to be confused about.*

Of course, it's not just about knowing who his "real" mother is—or even his father—it's about not having one single person in the world who is related to you, who is like you. He will have to do with his adopted family—with all its virtues, faults and foibles. Luke, do you have some kind of growing feeling your adopted and extended family seems to have a style that doesn't match yours? That you live in a slightly less familiar or comfortable psychological world? Do you feel a bit of an outsider with us now that you're older? I don't ask him that directly, but I ponder it, sometimes give him openings to register discomfort. Maybe that's why he hangs out so comfortably with his adopted Korean cousin Laura whenever they are together. They can share wry moments of reflections on the many foibles of their adopted families. Many years later, Laura will have her own first child, and will indeed comment on how amazing it is to see, for the first time In her life, someone who is actually related to her.

But Luke never says it's a problem; he has no grievances to convey on this score. He's not a great talker on these touchy-feely things anyway. We get him the book *On Being Adopted* which contains accounts of all kinds of adopted people from age ten to ninety, telling of the personal impact on them of being adopted—some minimal, some huge. But Luke doesn't really seem interested in reading the book. As a matter of fact, he doesn't really read for information in general—Prue keeps hammering this into me. "You go out and get a book when you're interested in something, but for Luke it's a turn-off. He's a doer, an experiencer." He'll read novels for fun maybe, but never for life info. He seems to shelve the adoption book, at least for now. So the Happy Valley revelation of these deep emotional currents inside Luke's happy-go-lucky exterior is a startling and rare insight.

And Luke's work at Happy Valley is going well. His grades are respectable. He's happy, and we're incredibly gratified.

But even the charmed valleys of Ojai cannot fully shield Luke from his past instincts: he gets caught sharing a cigarette with another kid behind the school. They give him a warning. He says firmly he wants to stay at Happy Valley. "Luke, a cigarette may not be a big deal, but you're really playing around with a great opportunity here, don't blow it." He nods, looks off into the distance.

But a few weeks later, a second smoking violation. Luke later tells us he and a number of other kids have also occasionally drunk wine behind the school. The school seemingly doesn't know about it. And then something much more serious: one weekend Luke of his own volition tells us that he has met this older girl, a senior, who has been making eyes at him. One afternoon she takes him into her bed in the dormitory; Luke has just lost his virginity at age fifteen. (As he tells it I note in myself a passing, immature twinge of envy that I didn't have such an experience at fifteen.) But the school finds out, or they think they have, because this is not the first time this girl—a reportedly stellar student and only a few months from graduation—has been involved in this sort of thing. The school reports its suspicion about the incident to us. In what was probably a big mistake on my part, I confirm to the school the incident which Luke had told us about, but point out that the older girl was the initiator. No matter, she is close to graduation and well-regarded. Luke is deemed at fault and will pay the price. He is expelled—five months after starting at Ojai.

So, on a somber morning bathed in southern California sun, we go over to Ojai, pack Luke and his stuff into the hearse of our station wagon, hearts heavy, and haul the remains home. Luke is silent, his mind seems far away, God knows how he's processing it, if at all. For days he lies in his darkened room, shutters closed, sleeping for long periods. He listens over and over to the haunting sounds of Enya singing *Orinoco Flow (Sail Away)*—a flow of sound now forever embedded into my own emotional psyche linked to this event. This dirge is the shattering dissipation of a dream, a castle of hope now seemingly made of sand that we had erected as a concrete symbol, for us and Luke together, that we were in the process of truly turning his world around.

Enya's haunting melody and lyrics still evoke the fleeting aspirations of sailing off into distant waves, "let me reach, let me beach, to the island of the moon."

Sounds wafting from his room carrying away dreams that once were, a longing for imaginary lost lands, a voyage across seas that could wash away the presence of failure. Was it my boat, or Luke's that we hear sailing off into the unknown waters, propelled by the song's rhythmic pulsations?

I can't hear that song to this day without tears welling into my eyes. They must speak too to Luke, even if subconsciously, of what might have been. He is gripped in a chastened mood for long days; a cloud of sadness hangs over us. An important door to a seemingly unbounded future has now closed. We take some time to pick up all the pieces, process them, rethink the project, lower our sights, lick our wounds, adjust to the latest splash of cold reality upon our faces.

Indeed, I'm not at all sure that Happy Valley wasn't indeed just the right place for Luke. A few cigarettes should not constitute the scrapping of a boy's future. (Luke said that surreptitious smoking was common—maybe so.) And he claims his first erotic encounter was not basically his own initiative. Indeed, Luke had always been slightly shy with girls, a quality which perhaps helps endear him to them. And he was much the younger party. But even the laid-back new age California school had its limits. We were far less upset at *what* Luke had done in itself; it was his playing with fire, the careless risks of predictable and serious consequences that were his mistakes—the same damagingly faulty judgment. Or was this simply an inevitable certainty in Luke's case—like a seed that will burst open, pre-programmed, at some unpredictable point—what in the Middle East might be called a fate that is "written?"

Even then, I couldn't let go of Ojai. I call up one of the instructors who had been kind to Luke and who knew him best and I invite him to lunch in town. What, I ask, did he think was really the problem with Luke? "Luke is basically a very nice kid," comes the answer. But is this merely a diplomatic, gentle response to a troubled father? He goes on: "Luke has a good brain, a lot of creative talents, and he gets along well with his classmates; I have never seen Luke mean or angry. He was a good citizen in the school in his dealings with his classmates. But he seemed too casual towards his school work, even though he was doing fairly well. He seemed *secretive* in some ways, hard to get to really know, behind the pleasant façade." Tell me about it.

"No," he says, "I thought that Luke could do well here. But maybe he needs a more disciplined environment that doesn't require quite as much self-reliance ... Mr. Fuller, have you ever thought about military school?"

*    *    *

So Luke is shoved down back into the loser chute of the local high school. I eat crow with the administration as I come in to re-register him. But I feel this is unsustainable, I'm hunkered down in thinking mode.

Meanwhile, one day Luke turns up with a tarantula he's gotten somewhere, "it's going to be my pet, Ba," he informs us. Is there some kind of symbolism here? Oh well, everything is grist for the mill; if it's a serious interest, even a fat ugly spider might have some redeeming features. Luke claims it was captured in the hills by a friend. Who knows, I stop asking about these things sometimes, a straight story is hard to come by. We go out and get a big glass aquarium to put the tarantula in. It's big and hairy, brown and black, eight inches across its body, huge furry legs, worrisome to look at. But it is Luke's friend, maybe consonant with his mood; he's comfortable with it, he shows us how he can hold it in his hands, a place it seems to find comforting. As usual I'm asked to suggest some original name—I choose Paooka—the Russian word for spider. Paooka it is, and now Paooka lives in his glass cage with a screen over the top in Luke's room. He/she—I didn't look—gets fed crickets from the garden as recommended by our local pet shop, along with live meal worms. We never witness Paooka's surreptitious eatings—just as well, and anyway tarantulas don't seem to eat that much. We also lower a shallow bowl of water into the cage from which she takes secretive and unperceived sips. (Does Paooka appeal to Luke's own tendency for furtive secretiveness?)

One morning Luke wakes up to find Paooka lying dead in the cage, upside down, horribly shriveled. He comes out in distress to tell us. We go in right away and peer into the glass cage. No, wait, it turns out that is not Paooka at all, she is not dead, she has merely shed her whole external skeleton overnight. Paooka is still very much with us, lurking behind a box structure in the corner of the cage, apparently incredibly vulnerable at the time of shedding her exo-skeleton when she can literally be badly hurt even by a cricket bite. She rises from the dead to a new life with new skin. Metaphors in unexpected quarters in Luke's very room.

One day Luke has Paooka out to show to some friends. Paooka suddenly runs up Luke's arm, up his face and into his hair. Luke loses his *sangfroid*, freaks and bats Paooka out of his hair off onto the floor. Paooka runs under Luke's very heavy dresser-bed combo that I made for him, and hides. We're afraid if we move the heavy bed, we could crush Paooka. We decide we may have to wait for her to come out. But Paooka doesn't want to come out. How do you tempt a tarantula out? Maybe the tarantula is more scared of us than the other way around. Luke is now nervous for the first time about Paooka lurking somewhere in his room at night, her furtive prowlings out of control like some Hollywood arachnid fantasy. In a display of parental cowardice we tell Luke to keep his door shut at night so Paooka doesn't start running rampant through the whole house. Paooka finally does appear from under Luke's bed a day later, maybe for a quick grasshopper; we recapture her with a small butterfly net and back into the cage she goes.

Paooka, face it, we'll never get beyond a highly ambivalent relationship with you. You are fuzzy but not cuddly. Your furry body dispels some of the grossest quality of insectness, but your inexplicable sudden motions when out of your cage are worrisome, unnerving. And I never really got into the task of catching crickets or grasshoppers which abound in our back yard, or can be bought at the pet store, and dropping them into the aquarium. Not that I identify with crickets that much either, but the idea of deliberately feeding one thing to another touches my liberal conscience. I feel like Renfrew in *Dracula*, the insane asylum inmate who over a period of time feeds a whole series of smaller things to ever bigger things to be eaten ... until Dracula himself comes along, excited at the blood-lust feeding frenzy.

When Luke goes away to his next school, we declare that where Luke goes, Paooka goes. So Paooka is recycled into a gift to an unsuspecting biology teacher whose professional qualifications make it an offer he can't refuse. And anyway, after these several months of hands-on spider experience Luke seems to move beyond his "tarantula period." Freudian implications? I won't even go there.

*      *      *

Luke still spends a lot of time in his room, often sleeping away the day. You walk into his room, it's dark, blinds closed mostly. You have to turn on the light or open the blinds to see much. Nothing too astonishing in a teenage boy's room. An absence of color. Clothes, mostly black, scattered all over the floor. A smell of cigarette smoke from his clothes; we don't fight him on cigarettes anymore, as long as it's not in the house. The room is a mess, although Luke is fastidious about his daily shower and wearing clean clothes. On the wall a Bruce Lee poster, a Pink Floyd poster. Remote control cars with myriad spare parts scattered around. Various controls with antennas. A bottle of pink model-car fuel. A few *Playboy* and *Hustler* mags sticking out from under the bed, no real effort to conceal them any longer. Scattered socks and crumpled Kleenexes. A number of fantasy and sci-fi novels on his bookcase beside the bed. Two *Far Side* cartoon books, a few school yearbooks from Hong Kong and Maryland. A big illustrated book on fishing. A book on martial arts, a book on reading palms. A boom box. Some CDs: Pink Floyd's *The Wall* and *The Dark Side of the Moon*, U2, R.E.M., The Beatles, a few older CDs of mine of 70s rock, *Bob Marley Live*. A chess set. A big gray stuffed toy tomcat from when he was small that he's never abandoned. A now empty fish/spider aquarium on his bureau. A small electronic keyboard. Hand squeezers for grip strengthening. School notebooks in the corner, scrumpled papers lying around with scrawled names and phone numbers, some not bad amateur sketches. A trumpet on the shelf. No TV, we have only one in the house, in the family room. Some *Game and Watch* electronic games, a joystick for video games, a track trophy. A tae kwon do trophy. A pair of new *numchucks*. A small Korean flag, a few crushed Coke cans, a dirty plate or two with chopsticks, from fried rice or noodles that he's cooked himself up, lying next to the bed on the floor. That's his daily life pretty much laid out all in one place.

\*　　　　　　\*　　　　　　\*

Fishing as communication—it's still a good way for me to reach Luke. I'm not sure why he really likes it since we rarely catch anything, and we had that rude spill into the freezing waters of Yellowstone Lake from the canoe. I'm actually surprised Luke is willing to sit around in a boat for several hours with limited action—and stuck with his old man. But I'm pleased at the option of doing something together. We usually go out to Lake Casitas, not too far from Ojai, a dammed up reservoir. We make the obligatory stop at the nearby bait shop on the way, more investment into worms, lures, lines, weights, flashers— none of which ever seem to translate into their weight in catch. We rent an outboard. Sure, Luke likes manning the tiller, but he's also happy to turn it over to Prue while he and I troll along, mainly looking for bass spots. We float around lazily in the middle of the lake, looking out at the golden-hued California landscapes and bare hills; but we also peer into dark murky waters in search of something elusive.

Sometimes we take Mark along as well, a friend of Luke's, a nice kid. Mark's presence in the boat, rather than limiting my exchanges with Luke, actually facilitates them in some way. He's a kind of neutral intermediary, helping the flow of conversation, making it more like three fishing buddies than a hierarchical father-son thing. I'm glad for the device of fishing during some of these more fraught days.

*Yeah, fishing is kind of boring, and we never really catch anything, but my dad likes it and it's a good way to hang out with him a little while without having to talk too much. It's cool.* If that's your thought, Luke, I appreciate it.

And I plot my next move.

# CHAPTER SEVEN

# SCHOOL SMORGASBORD: SPIT AND POLISH

*January 1990 - Thousand Oaks, California*

M r. Fuller, have you ever thought about military school?" I can't forget the suggestion from his Happy Valley teacher. For me this is a real psychological watershed. Military school has always seemed to me one step away from Nazi-dominated goose-stepping, sadistic hazing from hell. But, let's face it, that's me and my prejudices. "Remember," Prue says, "you're not Luke, you're different. What may not be for you may be just what Luke needs." I take her point. This isn't supposed to be about me and my vicarious trips. And besides, we've been the touchy-feely, casual, creative, laid-back, individualistic route at Ojai. We can't rule out some stark alternative in the quest to get this kid's shit together.

The idea marinates in my head—maybe it *is* just what Luke needs. He's drifting further in the direction of unhealthy friends, more indications of pot smoking. We warn him of the health, psychological, and—not to be dismissed—legal implications of pot use. We impose a number of periodic penalties, groundings, allowance fines. And we wheel up the big gun: we tell him we will not let him get a driver's license when he reaches sixteen next year, and we won't change our minds until such time as he seems mature enough to drive a car. Meanwhile he is still required to go to school, he needs a high school diploma. Why not give the military school a shot?

I notice I often tend to think of Luke as a free spirit—but I can't ignore that his free spirit seems to spin off the path entirely if the boundaries are too loose or non-existent. Maybe what I see as free spirit is something sadly much less than that: just a scatter-shot lack of focus and absence of any serious thought and direction. I broach the military school idea to Luke, anticipating instant rebellion. To my surprise, he poses no objections, he doesn't seem to view it at all as punitive; he even sounds slightly interested.

A catalog tells us about an Army and Navy Academy in Carlsbad, California, some thirty-five miles north of San Diego, a three-hour drive south from Thousand Oaks. Seized with this latest idea in my ongoing quest, I move fast. And so, in early January 1990 we drive off again on another venture, this time down to Carlsbad for interviews. Luke is fifteen. It's a college preparatory program, but has strong military discipline, a rigorous daily schedule of reveille at six fifteen, early formations and inspection before breakfast, programs in marching and military drills, everyone in uniform, strong emphasis on accountability, honor, integrity. To my surprise, the ever-inscrutable Luke seems actually pleased when he hears he's been accepted, he looks forward to the adventure. I can't figure the kid. I wonder if it maybe isn't distraction from *boredom* that these diverse challenges offer.

And again, we're thrilled when Luke regularly calls up from Army and Navy to report his doings. "Guess what, Ba," he says, "I'm getting to be one of the best marchers in my class and they sometimes let me lead the group. And I'm playing trumpet now in the school band. The track instructor says he wants me to join the track team, but I'm not sure about that." "Luke, that sounds great, you should do it, you're a good runner. How is the discipline going?" "No sweat, I can handle it," he replies. "The kids are great and I get along with everybody. I really like it here. When are you going to come down to see me?" Luke sends us a photo: There he is, his once long hair now shorn, posing proudly in his uniform, striking a Napoleonic pose against the backdrop of turreted military-style buildings and the Pacific in the distance. He has just turned sixteen. His roommate Kurt is an avid surfer, but Luke isn't part of the surfer crowd.

A month later we go down for visitor's weekend. I'm all psyched, this is a really gratifying moment; Luke seems almost at his most voluble with us, showing us around with a certain child-like pride, introducing us to people. "And this is Captain Brooks, Ba, he's my science instructor. And this is Sergeant Delvalle, he's my marching instructor." "Fine boy you've got there Mr. Fuller, Luke has told me all about your adventures abroad."

Luke imparts to us, almost shyly, little details of things he's accomplished, events that have occurred as we walk around the campus. We eagerly look forward to trips down the school, savoring the signs of how many things are going right. No way I'd ever have guessed this would be the right formula. When we're down there we sign him out of the school to go to an Asian buffet in town nearby for lunch. I can't quite believe all this—my son, the budding Marine.

But over the months, certain other more familiar realities set in. His academics start to present a very mixed bag. We go down for a parents-teachers consultation day. I'm surprised, worried at the discrepancy in comments among the various teachers, it sounds like they're each describing a different kid. Luke's got a Brahma-like visage with a hundred faces all in different directions at the same time. The classic question: *Which is the true face of Luke?* I devour the comments, take notes, combing them for clues, the shreds of reality that only outsiders can fully deliver that will help us to weave together a more comprehensive picture of this boy.

Two women teachers in particular are scathing in their characterization of Luke. Spanish, Mrs. Singleton: "Luke's attitude is 'don't mess with me.' He rarely does his homework, does the bare minimum for the course in general. He doesn't want advice, guidance or criticism from anyone. Luke is living inside a tight shell. He is sleepy in class. He's no longer an outsider in class, but he just doesn't care about anything. He's an enigma to everybody. Wants to see just how far he can go in pushing the system."

Mrs. Jones, English: "Luke is negative, defiant, obviously not doing assignments. He is disruptive in class. Very intelligent, but getting Ds and Fs on tests. Often comes to class without his books and unprepared. Doesn't like to be told what to do; he regularly gives me dirty looks, with a 'drop dead' message. He failed to complete his reading assignment of "All Quiet on the Western Front" in the six weeks that he had to finish it. Yet he is a good reader. He is totally sloppy in his approach to his work; I can't even read his handwriting. Even his signature is illegible. There is a bad group of Mexicans in class. They are rude; it may rub off on Luke. Why does he *want* to fail? Where is his self-respect? He often fails to even wear his glasses in class and so he can't read what's on the board. He is more a follower than a leader."

Mr. Jameson in History: "Luke seems to like history. But he often falls asleep in class, clearly a form of escape. He is socially active, getting along well with other boys. But he tends to associate with those boys who don't want to be here. He reacts less well to female teachers. Luke is well above average in intelligence but his behavior will damage him. If he's not careful he may not be asked back to school. He says he wants to study German. Interestingly, Luke likes Donald Horgeson, an exceptional student and natural leader who Luke often hangs out with. Luke should join the track team, he's a natural runner. Luke has genuine leadership potential but right now is a 'lost leader.'"

Math, Mr. Gurney: "Luke is getting all the work done, one of the best in the class in this respect. His work is accurate. He's polite. Sometimes late to class. His thought processes are correct, he can put his mind to work. He is not disruptive. No problems relating to students in class. Luke is interested in travel and foreign foods, restaurants."

Clearly Luke responds in very different ways to different teachers. Obviously something is wrong with his relations with women teachers, and we can't figure that out at all; both Prue and I agree that Luke has never had trouble in getting along with women, now or in the future. He is warm and affectionate towards Prue, if anything more ready to talk to her openly than to me sometimes.

We talk with Senior Master Sergeant O'Brian, a grizzled non-commissioned officer type, an old salt who has seen it all. He's in charge of the boys outside of academics. He's also in charge of Luke's disciplinary program. I tell him something about Luke's background, identity issues, adopted kid, etc. I toss in the current pop-culture phrase "low self-esteem."

Sergeant O'Brian looks me over and smiles. "Mr. Fuller, let me tell you something. We all come from different backgrounds. I hear a lot from parents about this boy and that boy and why he is the way he is. You know, I'm not really interested in what happened in Luke's past, I'm interested in his future. We're going to treat him like a man and make a man out of him. He's crafty on some things, but he won't get away with much here. He's a good kid, a smart kid, we can make something out of him."

But later on Sergeant O'Brian tells me he thinks he made a mistake: he shouldn't have put Luke together with Kurt, his roommate. He thinks they're not good for each other. Indeed, we will find out just how much they are not.

But despite periodic rule violations and small penalties that are fairly par for the course there, Luke likes the school. He sometimes comes back to LA on the train from Carlsbad and we meet him in the station. He tells his buddies back in Thousand Oaks that his school is cool whenever we overhear him talk about it. When we take Luke to downtown LA to put him on the train back to school on a Sunday night, we often stop off with him in LA's Chinatown right behind the station and get some good Asian food, which Luke always loves to do, and when he's always at his most talkative.

What is this with the fortune cookies? I've noted Luke seems serious about their messages; he almost tends to view them as possessing some mystical insight, as much as we try to disabuse him of it by telling him tales of the Fortune Cookie Factory. Luke regularly shows strange traces of superstition, a tendency to be attracted to ideas of special powers, special forces, even religious forces, both good and bad. He never saw a fortune cookie he didn't like. But they weren't always smiling on him.

And so Luke is really enthralled by the Carlos Castañeda books—*The Teachings of Don Juan* and *Journey to Ixtlán*—about the shaman figure Don Juan and mystical drug experiences—peyote, 'shrooms in Mexico, the terrifying miniature demon Mescalito. What is it exactly that seizes Luke's imagination here? Certainly the mystical, the mysterious, the other-worldly—and of course probably the drugs as a portal. Castañeda's view of the shaman as intermediary to another world, of shape-shifting, is common to many native peoples in America and Canada. Luke has a kind of superstition—or is it sensitivity?—to these things. Such tales continue to speak to Luke over the coming years, maybe providing an avenue of escape, maybe the chance of being something different than he is? A sense of another world? A sense that certain things have power over him? That he is not responsible for all that he does? I watch, I puzzle, I speculate.

*        *        *

Over the summer Luke gets a job at Taco Bell, and we get used to this new uniform, a temporary stand-in for his uniform at Army and Navy. He lets his hair grow again until the fall. He expresses more interest in music. We're pretty strapped for cash with our two daughters in college, and Luke at private school too, but we've noted his musical talent before; we feel we should scrape together what we can to buy him a used keyboard that he has his heart set on. He goes off to Wally's World in Thousand Oaks for lessons. Wally is an original, a bearded preserve from the sixties, a gentle guy, warm to Luke, impressed with Luke's seriousness in his playing. Indeed, we hear Luke make real progress in playing, including some classical music. He works impressively on the perennial piano student's assignment, Beethoven's *Für Elise*, a piece of music I now, emotionally, never fail to associate with Luke.

But at Taco Bell, he's sporadic at his job, sometimes late. He sometimes turns up at home with several bank rolls of coins—quarters, dimes—which I question. He claims he converted some of his money into coin rolls to use in fist-fighting if he ever needs self-defense. I'm skeptical, and Luke's not a fighter, but I'm not going to call up Taco Bell to inquire. Sometimes I just feel like don't ask, don't tell. No bad incidents over the summer. Things seem more on course. Army and Navy seems to be a stabilizer. Luke goes back happily in the fall for a second year.

22 October 1990: I am away on a research trip in the Middle East. Lightning strikes and the temple is rent asunder. Prue gets a phone call: Luke has been arrested on campus at Army and Navy by the Sheriff's Office of Orange County, California, on a felony charge.

From the Court Record:

*Circumstances of offense:*

*During the weekend of September 28 1990 the minor* [Luke] *spent the weekend at the residence of Kurt Black* [Luke's roommate at school] *in Orange County. On the evening of 28 September the minor and Black, at Black's suggestion, walked to a nearby golf course in order to ride the golf carts without permission. They arrived at approximately 10pm and, with a hack saw, took turns cutting through a chain to the maintenance yard fence in order to gain entry. Once inside the maintenance yard, the two hot-wired the ignitions to several golf carts and drove them around the golf course. They jammed the accelerator on the Marshall's cart, which went down an embankment and landed in a stream. The two then returned to Black's residence.*

*The next evening 29 Sep 1990, the minor, Black and third subject Devin Foreman all decided to go joy riding on the golf carts. They walked to the golf course and took turns cutting through a new chain that had been placed on the fence, by using a hack saw. After gaining entry into the maintenance yard, the three burglarized two or three trailers in order to obtain keys to the golf carts, and two-way radios so that they could talk to one another. All three drove approx 23 golf carts throughout the course of the late night and early morning hours. While playing bumper cars with the vehicles they drove a number of the golf carts into the water hazards on the golf course. They tipped one of the golf cars over and let it slide down an embankment. Several Motorola radios were lost on the golf course. Foreman kept one of the radios. The three remained on the golf course until approximately 5am.*

*On 22 Oct 90 the Orange County Sheriff's Department received information indicating that the suspects were the minor, Black, and Foreman. All three were subsequently contacted and related similar accounts of the circumstances as indicated in the above paragraphs.*

*Minor's [Luke's] statement:*

*The minor was interviewed in the presence of his parents and agreed with the circumstances as described in the police report. He indicated that he made a "stupid mistake" and that he should not have done it. He would like the court to know he is sorry for his involvement in the present offenses.*

"Sorry" won't cut it at this stage, Luke. This is a felony. Although the incident had nothing to do with school life, Army and Navy won't tolerate a student under a felony charge. Luke is out on his ass within a day of the arrest. I'm still half a world away so Prue drives the three hours down to pick up Luke from police custody in Orange County, and for the now ritualistic collection of his things from school for the long depressing drive back home. I get the news only a day or two later when Prue finally reaches me by phone in Cairo. A body blow ... But no, for me it can never be as shattering as the Happy Valley fiasco—at that time I still clung to the conviction that breaking out of the public school system and into the "right" hand-tailored private school would truly make the difference. How can I believe that anymore? If Luke lost his virginity at Happy Valley, I lost mine there, too.

We're into a deeper pattern of failure now. This is far worse: we're talking a clear criminal offense here. Luke's actions have irrevocably plucked him out of the loving protection of his family that could always try to make things alright and have thrust him into the cold calculations and objectively grinding wheels of the California legal system. We can't save him from himself any longer. He doesn't even answer to us anymore; he answers to the Law.

Furthermore, we're out of school options. We've tried touchy-feely and now the spit-and-polish approach. Neither was able to master Luke's problems, his colossal bad judgment and seeming incapacity to foresee consequences. I never liked his roommate Kurt who struck me when he came to our house one weekend as being surly, negative, furtive. But this was Luke's choice. And once again, Luke seems somehow puzzled, surprised, genuinely dismayed at being kicked out; he says he likes the school and wants to stay on. Sorry, Luke, but you've moved into a whole new world of hurt here; even if it just looks like stupid joyriding and contempt for rules and property to you, this is a felony. This is real world.

But how do we spare Luke from a potential conviction for a felony on his juvenile record? That's our key task right now. California law, cognizant of the problem, has an enlightened mechanism for assisting in this: the opportunity to "seal" certain juvenile court records to avoid sending the kids off into adulthood stamped with the legal mark of Cain.

And so Luke is now back once again at Continuation, the eternal dismal holding pen of a school in Thousand Oaks. But I'm determined that it won't be for long. We know this route, we've been there and we know it leads nowhere. We brood over events, plotting our next drastic move. I want to shatter this whole damn pattern with some kind, any kind of resolute, bold, swift, creative action. And none of this is cheap. Mercifully Samantha graduated from college two years ago and Melissa too has now just graduated from Macalester as well so with this year we no longer bear those heavy college tuition bills; they are both now on their own for any further education costs. We decide we will spend the money that we were saving for Luke's college education on some other course of action, anything that can break his trajectory off this path. God knows if there ever will even be a college in his future.

Even with a felony charge pending against him in the courts, Luke still can't manage to stay out of scrapes, minor and not so minor. He is again caught smoking at Continuation school—cigarettes, a charge which now seems laughably trivial to us, but rules are rules. By December he has gotten his fourth warning—this time for pot—on school grounds, and the notice that he will now be transferred to Independent Study. Translation: banned from the classrooms, do your own work at home or in a study hall, bring your work in to your teacher who will grade it, provide weekly ratings, and you will hopefully acquire points towards an eventual graduation certificate. Meantime, teacher ratings all parrot the usual "limited effort" by Luke, but strangely they also comment on his "good attitude." Maybe this is just dismaying insight into the even worse attitudinal issues among many others of the quasi-delinquents around him.

*     *     *

And yet it still doesn't stop. This kid is deaf, or on some kind of whacked-out autopilot. We receive a note from the Superior Court of California, Ventura Country, in this period not many months after expulsion from Army and Navy:

*In violation of Penal code Section 459, a FELONY was committed by the said minor, Luke Fuller, who did willfully and unlawfully enter The Ascension Lutheran Church School Bldg located at 1600 Hillcrest Ave in Thousand Oaks with the intent to commit larceny and felony.*

A church, for God's sake. In the end apparently nothing was stolen in this breaking and entering event and the felony charge is dropped; he is assigned to community service but with an understanding that this event will negatively affect his felony hearing on the golf course case.

I'm running out of ideas. We decide to consult a child psychologist on a longer term basis, to explore Luke in greater professional detail. We trudge up the stairs with Luke to the psychologist's small sunlit office in Thousand Oaks office park. He's a jovial, heavy-set bearish kind of guy, black beard, laid-back style. Luke dubs him Big Mike. He looks like he's good with kids. He talks with us alone, then he talks to Luke together with us, and then he spends many hours talking to Luke alone. He suggests that Luke take an IQ test and then an MMPI (Minnesota Multiphasic Personality Inventory) for adolescents.

I can't remember what Luke's exact IQ level was but he clearly tested well above average. No observer of Luke has ever questioned his basic intelligence. But the MMPI test was different, and was designed to uncover various elements of personality characteristics and potential disorders, all via several hundred true or false questions about feelings, desires, and attitudes such as, "Sometimes I feel the whole world hates me"—true or false. Or, "I would rather go fishing than go to a party"—true or false. Or, "Most people are inherently vicious—true or false." Following this test Big Mike privately delivers the blockbuster to us: Luke could be "borderline sociopath."

I am mortified, defenseless, ravaged at the very word, almost angry at Big Mike for bringing this clinically chilling term into our discussions of our son. He hastens to say that it is still an initial reading, at most a borderline case, and could go in any direction as he matures. Needless to say, we don't share these findings with Luke directly; I don't know exactly what Big Mike tells Luke and Luke doesn't go into details, but Big Mike's council to him is designed to encourage him to think more seriously and consciously about the implications of his actions.

Driven by growing anxiety—and yes, even fear—I turn to some basic readings in psychology myself, trembling about what I might uncover, about what a sociopathic personality, or psychopathic deviation might entail. And indeed, I find some worrisome overlaps with Luke's life. According to one account, in children with a potential antisocial personality disorder, three classical telltale characteristics are noted: a longer-than-usual period of bedwetting, cruelty to animals, and pyromania. I feel better on that score. While Luke did show an early fascination for fire, it seems to have lessened with age, and finally evolved into a simple fascination with fireworks—common to lots of young males. Bedwetting never fit, and mercifully, cruelty to animals was never present—on the contrary, his ties to Barney or other animals established by Prue are strong. So I had a slight sense of relief from that exploration.

But then I researched some other materials on Conduct Disorder that another psychiatrist later raised as a possibility. He told us that Adolescence Conduct Disorder is a common precursor to the emergence of a psychopathic or sociopathic personality—scary words. Conduct Disorder includes the presence of some, but not necessarily all, of the following criteria:

*Aggression to people and animals:*

*1. Often bullies people, threatens, or intimidates others.*

*2. Often initiates physical fights.*

*3. Has used a weapon that can cause serious physical harm to others (e.g., a bat, brick, broken bottle, knife, gun).*

*4. Has been physically cruel to people.*

*5. Has been physically cruel to animals.*

*6. Has stolen while confronting a victim (e.g., mugging, purse snatching, extortion, armed robbery).*

*7. Has forced someone into sexual activity.*

Thank God, not one of these most frightening and aggressive behaviors fit. But what if they had? What could we have done, how could we have handled nightmare characteristics like those with all their horrifying implications? But other criteria include:

*Destruction of property:*

*8. Has deliberately engaged in fire setting with the intention of causing serious damage.*

*9. Has deliberately destroyed others' property (other than by fire).*

Fire-setting, yes, but at a younger age and not repeated. Destruction of property was not a usual pattern; his paintballing and golf course spree seemed to have little to do with any sense of social resentments and more with grossly irresponsible joyriding.

*Deceitfulness or theft:*

*10. Has broken into someone else's house, building, or car.*

*11. Often lies to obtain goods or favors or to avoid obligations (i.e., "cons" others).*

*12. Has stolen items of nontrivial value without confronting a victim (e.g., shoplifting, but without breaking and entering; forgery).*

These all fit. That is disturbing. It goes on:

*Serious violations of rules:*

*13. Often stays out at night despite parental prohibitions, beginning before age 13 years*—nope, not Luke.

*14. Has run away from home overnight at least twice while living in parental or parental surrogate home (or once without returning for a lengthy period)*—not Luke again.

*15. Is often truant from school, beginning before age 13 years*—marginally applicable to Luke.

*B. The disturbance in behavior causes clinically significant impairment in social, academic, or occupational functioning*—yes, this definitely applies.

In the end, I'm left with an ambiguous pattern of behavior that resembles in some cases borderline sociopathy, but no clear match. No psychiatrist we saw was ready to make that firm diagnosis. On the other hand, as we were to learn years later, behavior due to a combination of Attention Deficit Hyperactivity Disorder and drug-driven theft seemed to provide a much more consistent explanation.

Yet Big Mike has raised some upsetting potential prospects. A dark seed has been planted in my mind that won't go away. I am scared. We are now on the edges of issues that seem potentially huge and destructive and beyond the capabilities of our home. How can we cope? How can we save Luke from himself? What shock can we deliver to his environment that will break a potentially destructive trajectory?

*      *      *

I am intrigued by Luke's strong interest in Pink Floyd's *The Wall*. He loves the album—why shouldn't he, it is part of the annals of classic rock—but his fascination with it seems to run deeper. He loves the animated film that was made for the music and he watches it a lot on VHS. We've seen it a number of times with him. Some great graphics and memorable scenes. I ask Luke why he likes it. It's good music he says, he likes the art in it. But that's about all he says. He draws a lot of the dragon-like creatures that appear in it in his notebooks. Good sketches, I note, some ability to draw.

But when you look into the story line of *The Wall*, there may be something that seems to resonate more deeply with him. It tells of a small boy who loses his father in the war, grows up unhappy and isolated at school, tyrannized by teachers in a kind of fascistic system who want him to conform. He is sensitive and can't take the pressure; he seeks to build up a wall to protect him from the world around him. As he grows up he gets into drugs as another form of self-protection, but his life turns to madness.

These aren't unique ideas of course, and many a teenager feels romantically misunderstood, oppressed by the process of growing up and facing society. So maybe it's just romantic sadness, isolation, rebellion that Luke feels here, but whatever it is, it speaks to him strongly through this album. I revisit the film periodically to sieve it for clues, even years later. I am distracted, spending ever more time and energy trying to track Luke's life, crack the code.

### December 1990 - London

A break, some real Christmas cheer. Samantha, and Melissa both join us and with Luke we all fly off to England on my accumulated air miles for two weeks to attend Prue's father's ninetieth birthday—"Pa" as he is known. Pa is Basil Handford, a Master of Latin and Greek at Lansing College in Sussex. The party foregathers at an old English country pub, dark timbers, stained glass, huge roaring fireplaces complete with hanging cauldron—the full monty—for a traditional, rustic, multi-course Elizabethan-style birthday meal.

A photo shows sixteen-year old Luke sitting at one of the tables wearing a party hat, engaged in conversation with other adults—something he's always been good at—a bit glassy-eyed, drinking a glass of hard cider, since English pubs don't seem to worry about drinking ages, holding his own in a non-adolescent environment.

We have fun walking around London as a family, the *de rigueur* photo on Westminster Bridge in front of Big Ben, our visits to a few pubs. Luke is great company, lots of wit and interest.

The ethnic character of Luke's adoptive family expands more vividly into Luke's consciousness with this first full dose of his English relatives on Prue's side, all together and on their home turf. Luke, this is your Auntie Ginny and Uncle William and Aunt Camilla. And these are your English cousins. Yes, Luke, along with your sisters you are "half English." Luke seems to take it all in good stride, clearly enjoys being in the UK. But how much does he really feel part of this cross-Atlantic family fest in which he finds himself? (He tucks this too away in his mental CV for future creative mining and posturing with new contacts.)

And the fiction of "family" is stretched ever thinner. I remember many years earlier when Luke, more innocent of the biological and genetic underpinnings of familyness, delivered an oral report in third grade in a session dedicated to sharing ethnic origins. Luke told his class that his family had "come to the US on the *Mayflower*"—only to be jeered down—"Come on, Luke, there weren't any Koreans on the *Mayflower!*" (There was a Fuller on board, no clue as to whether he was related, but Luke liked the idea.)

All Luke's English "relatives" seem to take to him. He's not a pimply adolescent, sullen and retiring, but a seemingly confident, good-looking young man comfortable in the company of adults and enjoying drinking with them. He's acquiring social skills. Prue and I instinctively collude in not passing along to most of the English relatives Luke's darker side, other than a few references to his occasional capacity to get into trouble. No one pries. But Luke's sisters are well informed about his doings; they are angry about it, observing the toll it takes on us.

And then another revealing insight into Luke's thinking, rarely vouchsafed to us: that night Luke and Larry, Samantha's significant other at the time, bunk down in the living room at the bottom of the stairs in Pa's house and they stay up late talking. The next day Larry draws me aside and recounts a conversation he had with Luke the night before. Larry had asked Luke about his biological father. Luke says he doesn't know anything about him. But, Luke says, he's imagined a situation where one day his father will come driving up in a fancy car, call out to Luke and say, "Son, I'm your father. Hop in." And Luke said, "You know what, I'd just laugh at him, turn around and walk back into the house." Wow! Does Luke mean this? He surely can't say it without some degree of pain. Luke has never shared this particular fantasy with us. In fact, he's scarcely ever mentioned the idea of a "father" at all, even though the subject of his mother has periodically come up. But still I can't help but speculate about what may go on in Luke's mind, what he maybe didn't spell out for Larry or us:

*My father is bound to have a big fancy car. He may not have cared about me, known about me even, but he wasn't a loser, not just some guy who happened to screw my mother and get her pregnant, but somebody who matters, who would have a fancy car, man about town. Maybe my father was a kind of Korean yakuza, a big-time underworld leader who ran whole parts of Daegu. Is he still alive? I wonder if he knows I was born, even conceived. Did he care? Would he think about looking me up someday if he could, track me down as his son, find out where I'm living? Would I really tell him to get lost if he found me? Who in hell do you think you are, I'd tell him, abandoning me to my fate? Why did it take you seventeen fucking years to get around to finding your own son? Well, I've got news for you, I've got a new family in the meantime, that does love me. Or if he showed up, maybe I would want to sit down with him and have it all out, maybe trying to make it up, forget the pain and mistakes of the past. Will he ever show up I wonder? But even if he does, I am now my own person, I don't need him, to hell with him.*

*And what does all of this make my mother? Was she a young girl who had a fling with this guy and got pregnant and couldn't handle it? Or, much more painful, was she just some slut who slept around? What would that make my father? Did my mother weep as she left me in a police box, upset that she couldn't take care of me? I can imagine how guilty she must feel now as she wonders where I am, where I went, whatever happened to me. Maybe she even tried to find out where I went after she left me in the police box, but the orphanage wouldn't tell her, just told her I'd gone to America. Or maybe she didn't give a shit either.*

*And she could never find me anyway. She wouldn't even know my name ...*

*Maybe I should just be grateful that she gave birth to me ... Is that a favor? How can I ever know these things?*

\*　　　　　\*　　　　　\*

We return after Christmas from our warm overseas flight from reality. We're barely back home a few days when on 3 January 1991—why am I not surprised?— Luke is again detained by the police and, incredibly, charged with involvement with two other people in what might be termed attempted theft of a vehicle. My notes from the arresting police officer:

Luke was involved with a guy who lives off forged credit cards. An attempted burglary took place at Oak Park. One of the three men says Luke was with them during the burglary. Luke and another allegedly tried to steal a

Jeep. The owner intercepted the action, and the guys ran off. The owner remembered a young "oriental" and quickly thereafter identified Luke from a police photo. Charges were later downgraded to attempted theft and Luke's role turns out to have been only as a bystander to the older guys. The arresting officer says Luke initially denied all involvement, yet hung his head and looked at the floor. But the officer feels Luke, unlike the other two, is redeemable, well-spoken, intelligent, can figure life out, was cooperative, polite with the authorities.

So Luke will serve instead as a witness for the police to the actions of the others. In the end, he is mercifully let off for playing no substantive part of the incident, but put on probation. But how in hell does he come by these companions? Does he feel this is his natural environment, for God's sake?

What are the possible alternative mindsets in Luke's head behind all this— as he gets drawn into these unsavory incidents and associations?

*Screw my parents. I'm going to do what I want. All that matters in this world is me. I want mine. I don't owe the world a goddam thing. It owes me.*

But that just isn't Luke in our view. By all indications he does care about us, and he doesn't seem to be all about acquisition, he doesn't seem angry at the world. He doesn't express bitterness about life; on the contrary, he's fairly sunny except when he's coming off pot, when he can be sometimes surly.

*I'm bored. This is exciting. I'll take it as it comes. Right now these guys are into some cool shit. I can learn some stuff about how to deal with stolen credit cards that might be useful. They're good to have some kicks with. I don't have to spend my life with them. They're not that smart. And I can pick and choose what I get involved in. I want to be spontaneous, live for the moment. Let's go with the action. I don't think I'm going to get caught. I'll try to keep my parents out of all of this.*

Yeah, that one seems to fit more closely. That's maybe as close as I can get to the rationale of Luke's mind, for now. But what does Luke have to show for all of this grief—no loot, no toys, no money, no car, no girlfriends, no fun in life—what is he getting out of it? Or is he just reacting to what comes down the pike, no plan, no consideration, just impulse? Is this the best he can manage for himself right now?

By God, I'm determined I'm going to break this pattern wide open.

# CHAPTER EIGHT

# BE FREE

## *1991 - Thousand Oaks California*

It's eight on a January morning in 1991 and I'm not looking forward to the day. Prue, Luke and I merge onto Freeway 101 heading north to the county seat of Ventura. We turn into a huge parking lot in front of a soulless granite building whose gray federal-style architecture houses the machinery of Ventura County's legal system. The Law moves more slowly than Luke does, but it does move and it's drawing us into its orbit ever more closely.

The Law has now formally assigned Luke a probation officer whom we are about to meet. I had never really expected that I would come to develop a certain expertise on the workings of the juvenile legal system in California. Or its drug prevention programs. But this officer is just a piece of a larger order of the Law's acolytes and priests; we are gradually being introduced into their presence and their rituals. And they—increasingly, collectively—start to preside over Luke's fate.

We walk through the central pavilion past the armed security guards, trying to make sense of the maze of corridors as we slink down the halls of marble, past the rows of intimidatingly high solid wooden doors, all identical, numbered, and closed, concealing behind them their dismal proceedings. The corridors are populated by sullen, unhappy, intimidated teenagers, many in hip-hop outfits, pants sagging off the hips, boxer shorts in full display, bunched-up dragging cuffs, black woolen caps. But there's none of the 'hood's cheekiness, strut and self-confidence here, no spirit of confrontation; they feign disinterest in where they are, lounging along wooden benches, half asleep if they can manage, as they wait for their judgments to be reached in the chambers within. Alongside them are parents—actually mostly just mothers— faces sad, tired, lined, fulfilling their biologically-assigned role of comfort giver, protector of family and conscience of society; their very presence is an acknowledgment of the propriety of the Law's demands. Perhaps, like us, they are all desperately hoping to save some semblance of family honor as well. Many exchanges are in Spanish. Our family isn't from the 'hood, our lives have perhaps been a good bit luckier than many who live there, but I'm kidding myself if I think we're really any different. Adolescent trouble is an equal opportunity affliction. It's the great leveler, even if Luke's case is probably not as grave as those of some of the other teens here. We are just like them; we're fully part of the scene, just another set of parents whose boy is in trouble with the Law.

We find room 232 and knock on the paneled door marked with a plaque: Probation Officer, C. Gonzales. We enter and a middle-aged woman rises to meet us. Ms. Gonzales is a small, alert, sensible-looking woman who looks like she knows a thing or two. We fill her in briefly on Luke's legal problems. She nods impatiently, "Thank you, Mr. Fuller, I've read the file and I'm aware of the basic facts. This is a very straightforward matter right now. I'm here to let you and Luke know the terms of his probation. I'm also aware also of the more serious charges pending right now in Orange County on the golf course case. But today we are here for the marijuana charge in Luke's file and its legal consequences." Without further discussion Ms. Gonzales directs Luke to fulfill thirty-two hours of community service. Luke, of course, has been that route before.

But there is more. "Luke, because you have been detained on a charge not only of possession of marijuana, but also involvement in selling it to others, you are now required, by law, to attend a formal substance abuse program designated for youthful offenders. In place of pressing formal charges I am mandating your attendance at a local program in Thousand Oaks called Be Free, starting immediately."

This is the first we have heard of Be Free. I don't realize it yet, but Be Free will demand more of our time, attention and our very selves and our lives than we had ever anticipated. Meanwhile, there is really nothing further to discuss here; the offense is evident, our marching orders are clear. Ms. Gonzales reminds us she will monitor Luke's progress in the program. We are now to proceed immediately to the Be Free office in Thousand Oaks to register.

We are not the only family in the reception area—it seems to be a commonly frequented, not to say popular program. We sit down with a psychologist who briefs us on the particulars. "Luke, you will be required to attend Be Free meetings every Tuesday and Thursday evening. That's every week. Meetings will run about two hours and will include group discussion among kids your own age. I'll be seeing you regularly in the sessions … And you, Mr. and Mrs. Fuller, are also required to attend Be Free meetings on the same evenings. Luke may be the one on the drugs, but you as a family are all afflicted by a drug problem. We are looking at the impact of drugs upon the entire family. Your meeting with the parents of the other kids is held simultaneously in the same building. We expect both parents to attend. If you do not attend regularly, Luke will not be able to obtain release from the program."

A twice-a-week drug program for us? I expected as parents to be interested and involved, sure, but not like this. The seriousness of the program sinks in as the psychologist asks us to read, acknowledge and sign a series of eight stark propositions about our own circumstances.

• *We admit that mind-altering chemicals have caused our families to become unmanageable.*

• *We recognize that our usual resources are powerless to free our families from the abuse of these chemicals, and that our old solutions are not working to resolve our new problem.*

• *We seek to be empowered as parents; we resolve to take charge of our households.*

• *We open ourselves to strength from a higher power and the support of the group.*

• *We will make a searching and fearless inventory of our family dynamic.*

• *After fearlessly examining our family system, we are willing to change what needs to be changed, starting with ourselves, and reinforce the current strength of the family.*

• *We continue to look at ourselves and, when wrong, promptly admit it.*

• *Helped by a higher power expressed through the group, we willingly help others through understanding and love.*

Luke is sobered as his future life is rolled out in front of him in detail. "Man, this is going to be a real drag," he groans. But he doesn't seriously resist. Nor does he have much choice.

And promptly, next Tuesday evening, Prue and I find ourselves walking into a classroom at the local middle school to join with some eight other couples sitting around in a circle. Each of us is seated in an individual student desk, slightly undersized, maybe appropriate to our reduced status and options. The smell of the cleaning compound in the hallways, the posted signs, the green chalk boards, the smell of chalk and the class-room setting— all spark a flashback to my own years as a middle school student, seated before an authority figure. Having failed as a family in the real world outside—at least in this part of our lives—here we are all back in school again, learning how to manage our family lives and handle our kids. Luke is in the classroom next door, at his own meeting with his peers.

A woman in her mid-thirties in blue jeans and a light sweater steps forward. "Hi, I'm Suzanne. I'm a family psychologist and I'll be in charge of this meeting tonight." Suzanne looks professional but makes an effort to be casual, welcoming. There is a male psychologist present as well who is introduced as a specialist on addiction. Suzanne welcomes Prue and myself, asks us to introduce ourselves to the group. People greet us by name in response: "Hello, Graham, hello, Prue." Suzanne asks us to present as candid a summary as we can of our own situation with Luke and how we got here. Not quite "Hi, I'm Graham and I'm an alcoholic," but not too far off. "Hi, we're the Fullers and our son is getting more and more deeply into pot, maybe even something heavier on occasion. He's gotten into trouble with the law as a result. It looks like he may be drifting into theft to support the habit. We no longer feel we know how to handle it." I sketch out Luke's background, his history with drug use as we understand it. Several parents nod sympathetically, "Yes, that's like what we experienced with Josh at that stage," one says.

Then come a barrage of questions—not from Suzanne or the addiction expert, but from the other parents—how old is Luke, how old was he when he was adopted, when did he start smoking cigarettes, smoking pot or drinking alcohol as far as we know? How are you guys feeling about being here? The questions are direct, but the faces and voices are sympathetic, supportive, open; they sound like they have all been where we are.

Suzanne quickly reviews the philosophy behind Be Free. "We don't see the kids alone as the whole of the problem. Each family, in the presence of their kid's substance abuse, has frankly now become a partially *dysfunctional unit.* Each of your families has its own particular dynamic from which the problem emerged. So the problem requires analysis and treatment as a family unit, not just the problem child alone." *We have become a dysfunctional family?* Yes, demonstrably—we're having trouble with Luke and the Law, that's why we're here. "We're going to ask you to openly examine yourselves in a group setting just like our kids are doing on their own next door," Suzanne informs us.

Each of the families updates their report on how their family, including the problem kid, is doing since the last session. We soon learn the names of all kids involved and the family circumstances around each of them.

"Ricky relapsed this week. We were sitting outside the house and caught a whiff of pot coming from his open window. When we confronted him, he stormed out of the house and didn't come back until well after midnight, clearly drunk as well. He gave us a lot of lip, said that he had a right to live his own life as he wanted ..." His mother stares down at the floor for a moment. "We're really very disappointed. You remember how things had been going pretty well in the previous weeks on the new discipline. We're not sure how hard to come down on him at this point. But he's missed three days of school."

"Well, that's like what happened with Maria a few months ago," a man across the circle says. "But since it came after a long period of good behavior, we didn't throw the book at her right off. We did warn her that we will have to renegotiate the rules if it happens again. That seemed to have taken care of it for now … Sometimes it pays to avoid confrontation if you can."

"This has been a good week with Carl. He's been at dinner with us each night, been in a good mood, talked about high school, and actually did the dishes. He's getting back into his sports more. He's been making an effort not to quarrel with his brother, and he's dropped some of his sarcasm. We're feeling better."

"Well, with Jonathan, this program has so far been great for us. But we worry about the type of friends he hangs out with. None of them are in any program. I don't think half their parents are even on top of the situation. We think Jonathan can do OK on his own, but these friends are no good. We're afraid it's a matter of time before they drag him into pot again. But how do we break him away from them? We're not sure how to do it … At least Be Free is helping re-orient his social life—for part of the time."

A single father speaks up. "In our family we don't see any way of pulling Jenny out of the grip of these drugs—other than sending her off to the closed rehab facility in Utah. She rejects all our efforts to establish rules, and our framework of agreement. She refused to come to the meeting again tonight. If she were in Utah she wouldn't have the freedom to quit the program. I've tried everything else here, but it just doesn't seem to work … she keeps falling back into the same old habits. I haven't seen any actual evidence of pot use this week, except she's gotten very sullen and uncommunicative again… I'm scared there are some indications that she … well, she may be trying heroin. I don't know how far I can press the discipline without breaking my control over her. Such as it is."

Most of the kids involved are boys, but there are a few girls as well. The families are almost all white upper middle class professionals. Where are the racial minorities and lower income families? Maybe they're into a whole different social environment. Many people may not be able to afford the program either; it's not cheap, although our medical insurance program, as with the other families, will cover a significant portion of the cost. We're learning: if it costs money to buy drugs, it costs a lot more to stop buying them.

Two hours go by before I even notice—time is up for tonight. We're reminded of the Saturday night social get-together on the weekend—mandatory—of all the kids and families and who will be hosting it. We then all stand up and form a circle in the middle of the room. Watching the others, Prue and I awkwardly extend our hands to the person on each side of us as we hold hands for a moment of silence. We thank each other collectively for the help offered to each other. Then we recite the Alcoholics Anonymous Prayer: "Grant me the courage to change the things I can change, the serenity to accept the things I cannot change, and the wisdom to know the difference." I'm struck by the formulation of the prayer. Whether or not one is religious, this is a pretty good summation of our need. I really feel like I've been through an emotional experience here tonight. It's hard not to feel some comfort in the warmth and purposefulness of the group—a kind of instant bonding with strangers. We are not alone, nor are we unique.

Out in the hallway a few minutes later Luke bursts out of the door with his own group, all fairly boisterous. He seems in excellent spirits. He says goodbye to many of the kids by name, "Catch you next session, man." High fives. As we ride home, I can feel the positive vibes coming out of him. "How was it, Luke?" "Oh, it was cool," he says, "and I liked the kids. They were really friendly." "So what did you talk about?" "Oh, we just all talked about this and that, what drugs we had tried, and, you know, like the problems we have from them and stuff—and the problems for our families … I didn't know what to expect, but I like the kids in there and there was no bullshit, not even from the psychologist … How did you guys do?" "Pretty good," I say, "a lot of concerned parents who don't have very many answers to their kids' problems, but are struggling to find them … and thinking about how we might have screwed up as parents, too." Luke takes it in. "Yeah?" Then a moment later, "I am kind of worried about the Saturday night party, though, Ba," he adds, "it sounds like it may be kind of lame." "Well, we'll find out," I reply. "I'm not sure it's going to be all that fun for us either … You know the parents aren't supposed to drink at the party either." "Really?" Luke comments, "Wow, that's hard core."

*     *     *

Welcome to the world of the piss-test. Like other parents we're regularly taking Luke off to the local lab for urine sample tests for pot. Be Free cannily adheres to the old Ronald Reagan maxim on nuclear agreements with the Soviet Union: trust, but verify. Luke's file is now filled with lab test reports, the parents' copy, appropriately, on yellow paper, documenting the chemical content of his latest offering. Luke grumbles but submits; the results show periods of testing clean, punctuated by occasional lapses. Luke is also learning the lore of piss-test deception from his friends; he tells us all about it quite openly and with amusement—marathon glasses of boiled goldenseal herb tea consumed twenty-four hours before the test supposedly wipes away traces of lapses. Just urban legend, says Be Free. Luke is amazingly open on all of this, talks at length about his group and what people are serious and who is cheating; he seems almost to be *enjoying* being part of it all.

These Be Free sessions aren't easy. Many of them involve examination of particular facets of ourselves, our family situation, our overall predicament. Our discussions are blunt, intrusive, sometimes raw. At one session we examine our marriage relationships as they affect the drug situation.

"Graham," the psychologist asks, "are you, or is Prue, the one more likely to 'defend' Luke or to downplay the seriousness of his condition?"

"I guess it's me," I say.

"It's definitely you," Prue comments: I am too unwilling to take the bad news seriously enough, I defend him against some of her expressions of concern, or from the anger of Samantha and Melissa when they are around.

"Do you quarrel between yourselves over how to understand his condition? Or how to handle it?"

"Yes, sometimes we do quarrel about it."

"How does Luke's situation affect the personal relationship between Prue and yourself?"

"Well," I say, "it can create anger, frustration. Sometimes even blame about what one or the other of us should be doing."

"Yes, Prue adds, "I feel like I'm sometimes afraid to talk about it with Graham anymore, for fear of getting into an unpleasant fight."

"OK," I say, "I do feel sensitive on the issue ... and trapped, and I don't know what more to say ... But I'm listening, I'm trying to listen. I don't think either of us believes there's any magic answer out there. And maybe, maybe this problem helps bring us together in another way ... as we realize the seriousness of our problem, so we can try to work for solutions."

We are asked to consider what quality most requires change in *ourselves*. This really requires a lot of examination. I need to open my eyes more, be more beady-eyed, more suspicious. "I think we should be stricter on penalties," Prue says, "but I agree, there's no easy way to enforce rules ... Maybe some of them we can't even enforce." These questions are all examined as a group. Our collective anguish and helplessness are laid out for all to see, shared.

Prue and I have never been in a group therapy like this before. We find ourselves baring our souls to others, saying things that we may not have even said or admitted previously to each other quite that openly. Our angers, fears, acknowledgment of shortcomings, weaknesses. "You know," Prue says, turning to me, "you can be a domestic dictator, that doesn't help in this problem. Sometimes you dismiss my proposals, or even ride roughshod over my space." "OK," I sigh ruefully, "you're probably right, I accept that. I'm sorry. I guess I do have that tendency and I try to fight it. But I also get frustrated when you don't communicate your own feelings and preferences enough to contribute to a solution. If you want a stronger voice in this then you should be asserting your own role more, more ideas of your own. I feel sometimes like I am the only one to bear the burden, to come up with the ideas."

It comes pouring on out. "And I'm concerned," Prue says, "that our daughters sometimes get the short end of the stick in all this, given the time and attention and traumas with Luke in recent years. I think they feel partially left out of your range of concerns, especially before they went off to college. And I think you're sometimes naïve about what Luke is likely to do ... You know, you push Luke hard to 'talk' about these things, but talk isn't always the answer. You can be too talkative, you love to theorize, and you can wear people out with your enthusiasms and your new schemes for Luke. Sometimes you don't know when enough is enough." I melt back into my chair in silent pain.

But at home we acknowledge that the Be Free process has strengthened our marriage, it lets us speak with greater frankness on core issues than perhaps we ever have before—and may not again to quite that extent. Be Free at least gives us permission to talk openly, to know that, in the end, we cannot manage the life of a druggie. All we can do is try to manage our own lives, our own ability to cope, persevere, and to create the best atmosphere for Luke to help himself. The strange liberation of facing reality.

Other families talk about their own dynamics. Of course they all come from differing backgrounds, different experiences and circumstances. But we're all on level ground here; one family's success offers an insight for the rest of us. Interestingly, nobody gives a damn about each other's professional personas or credentials here. *Our problems are who we are.*

"You have to realize that a drug user in the family affects *all* the interrelationships of the family," the psychologist reminds us. We try to inventory how it has affected the other kids in our families. At another session we are all urged to consider what parts of our own family lives might have contributed to our children's turn to drugs. One father admits that he is too much of a workaholic, that he probably hasn't devoted enough time to being with his son. "I hate to say it, but I'm not sure I always feel comfortable with my son, I don't know what to talk about with him." Phil says, "My son is surrounded by bad friends, that's the problem. I mean it really bugs me … I can't stand them, I feel like they're mocking me … they humiliate me with their smirks. They're the ones dragging him into this stuff." But our group, ever able to scent the self-serving line, suggests that maybe his son is *choosing* the bad friends. We see that in Luke, too. *What* bad influences on Luke? Maybe Luke is the bad influence.

A new couple joins us one night; the wife weeps as the father tries to explain the situation. "I'm not sure we should even be here. Our kid has tried pot only a few times, it's nothing serious. We've warned him, and I don't think he'll do it again." They don't really have a problem, they protest. They don't want to be here, they were just required by the court to come to the meeting, which they hope to get over and done with soon. Man, they are asking for it. They don't even realize how they're tossing out big hunks of juicy red meat before us hungry lions. By now we're hard-schooled, and one by one we interrogate this couple about their realities. We know all the stories, the alibis, the telltale signs, all the rationalizations and justifications; the psychologist running the meeting doesn't have to say a word, she just sits back while we let the father have it. We tell him he's in denial, he's got to face up to some hard facts. He squirms. And they don't come back again to the next session. But that's unusual, most parents hang in.

The term "in denial" is of course now part of our society's psycho-babble culture, working its way out from the psychiatrist's couch onto Oprah. It can mean different things. Am I in denial about Luke? Surely not, I know we have a problem, we go to court, we put him in programs, schools, talk to psychiatrists, try multiple approaches, I'm thinking about it all the time. OK, the psychologist says, but am I kidding myself about my own ability to bring about change? Am I really denying, as one of the Be Free propositions puts it, that my "usual resources are powerless to free our families, that our old solutions are not working to resolve our new problem"? I plead guilty. But I still think I can find some way out of this.

The program grinds inexorably on week after week, biting deeper, bruising egos and aspirations, touching our personal lives—and providing some laughs in the midst of all this rueful self-examination. One evening we examine our own relationships to "mind-altering substances." "Come on, now," the psychologist says, "let's bring it home. Do we smoke cigarettes? Are we hooked on them? Or do we sometimes have a little 'picker-upper,' our little glass of scotch when we get home from work at night before dinner? Maybe every single night? And is it just one? Even if it is only one, don't we look forward to having it? Just *how much* do we look forward to having it?" At that point we've clearly stumbled across Arnaud's red line of irritation—"Look, come on, that's not being hooked, it's just a harmless pleasure. Why not?" "OK," says the psychologist, "but what if you couldn't have your little pleasure for a whole week? Or a month? Is it possible that we are perhaps sliding subtly into some form of 'dependence' ourselves, however slight, in the way we define having a good time?" The discussion busts wide open. Tony weighs in with some vehemence: "Look, let's get something straight here; it's one thing to use these 'substances' as you call them. But don't forget—we lead normal lives. We're productive citizens. We're handling these things with moderation. It's another thing to be hooked on them like our kids." "OK, fair enough," the psychologist rejoins, "I'm just trying to put it into perspective for you a little bit, make you look at it a different way. But just remember, our goal here is to keep our kids *totally* clean, drug-free. In their condition there is no such thing as a 'moderate'' approach to drug or alcohol usage. Zero tolerance is the goal."

Cigarettes are the program's only compromise with reality; there has to be some kind of outlet for the kids, and there's a lot of smoking going on among all of them. Luke has been smoking cigarettes now openly since about fourteen; we don't like it for many reasons including health, but we know we can't really stop it, except inside the house. His clothes all reek permanently of smoke.

Then the psychologist really sticks it to us. "Maybe we might get a better idea of what our kids are going through," he suggests, "if we considered remaining 'clean' ourselves for the duration of the program, if only as a sign of solidarity with them. No booze … Strictly voluntary, of course." "Wait one goddam minute here," Ralph says, "I'm not the one who's abusing substances, I'm not the one in trouble with the law. I don't even drink that much." "OK," the psychologist responds, "then it should be no biggie to come home from work and give up the occasional picker-upper before dinner. Or when you go out to a restaurant on Saturday night to completely abstain, maybe for the next few months?" "Let's get real," Tony protests, "this program has already placed big demands on us in time and effort. This is just too damn much. I don't think my son is going to change his behavior just because he sees me giving up a scotch and water every evening for a month. I don't think this is central to the program and I, frankly, don't want to go there." "No problem," the psychologist says, "just a thought." But after we get home, Prue and I talk it over and agree maybe we should give up alcohol for a while as a self-challenge, just to get a sense of it, and to show Luke we're committed to the program.

So it is with a small degree of concern that I, as a really mild drinker, a glass or two of wine or beer once or twice a week at most, note that abstention from all alcohol *does* seem to negatively impact my full sense of enjoyment, especially when we go to a restaurant, and I can't have a good microbrew or a glass of Chardonnay. This is unnerving. Is my pleasure at the restaurant psychologically dependent upon this substance called alcohol? I feel I might be getting a glimpse into what it means to be dependent, however slightly.

And then, yes, there are the Be Free Saturday nights. Saturday night—the very words redolent of the big night on the town, big time good time. But no more. Be Free has co-opted the institution with its own Saturday evening socials, where our parent group comes together to party—soberly—with their kids.

Tonight we're going to the Inderfurths. We really like them, they're both artists, creative people. They have a rustic home, much of it in adobe style, with lots of rough natural wood Mexican-style furniture, Native American-style rugs on the tile floors, cactuses and vines growing around their house; it perches over a small canyon in the back. Their oldest son is gay, not a big deal, but, heartbreakingly, he is in prison for third degree murder, for knifing a man in what seemed like clear self-defense when he was being harassed and beaten up by a homophobic group outside a nightspot. It is a painful burden for them as they go and visit him in prison on weekends. But it isn't their son in prison who is the problem now, but their fifteen-year-old son at home who has been traumatized by events, the one who is using and in the Be Free program. These are wrenching human stories whose endings have not yet been written. How does this painful shadow of murder and prison impact this family and the younger son?

But, despite the somewhat compulsory character of the evening, we do actually have a good time. The party is potluck (an ill-chosen term), and we've each brought a dish. The Inderfurths put out some good Mexican-style cheese and olive dips and eats and we sit around the big rough-hewn table. There are a lot of laughs at our predicaments. "I'm afraid I don't dare mention at the office how I spent my Saturday night, it's not good for my swinging youthful image," he jokes. Another father wonders, "Am I punishing my son, or is he punishing me? Or maybe we're just bonding over common mutual misery."

And our talk also turns to many other things beyond the obsessive focus about our kids and drugs.

Rock music is playing in the background and the kids too crowd in around the table with us for some food. They actually do seem to be having a good time, and are bonding as they go through these intensive sessions of self-revelation together. It's interesting to meet face to face with all the other kids whose lives, intimate secrets, vices and peccadilloes we all now know a good bit about. Nearly all of them seem like "good kids," nice to talk to, responsive, fairly open. Quite a lot of the parents spend time with some of the other kids present, as we do. Part of the point of these socials is, of course, to keep the kids away from darker pursuits and shady pals and to demonstrate that it is possible to have a good time without any "chemical support." Some of the kids are dancing, playing music, board games. Even the addiction of TV is absent here tonight.

A few weeks later we sponsor the Saturday party at our house. Luke is all psyched up to arrange it, and he whips out pans to do a lot of the cooking for it himself. Luke is in as good a mood as I've seen him in quite a while, warm to us, happy-go-lucky mood. "Check it out, Ba, taste these Korean burgers I made." Aside from the potluck we have a barbecue, play guitar, sing, kids swim in the pool, sit around and tell stories. Nobody hangs back in sullen isolation.

So what is it? Artificial, phony togetherness? Mr. Clean fantasy world here, everyone reveling in the questionable joys of good clean fun? Was a good time had by all? Sometimes I think what *Saturday Night Live* could do with an evening like this, adults sitting around with the strained smiles pretending to "have fun" without booze. Like standing around in a nudist colony with everyone pretending not to notice. And it does on occasion seem slightly unreal, a little forced—but the task at hand is deadly real, that's why we're here, for God's sake. "Yeah," says Simon, "probably most of us would rather be sailing, as the bumper sticker says. But we'd rather our kids were clean too, and not blotto or in jail." This cloistered artificial world that we have willingly created for ourselves in Be Free is not a flight to a Peter Pan Never-Never Land; it's simply the cost for a lot of committed people to attain goals that are important to our families' survival. The bonding is powerful. That's what prevents these Saturday night socials from becoming smirky little pretends that we're all having fun. Fun is *irrelevant*.

I'm amazed I don't even find the kids cynical about all of this zealous undertaking. Luke doesn't roll his eyes when the meetings or Saturday socials come up. He's happy to go off to them. I wouldn't think it's any kind of cool scene for the kids here, but most of them know that some kind of serious shit is going down in their lives, and that they are in need of help. Would they all split from the program if they could? Possibly. But it doesn't seem to take much to keep them in the program, at least officially. Luke knows we're not just packing him off to "his" meeting. It's "our" meeting—and yes, we too could think of better things to do with our evenings, all other things being equal.

Bit by bit we learn more of the stories. The daughter of the Spauldings is only fourteen; she has been into really hard stuff including heroin for a while, out of control, had to be physically restrained. She has been in a local resident rehab session but she skipped out of it and took up drugs again. California will not allow a minor to be physically restrained or locked in except by a judge's decision. So she has now gone off to a "closed" facility in Utah, where it is permitted, because she isn't responding sufficiently to the lighter hand of Be Free. Her father says she accepted it willingly; she too wants to get out of this snare she's in. But he keeps coming himself to the meetings to keep us abreast with what's going on with his daughter, and to maintain membership—and even the moral support—in the group. Actually, compared to some of these cases, Luke seems to be in less desperate circumstances.

The son of the Birnbaums is heavily into alcohol and pot. He is fifteen. The deeper family tragedy is that his brother committed suicide two years ago, at age seventeen. The boy Josh was traumatized; it's hard to know how much this is the issue that is behind his drug use. The parents understandably writhe in anguish and terror that their second son might take a similar path. They are hungry for ideas, suggestions from any of us.

The Dalton's daughter has been smoking pot "recreationally" for some six months now. She is still doing pretty well in school, and is a very poised girl from what we can see. Her parents hope that preemptive measures will keep her case from getting any further out of hand. They think participation in the program and its heavy intervention into her life will make her get more serious about it, realize the potential costs.

Another father, Ralph, tells me he's impressed with Luke. "I think you've got a good, decent kid there," he says. "I like his directness and his humor. He seems comfortable talking to adults. I think he's going to make it." I swell with pride, like I've just received a dispensation from the governor of the state.

Few stones are left unturned as we search for techniques that work. One approach is to draw up actual contracts with our kids, a key Be Free technique. These aren't just guidelines, "thank-you-for-not-doing-drugs"-type things; they're firm, clear, explicit terms of agreement—"you-deliver, I-deliver"-language, with built-in detailed incentives and penalties spelled out for violating agreed-upon family rules and procedures. It's designed to take away some of the guesswork, to spare us and our kids from having to wing it on every behavioral situation that comes up.

"You know what we ended up doing?" one mother offers. "We warned Josh that we would take away his phone [the land line—mass cell phones weren't yet around] if he didn't start shaping up. And we did have to take it out. He was really pissed, but he got the message and things started to change. You might also tell Luke, if you think he is dealing in drugs, that you are going to listen in on his calls. Believe me, it will crimp his style. For that matter, all this technology, TV in his room, CD players, whatever, they are all items you can threaten to remove. These items matter to kids."

I'm not sure I like all this police state stuff, but if that's what it takes, we're going to have to consider it all. "We went further with Jonathan," a father offers. "We first took the lock off his door, especially when we thought he was sometimes smoking pot in his room. When that didn't work we actually took the door off its hinges. It was a devastating loss of privacy to him to have no door, but we got his attention. Shortly after that we were able to negotiate a 'deal" to get the door back on."

"And clothing," Arnaud mentions. "One psychologist we saw said that in many rehab institutions none of the kids are allowed to wear black. He said kids see them as some kind of a symbol of darker drug culture. You can show how bad you are by dressing up in a goth uniform to upset bourgeois-minded adults. So you might want to consider not letting your kid wear black as his daily uniform. I think it does kind of promote an anti-social attitude that works against this drug program." Prue and I later consider whether we should try to discourage black clothes for Luke—his favorite. But do we want to take on color of clothing in the midst of a lot more urgent problems? Same with hairstyles. While long hair (at that time) did express a certain attitude, we were quite willing to let it go in favor of the bigger goals.

In the end, it's like fishing. All of these penalties and threats are really just like using a light-weight line. You need a deft hand and a gentle pressure—first yielding and then cautiously reeling in, yielding again and reeling in again, making sure the hook is always set. If you pull too hard, use too much strength, the line breaks, the hook tears out, the fish is gone and all the strength in the world is of no avail. Same delicate balance with these contracts and penalties with our kids. Do you have the sensitivity to feel the limits beyond which even parental authority cannot be pushed? Whatever little modest moral authority we have is easily squandered, wasted, can get mocked, shredded, irretrievably lost. But how can I know whether our guidelines for Luke are enough to save him from himself? Does an ideal tension on the line even exist—one that will give him the freedom he wants and yet protect him from catastrophe? Seat-of-the-pants navigation here.

One day at one of the private sessions with just Luke, ourselves and two psychologists present, we are asked what gift we would give each other if we could. "That's a hard one," I say, "but Luke, I guess I would want to give you a strong sense of curiosity." Perhaps not a very exciting gift in Luke's eyes, but it may sum up my sense of how to approach life, with a thirst for experience, zest for knowledge, and an interest in everything around us. It's the opposite of apathy and boredom—those demons that I see lurking in his soul, sapping his energy, his self-control, sense of direction and purpose. "Luke," I say, "that's what really bugs me about this booze and drugs, they don't stimulate an excitement for life at all, they just inhibit it, drown it. I'm afraid I see you as a cork bobbing on the waves, going where wind and currents take you, and not because *you* want to go someplace. I wish you would decide what *you* want." Prue says she wishes for Luke a sense of peace, to escape from being driven by his demons. "Luke, what about you, what gift would you give?" the psychologist asks. "I don't know … I guess I'd like to give my parents the freedom not to worry about me," he says.

Strangely, we are never at loggerheads with Luke at these sessions. No shouting, no mutual recriminations whatsoever. We feel close, it's more like sharing a mutual pain imposed on all of us.

And Prue always sees me clearly in my limitations, especially with Luke. Sometimes I get just plain pissed-off when I'm trying to get close to this kid, understand him, fathom his motives and thoughts, but he often remains elusive, fobs me off with generalities, or brief responses, avoids a good emotional/intellectual wallow, tell-it-all, articulate your feelings in depth, blah, blah. That's probably precisely his goal: he's shielding himself, keeping me from getting too close to his inner life and its secrets.

For better or for worse my genes come from a really talkative family that loves to articulate things. With Samantha and Melissa I can sit down and talk for hours about books we've read, ideas we've had, events we see, movies, discussions about the nature of the world, politics, a lot of easy laughs and interchange, including some issues of personal feelings, discussions of why people behave the way they do. And, as I've gotten older, I find it slowly easier and more vital to get into talk of emotions as well.

Ironically I find my own slow, painful learning curve here also starts to affect my relationship with *my* father. He's become slightly more open after my mother's death. But still I feel growing irritation with him; he seems simply unable to bridge that boundary of the intellect, however loving he is in his own way. He always seems to make sure the conversation focuses around objective things out there in the world—mostly about his life in the arts and feeling about movies, or books or politics, but precious little about his feelings. My grown daughters will now still fault my parenting style as having been sometimes emotionally aloof, even while being hands-on engaged in all other details of doing things together, sharing their interests. But low on the intimacy.

And yet, knowing all this, I find myself on a few occasions slipping into an immature, almost petulant state of mind with Luke; when he won't communicate with me, by God I'll give him the silent treatment back, I won't volunteer anything anymore, I'll answer his questions with only the briefest, coolest of responses or remarks, avoid interchange. Then he'll eventually come to Prue and say, "Why is Baba pissed off at me?" And she says, "Because he wants you to talk to him, and you don't." Luke is a bit puzzled by all of this. What's this big urge to talk things out ad nauseam? He isn't a Fuller anyway, with a deep urge to say it, to derive pleasure from the sheer articulation of it all. Prue keeps telling me, "Remember, Luke's not you!" Good advice, I intellectually understand it but emotionally it's different; I feel deprived, her admonitions require constant reiteration. It's this kid's misfortune that chance landed him up in the midst of a lot of compulsive talkers—word people. And three goddam psychologists in the family as well. I guess I'll have to settle for the physical, matey slow-punch to the gut from Luke and read volumes of affection and words into it.

*      *      *

OK. I'm going to get off this kick of wanting to talk issues out. It's clear that *doing* things with Luke is far more beneficial. I find out there's a course in scuba diving offered nearby in Ventura. Prue and I had learned to scuba dive when we spent three years living in Jeddah, Saudi Arabia, just after Samantha and Melissa were born. While we never took a formal course of accreditation, we logged hundreds of hours diving in the company of experienced divers in the Red Sea. We'd told Luke tales about our diving exploits in Jeddah, our occasional shark encounters and shown him some of our underwater slides, including one of Prue with her anti-shark bang stick while a shark hovers in the background. "Way cool," Luke says, honoring us.

What better bonding experience with my son, now seventeen? Luke is enthusiastic so we sign up. Unfortunately, I'll have to miss the first and second class of the twelve-week course since I've got to be in the Middle East on a RAND project. But with my many years of diving experience—even if it was twenty years ago—it should be no big deal to miss the opening.

But it is a big deal for the instructor. When I show up for the third class, it turns out much of the equipment is new, unfamiliar to me; I'm not doing it right, and even though the first half of the course is all in a big municipal pool, I'm much less quick at these things than I used to be. The instructor rides me hard in front of the others: what makes me think I can blow off the first two critical sessions of the course? He says he may force me to wait till the next cycle of the course to start over. I apologize, tell him I really want to do this with Luke, it's important. He relents, but he's still tough on me.

Luke is my diving buddy for the class—everybody has to have a buddy. Luke's a natural at it, takes to the equipment fast. But typically he's somewhat slap-dash at the written work—calculating dive tables, how long you can safely stay down at what depth, what chemical changes take place in the blood stream that might be dangerous, how to avoid getting a fatal embolism in the blood stream—boring life-or-death stuff. I point out to him too that pot and diving sound like a bad combination. "Don't you think I know better than to do that?" he says. He's amused at my slowness and clumsiness on some of the equipment, but he is patient, caring and helpful with me and attentive in helping keep the instructor off my back. Am I having fun yet? No, not much with the harassment of the instructor, but it's great doing it with Luke and we have a good time together. It's great that this is something *he's* good at, even as I flounder, struggle to keep up. He's thoughtful, solicitous of my predicament, gives generously of himself in imparting his skills to *me*.

For the last four weeks of the course we go down to the beach in Ventura each Saturday morning, before the mist is even lifting off the gray sea. Man, ass-freezing water. I don't take to cold water, I chill fast. The waves of the Pacific are high and rough, nothing like the gentle, tepid waters of the Red Sea. We have to wear full body suits, rubber helmets, gloves, booties. The first thing you feel in the sudden cold is an urgent need to piss, and pissing in the wet suit is standard operating procedure, says the instructor. Yes, the suits are washed and soaked after each usage. OK. Luke and I share a certain male ribald humor at all of this when we get back to the dive center and strip off all the rubber equipment and soap down, luxuriating under the hot water in the steamy shower room at the end of each dive and wash out our rubber suits and equipment and ourselves.

Our last two classes are spectacular dives around an old wreck off Catalina Island—a great finish. Luke gets high marks in the course. "Is this more fun than kicking back and smoking weed with your friends?" I ask. "Yeah, actually I think it is, Ba," Luke grins. And he's gained a skill, gained some confidence in himself. It's been great for the two of us. We have a hearty affectionate relationship, somewhat physical in delivering the soft pulled punches into the gut of the other in typical, inarticulate, gruff, matey male bonding patterns. No doubt, for effectiveness in communicating with Luke it beats talking, my forte. And I begin to recognize: talking may be *my own* default defense mechanism, protecting against too much emotional or physical expression. I need to do more stuff with Luke.

I realize that that's one of the things I love about the Middle East: I have often felt at times like I'm trapped in an Anglo-Saxon body and temperament, that I'd really prefer to be more physical, emotional, volatile in personality. I like the social conventions in the Middle East when I deal with Arabs, Turks, Pakistanis; it is expected that you stand close to someone when you talk, touch them frequently in expressing frankness, friendliness, intimacy, trust, embracing, holding a handshake for maybe a full minute while exchanging greeting or farewells. I'd like to be more spontaneous. Luke helps me in that.

Prue is of course English, from a caring but totally unphysical family where hugs, kisses, embraces, touching, expression of great emotion are just not done. She's come a very long way herself in this respect; my side of the family is more physical in its embraces than hers, and we've both gotten to appreciate the physicality and emotional openness of the Mediterranean and the Middle East. It wasn't the natural mode for either of us, but it's a way that we have come to appreciate and adopt. My relationship with Luke as buddy is a nod towards the Middle East culture I know. These unspoken bonds of mild physical relating overcome a lot of things that we can't/don't/won't say.

Luke and I get to practice our scuba in a new venue. Prue, Luke and I fly down from LA on a four-day package deal to Puerto Vallarta on the Pacific coast of Mexico. We stay in a little beach cabin. I think Luke was rather aspiring to grander accommodations, more on the scale of an Acapulco. This is no Acapulco, but it's still a resort even if a bit more of gringolandia than I quite care for in Mexico. But it has scuba facilities.

We're still working Be Free and we try to keep Luke on a fairly short leash, so he doesn't drift off into town and employ his powerful homing devices to zoom in on a local head-shop where he can score some weed. We sign up for a local dive, from a boat. The spot is nice, we have a great time, but the water is somewhat cloudy. On the beach Luke meets some guy who has a yacht and who is going diving way off shore the next day with some friends. Typically Luke strikes up a friendship and gets invited. I wonder to myself if pot is part of it, but I can't control the scene. He's gone for the day, comes back with tales of good diving, and I don't see any signs of pot use.

That last night we're really feeling good. Luke has been good company as he often is on the road, witty in some of his tales, affectionate. We're sitting in a nice little rattan type cabana, tropical flowers all around, cool evening breeze and moon out over the Pacific, smells of spicy food drifting in. It's nice having Luke with us, we've had a good time and some laughs. I'm feeling mellow and it's been a while—I decide I want a beer. Luke looks up. "Can I have one too?" he asks. I hesitate ... What the hell. We're on vacation, he's seventeen years old, he's been good, disciplined, he's been pretty diligent at Be Free, I don't think he's been smoking any pot recently. This is a one-time event here in Mexico, he's under our supervision. It's not like he's never had a beer before. We're having a good time together and I say, "Sure." Why shouldn't I cut him some slack for once, right?

Wrong. At the next Be Free meeting, after my account of the successful bonding aspect of the trip with Luke, I fess up rather casually that we did have one beer together. But bonding is not Be Free's bottom line. Sobriety is. All hell breaks loose. I get lacerated, tongue-lashed by everyone, a strip taken off my hide. I have broken a fundamental trust. I have set the wrong example. I have facilitated. I have set him back who knows for how long. I have demonstrated that I too can't have a good time without alcohol. The supervisor warns me that our family is now in serious jeopardy in the program, that we may be expelled for willfully and knowingly breaking the rules, the trust, the commitment. Nothing could be worse than a parent setting the wrong example.

I apologize, I'm humbled. How could I have been so stupid? I remember that Be Free is a true believer world. This means zero tolerance, no room for interpretation, no situational ethics, no bonding over a beer, no slack for a bit for good behavior. Who am I to say this hard-ass approach isn't right? I'm here precisely because my own methods didn't work, did they? They didn't save Luke from arrest, expulsion from school, smoking pot, or slipping into the loser track. The Law wants me in the program. But I also wanted to enjoy myself with my son, didn't I?

And even Be Free casts no magic cloak over Luke. Despite his pretty good standing at Be Free sessions, neither they nor we can monitor him twenty-four-seven. We get a note from Thousand Oaks Continuation School: Luke has been apprehended with possession of drug paraphernalia: "he appeared to be involved in drug transaction—possession of marijuana—he was cited by police and released." I wave the Be Free program in front of Luke's probation officer—we and Luke are already regularly attending the substance abuse program with Luke as directed. But it is still a violation of his probation, one more entry in Luke's file that will not sit well in later hearings.

# CHAPTER NINE

# QUESTIONS OF BLOOD

Luke has almost never brought up adoption issues, but one day we go out with him for sushi at our favorite local Japanese place—a nice venue where Luke is at his chattiest. As we look through the menu and sip our green tea, he turns and suddenly says, "I know why you adopted me." Right out of the blue, years down the road from earlier discussions.

"Oh, why?" I casually ask.

"Because you needed a boy to continue the Fuller name."

Wow. I put down my tea cup, I'm not sure how best to respond to this. Luke's right in one sense, he's seventeen, old enough now to discern that the immediate male line of the Fuller name is in fact coming to an end. Prue and I have two biological daughters, and my brother David has two daughters. My sister's sons don't of course bear the Fuller name. Luke's got that much right. But somehow this has never seemed that big a thing to either my brother or myself. Or even to my father as far as I can see. A minor regret perhaps in seeing this immediate Fuller line legally fade out, but not something we give much thought to. I mean, we're in the late twentieth century here, it's not like dynastic lines of power, authority and property are involved. More important, our daughters are clearly continuing the Fuller blood line, even if not in name. If there was no continuation of the family genetic line at all, I might be more regretful. But family blood line doesn't have to be via the male line.

"Hmm, Luke, we certainly wanted to have a boy to help balance the family, but you know what? I'm afraid that to people who trace family lines, it has to be the blood connection that matters for genealogy. So it's great to have a boy in our family along with two girls, but continuation of the family name wasn't really the issue. We wanted you for you, Luke."

"OK, but if I'm not part of the family line, then why did you want to have me be part of the family then? I'm separate from you."

"Luke, we love you for you. You're you, that's what matters. We'll be interested in your future family, your own wife and kids. You are part of us. If the family name had mattered that much, David or I would have kept on having kids until we got a biological son. You know we could have had more kids. It just wasn't that big a deal to us."

Luke sits back, takes this in. Clearly it's something that's been simmering on the back burner, just one more mystery for him. He *has* been thinking about adoption. *I don't know who my biological parents were and why they abandoned me. But why did these people adopt me? What are their motives? If I don't have the genetic connection, how does that affect the way they view me, or accept me in the broader family? What about my so-called uncles and aunts and cousins—aren't I an outsider ultimately to them? Where do I look for genuine belonging?*

*       *       *

Genetic connection—it's a spectral concept that begins to creep in more seriously around the edges of my mind. Just in periodic flashes, but still too conscious to be dismissed. I had never gotten over the ugly suggestion—just a suggestion, mind you, a psychiatrist had made a while back—that Luke could be a "border-line sociopath."

And one day I'm browsing the bookshop at Dulles airport while waiting for my flight back home to LA. Luke is on my mind, even from afar; we have another court session coming up, a serious one, the day after tomorrow. My attention is drawn to a book on the shelf: *The Fifth Child*, a novel by Doris Lessing. I read the blurb and it rings some kind of bell and I buy it for the flight. As I read I find myself growing claustrophobic in the narrow cabin, in the rarified atmosphere of 35,000 feet; the book scares the hell out of me. It's about a couple whose fifth child demonstrates early signs of being abnormal, even brutal. As he grows up "troll-like and alien" in her words, he creates a deep sense of abiding fear, even entrapment in an otherwise happy family. There is no way out, the evil is upon them. There was a similar kind of book a decade or two earlier, *The Bad Seed*.

Despite the horror and sense of helplessness evoked by these terrifying fictional children, mercifully I recognize that both these descriptions seemed distant from our problems with Luke. He isn't "troll-like and alien" at all; he is generally affectionate towards us. At least so far. But where are we heading?

As I look out over the frozen snows of the Midwestern prairie below I run the known facts through my head in a quick reality check. Irresponsible, yes, ethically insensitive, unthinking, impulsive, poor judgment, immature—all those things. But now that we are into the drug scene, forced to publicly acknowledge our own inability to control the destiny and choices of our son, are we into a new jungle? Already we see some early signs—someone whose drug needs ultimately may begin to cause him to financially victimize his own family—yes, all of those things, all that is possible. But evil? I cringe at these implications, something that will reach out and touch me at my most vulnerable, at a restless three am of dark thoughts intertwisted with the bed sheets of insomnia: could a faulty mental wiring, a genetic poison-pill left within Luke, eventually impel him into conduct that is truly sociopathic, vicious, evil? A malignant seed has been implanted in my own mind. I can't fully banish it.

I will not share this novel with Prue when I get home. I will leave it deeply and safely buried at the bottom of the seat pocket on the plane.

But I want to reassure myself, even then. Late the next night Prue and I talk about our court hearing in the morning. I decide to bring it up. "Do you ... ever think there might be some genetic factor here with Luke, you know, making him behave the way he is, even beyond our control?" I ask. "Could there be perhaps something fundamentally 'wrong' with him—something genetically damaged or flawed that was beyond our ability—even his—to alter?" Prue shifts in her seat, puts down her book. She speaks slowly, searching for words. "I don't know. Yes, I do think about that sometimes. But I think ... basically ... he has been a caring person. He's generally kind with others ... except when the drugs are talking. But I do worry when the drugs take over. They seem to drive almost all warmth from his heart ... But no, we haven't ever seen him inflict physical harm on others. I think he's confused, no sense of real values, but ... not mean-spirited."

I hear her, but I press on into the pain realm. "Have you ... have you ever felt afraid of Luke?" I ask, worried about what I might be invoking. Prue hesitates for a moment. "No," she says, "no. But I feel afraid *for* him."

We talk rationally of these things but we both know how deeply disturbing it is to have to run these calculations through our minds, to flirt with the unthinkable, the fear of future unknowns. This term "sociopath"—isn't this just a more scientific, less emotional and less moralistic term, but no less real term for "evil?" These are mysteries: Luke's origins, his early family conditions, his fate encoded in genes, designed in the careless coupling of two flawed beings, passed down to him as an unwanted, undeserved fateful burden. And fate delivers him to our doorstep, into the bosom of the family.

I consult with a close doctor friend of mine, an old classmate who had also adopted a Korean daughter among five other kids of his own. "Jerry," I say, "we of course knew from day one that elements of a roll of the dice with an adopted child are always present. Do you think this is a problem with Luke?" "Frankly," he says, "it's pretty clear the potential for problems with adoption are probably higher. Clearly *some* kind of undesirable sequence of events lead to the abandonment of a child. And certain kinds of behaviors—especially drugs and alcohol abuse by the biological parents, especially the pregnant mother—can never be known."

"OK, but do you think Luke has suffered from some kind of fetal alcohol syndrome in his seeming inability to understand the consequences of actions, the impulsivity?" "It's hard to know," Jerry says, "but I don't see any overt signs in Luke of classic fetal alcohol syndrome—you know, the slightly mongoloid features, high forehead. And he doesn't show any signs of mental or physical retardation. But that doesn't rule out some other kind of inherited genetic damage."

But then, isn't there *always* a roll of the dice inherent in every arbitrary new recombinant of parental DNA? Our experiences in Be Free demonstrated how one kid out of three biological children within a single family, all with fine caring parents, could be deeply enmeshed in drugs and all its wrenching consequences while the other two were fine.

And what about Luke? Mustn't he himself suffer torment over these same issues in his own way, in his own mind, in his own bed in the same wee hours of the night as I do? In pot-tinged speculations and fantasies? *What is happening to me? Why do I act the way I do? What were my father and mother like? Was there something wrong with them that they abandoned me? Or was it me? Is there something that is still wrong with me? Why am I always in trouble?*

Of course Prue and I never dream of raising these most toxic of issues with Luke directly. To discuss any hints of "genetic poisoning" would be cruel and pointless; we recoil from going there ourselves. But Luke himself must now feel weighted with such questions as the consequences of his actions, for himself and his family, come rumbling in like dark tsunamis whose presence is not visible way out at sea; it is only as they approach the shore that they deliver their devastation. Luke is silent on these issues, but it may be the silence of fear. If only he would break down, open up, cry, share his inner fears with us.

*       *       *

But he doesn't. It's just more of the same. We get another negative report on Luke from his supervisor at Continuation, what he's not doing right in school. "What good is this so-called education process doing Luke, anyway?" I rail at Prue, venting at the world. "Why should we go along with this farce? Is it just about stuffing basic facts and data into his head so he can function in society? Screw it!" I'm convinced this schooling system is little more than a holding pen for the alley cats of the adolescent mind while the worst of the hormonal waves wash over them.

By now I really don't give a damn about the academics for Luke. The kid can read quite well when he wants to; books on occasion even provide a form of escape for him. What I'm really looking for are ways for Luke to *grow up*, to think things through, to understand choice and consequences. And in a better venue than the state pen.

It's probably no help that Luke has two high-achiever sisters. This comes home to me when in late May the three of us fly to St. Paul, Minnesota, to attend Melissa's graduation from Macalester College, where Samantha had graduated two years earlier. Melissa receives a special honor there as a star regional debater. The broader Fuller family has always been drawn to debating and arguing, sometimes tiresomely so, and Melissa is razor-sharp at her trade. She aspires to be a lawyer—an aspiration she later abandons after getting a closer look at the profession.

But none of this is Luke's world at all. We all know it; we joke with him about our family verbal diarrhea; he tolerates our foibles with a smile. He is certainly bright enough, but he knows in his heart there is no Macalester in his future—it is alien to his sensibilities.

As I look back at the picture of him sitting next to Melissa with his arm around her at her graduation I can almost sense a fear in his eyes. Or is it an emptiness? A feeling that he is a poseur? That he can walk the walk and even talk the talk a good bit—he's grown up in an articulate environment—but that he knows he is in over his head? I fear sometimes he is desperately treading water in an environment that accepts him but which he knows in his gut is not truly his. The pretense may be getting exhausting.

Or is there another way to look at it? Is he learning to let all this roll off like water off a duck's back as he confidently asserts his own true self without apology? Trouble is, I don't really see that either, it doesn't ring true. I see wearying and exhaustion. Yes, Luke seems to take genuine pride in his sisters' accomplishments; we know that he sometimes boasts to others about them. *But I know this place is not me, it is not my world.* What is your world to be then, Luke? How do we discover it?

Something snaps in me. "You know what?" Prue is familiar with my periodic rants and impulsive projects of the moment, "As long as Luke is engulfed in this goddam toxic teenage mall world he's not going to make it. We've lived all around the Third World. They don't have teenagers there, I mean as a special social class. They're just part of normal society. It's here, here in America where we invented the teenager. It's just a bloody socio-economic invention of the market. And it's been such a roaring commercial success we're now exporting it abroad." Yeah, I'm feeling frustrated and angry, and my rant shows it, but that makes it no less true. American teenager-dom packaged as a distinct class, economy, language, tribal dress, customs, values, rules, accoutrements, code of honor. And distinct penalties.

And why not? For a lot of kids, the teen-pack represents a comforting clan, a safe, isolated social space away from an adult jungle. Only a few brave adolescents decide to break away from that protected isolation, to bushwhack their way back early on into the adult world with its pleasures and hard demands. For Luke this whole enforced sojourn in high school business isn't doing anything except deferring maturity.

Dammit, I'm Luke's father. I have the duty and, yes, the presumption and determination to put an end to his mindless drifting around the blank spaces of the teenage world. I'm not going to deal with the system here anymore. I want to plunge Luke into some totally new physical environment, some alternative form of coming of age.

Prue too is open to trying anything. But at the same time she is slowly developing her own darker sense of Luke's possible longer term prospects. And as it happens, she's been the one, when I've been away, who's had to spring him from various Maryland and California police stations—much more often than I have. Hanging out with the police, she says, is not her thing.

But can we find a radical new game plan?

# CHAPTER TEN

# OUTWARD BOUND

## Summer 1991 - Bethel, Maine

In almost a belligerent, exhilarating high, with a rush of power at remaking the realities around Luke, I march into the high school and inform them we're yanking Luke out. For good. He's old enough to quit high school now. We're taking destiny into our own hands.

But to do what?

We've gotten word of an outfit called Outward Bound that runs a series of challenging wilderness programs. They're designed to test the individual in an outdoor environment, to call forth new-found personal resources and inner strengths to cooperate with others for survival in tough environments. Intriguing. Confronting a radical adult experience like this might just offer a turning point for Luke. I've always been impressed with Native American culture and the potency of their coming of age rituals. The modern men's movement in the US also emphasizes the importance of being in the wilderness, the mentoring of teenagers by adults who are *not* their parents, in challenging ceremonies and spirit quests for self-discovery.

Luke perks up; no groan, he says he's totally up for it. We apply—and Luke is accepted! He's seventeen, so it's a special Outward Bound Youth at Risk program—out in the wilds of the Maine woods. I contact Luke's parole officer to get permission for him to go to Maine in lieu of the Be Free program. Be Free sends me a letter indicating their unhappiness with our decision to take Luke out "before he has completed the program; we urgently recommend he continue to seek immediate treatment in the form of twelve-step meetings such as Alcoholics Anonymous, Narcotics Anonymous, etc. In addition, we recommend the family continue to seek family therapy." OK, I've been impressed with the dedication of Be Free, but I don't think Luke sitting around in the local losers' high school between Be Free sessions is constructive any more. I want a clean break.

Luke learns he will be in for a program of camping, orienteering, canoeing, portaging, hiking, rock climbing—all far from the sight of civilization over one month. The highlight of the course is a solo exercise in which the student sits on his own somewhere out in the woods, all alone for three whole days

106

with limited food and water, to just exist and contemplate reality around him. How will Luke react to such a period of isolation, with no entertainment other than his own mind and the quiet incessant workings of Nature all around him?

Filled with vicarious excitement, we put Luke on the airplane for Boston. "Luke, be aware they're pretty likely to shake you down before you head out into the woods—drugs, even cigarettes are totally out during the program." "I can handle that Ba, no problemo," he assures me.

And he goes off for the whole month of August—out of sight but still the obsessive magnet of our thoughts every day as we spin visions of him off on his own in the wilderness of reality recovery. We permit ourselves some modest infusion of hope in this long-shot adventure we have charted for him. Luke, how are you doing out there in the boonies right now around the campfire, as we eat supper in the comfort of home? Is it coming together?

And then, a month later, the long-awaited moment: Prue and I fly to Boston for Luke's "graduation." We drive up into the great northern woods of Maine to the small town of Bethel, only a few hours from the Canadian border. It's a sparsely populated area, well suited to a retreat adventure. We stay in a local B&B that is familiar with the drill of parents coming up for just such emotional occasions of Outward Bound graduations. In the evening from behind our beflowered pendulous chintz B&B curtains I peer out into the woods with its choruses of tree-frogs. Inside the room I'm surrounded by the little bowl of potpourri lavender petals on the window shelf, the crochet pillow cases, the needlepoint rural scenes on the walls, the cheery framed rural mottoes, the high bursting bedclothes of the overstuffed four-poster double bed: I am encapsulated in propriety and preciousness. And I realize that at this very same moment Luke is out there in the dark, surrounded by the wilds, lying in his sleeping bag on the leaves in the woods; he is not too far off from us anymore, but probably grimy, seasoned, older, poised for reentry into civilization at the break of dawn. At sun-up they will do a final ten-mile "marathon" run back into camp headquarters in Bethel where we await them. Will the boys who set out into the elemental reality of wilderness one month ago be the same ones who now come back in?

We're up at first light, descend for the fussy, ritual hearty breakfast of eggs, ham, homemade muffins and scones, country butter, homemade jellies, little glass crystals of jam, special breads, embroidered cloth napkins in painted wooden napkin rings with deer and pine trees on them. We pass the cloth-wrapped muffin basket and the beflowered tea pot in its tea cozy along to the other sets of parents; we all nourish similar anxious and gentle hopes for our sons. Their own unspoken anxieties bring us together over homemade hotbreads in this remote meeting-place where woods cure souls.

And outside it's a beautiful crisp northern Maine morning. We make it to the campground base well before seven to wait in quiet anticipation. Then, minutes later, still quite some distance away, we spot red and blue and yellow running shorts flashing in the slanting morning sun between the trees, moving up the dirt road. Then, finally, there they are! Can it be? We think we see Luke near the front of a long and straggling pack. He is! He is number two over the finish line out of forty-one boys! He collapses into our arms sweaty, thinner, glowing with a pride that is more than matched by ours. "Did you see me Ba? Number two, pretty cool!" We stand around as all the other kids come in, all telling their tales of the run. We choke back emotions, as do the many other parents there, whose stories about their own sons we can only guess at.

There's the photo: Luke between Prue and me, looking fit, panting, tired but exhilarated in his Outward Bound running shorts, bare-chested, arms casually flung around our shoulders, looking happy and triumphant.

This is the boys' last time together, and parting is in some ways hard for them. They've shared an intense experience, bonded in the challenges of a wilderness heretofore unknown to most of them. Flurries of info and notes are exchanged among them, addresses and phone numbers, great job dude, hang in there, stay out of trouble man, don't do anything I wouldn't do, high-fiving all around. Nicknames rule as his wilderness buddies are presented to us with lots of in-jokes. Finally they all head off to shower, pack, and the trip back out. I am jubilant. Outward Bound has delivered.

I get in a few words with the councilors on the expedition. One of the councilors, Sarah, said she'd be happy to talk about him more if I want to give her a ring next week after we get home. Overall they speak really well of Luke. Reinsert him back into real life only slowly, they counsel: the intensity of wilderness immersion and the experience of remoteness from civilization can make reintroduction into the daily world an unreal experience, even a shock. That's fine with us. The "real world" hasn't really been our closest ally in working with Luke.

On our way back to Boston we stop off in Freeport at the big LL Bean store where we let Luke choose a nice compass and altimeter as a prize; at lunch he chooses a shrimp cocktail to break his wilderness diet. After lunch he lights up a cigarette, his first, he says, since the program began. "It wasn't so hard, I didn't think much about cigarettes out on the trail," he claims. "Maybe now might be an easy time to quit," I teasingly venture, but Luke pats my arm reassuringly, almost patronizingly, "Nah, don't worry, Ba." It's his day. But we don't have a beer.

Luke later receives a letter from Outward Bound.

*Dear Luke,*

*Congratulations on successfully completing your Outward Bound course! Now that you are enjoying the comforts of home, Luke, remember this is where you can draw upon all that you learned and experienced here at Outward Bound. You can be proud of all that you accomplished in the 28 days.*

*If you think back, the course began with three days of tough bushwhacking which led us up to some of our finest beautiful views of the western Maine mountains. The next two days were spent challenging ourselves rock climbing and on the ropes course. We then transported to the Rangeley Lakes where we canoed for three days and completed a difficult four and one half mile portage. Luke, you also completed a three-day solo during an epic rainstorm. There was Final Expedition with challenges and obstacles that you overcame—and don't forget Hurricane Bob and the moons over the Mahoosuc Mountains.*

*Physically you excelled. While bushwhacking and trail hiking, you were consistently in the front setting the pace. On the ropes course and rock climbing days you pushed beyond your physical limits. You challenged yourself by climbing blindfolded and attempting to negotiate obstacles on the ropes course with new and interesting variations. While canoeing Luke, you learned the various strokes and used them to become a strong, competent paddler. The marathon was also a great achievement for you. You pushed yourself and finished in second place, out of a field of 41 other students. Good job!*

*Luke, your acceptance of program responsibilities improved as the course progressed. During Training and Main Expeditions you had to be asked and reminded to perform your group responsibilities. During Final Expedition you contracted to take the initiative to keep the group focused on their daily activities. You followed through on your contract and displayed very good leadership qualities. You also volunteered to be navigator several times. By taking on this responsibility you empowered yourself and the group to run Final Expedition which contributed to a successful course.*

*You were a well-liked and respected member of the group, Luke. You were a good role model, communicating in a constructive, healthy manner. You also reminded the group throughout the course to be non-threatening and non-aggressive in their interactions with others. Luke, on day 20 at Full Goose shelter you displayed compassion when Andy was down and felt like quitting. You made the effort to encourage him to hang in there and not give up on himself and the course.*

*Your relationships with the instructors were generally good. You responded and interacted with us in a friendly, respectful manner. We truly enjoyed our conversations with you about experiences you had and knowledge you acquired while traveling and living in foreign countries. We also appreciated your kind acts of filling water bottles and your "friction therapy" as applied to sore knees. Thank you.*

*Overall Luke, you displayed good leadership qualities, self-motivation, the ability to push your own limits and compassion. Now that you are home your biggest challenge is to continue on with your life. You are seventeen and have some big decisions to make. Outward Bound was only the beginning, now it is up to you.*

*Good luck,*

*Signed . . .*

This letter is balm for our souls as we see the rough outlines of another kid trying to shine through the gloom of failure and the looming Law. Luke beams as he reads it; I think it really bucks him up to find some recognition of positive qualities. I'm determined to dig down further beneath the surface. I call Sarah the next week and tell her briefly about Luke's background. "I'd really value your personal impressions of how Luke was under the special conditions of the course. Frankly, he is something of a mystery to us at times but with outsiders he may be different."

"Mr. Fuller, Luke did mention that he had gotten in trouble with the law on several occasions. But the boy that I saw was fairly on top of his act. He was a definitely positive member of the group. He did what he was supposed to. He was dressed and ready to go on time every day. He didn't resist the program. He wanted to make things work."

"Did you generally find him communicative?"

"You know, Luke was always talkative, especially with other kids. Sometimes he could talk too much, distract us from some of our focus. But his contributions in discussion of group issues were always good. He could be funny. He always stayed calm and had constructive things to say. I valued him in the group. He communicated effectively on the daily challenges we faced and offered good ideas on what we should do. The other students liked him and often looked up to him. They saw him as calm and helpful."

"That's great to hear—sounds like a different Luke almost. But if you had to critique him, what would you point to?"

"OK, Luke didn't always take the course seriously, especially for the first week or two. He joked at inappropriate times, sometimes talked too loud at night. When it came time to do community work he tended to skip out on that type of activity. He sometimes liked to provoke some kids into mischief, but nothing serious. But by the second half of the course he got much more serious and responsible. He grew."

"So he really stayed out of trouble?"

"Definitely. He worked to keep the group together, especially when one of the other kids freaked out and wanted to drop out, Luke helped keep the boy on board. He treated other people with respect. He really was a calming influence."

"I've always been intrigued by the three-day solo, how did Luke do at the 'spirit quest?'"

"His turn came up in really bad weather, lot of wind and rain. But he stayed put. He said he thought a lot. He talked a lot about that, and I don't remember all the details, but he said he was worried about his future, knew he needed to get out of the drug scene. He said he wanted to do better by you guys, he said that you stick up for him pretty well. I got the sense that he knows what his problem is, and he wants to do better."

Wow, we're impressed. This sounds like he has the raw material to do something fresh with his life. Dare we hope that we see strong flashes of potential maturity here, an ability to get it together, a sense of group responsibility—at least under these controlled circumstances? Maybe this is just the type of challenge he responds to most. We note that Luke seems more sober and reflective since coming back, a lot brewing beneath the surface as he quietly processes the experience. As usual he doesn't verbalize it too much and I'm trying to learn not to grill him too much in my eagerness. But that he could sometimes "talk too much" on his expedition? Amazing!

After we get back home to California, I have to take off for the Middle East again for two conferences and research. I'll be away from home altogether three weeks, an unusually long time for Prue to tend the potentially volatile home fires. I worry about what might happen while I'm gone. But maybe he will be more stable now. Meantime, the post-Maine Luke is back at part-time fast-food jobs while we actively seek ideas on where to go next.

### Fall 1991 - Utah

Yes! Luke does stay out of trouble with the law after Maine, even while I was gone. But we all have to go off to Orange County to attend another interim hearing on the golf course case. The bad news is that in the meantime we note that his marijuana use has not dropped off. He is often coming home in the evening after seeing friends with that classic glassy-eyed appearance. We decide we need to go further in the direction of radical drug therapy.

We hear from some of our Be Free friends about a six-month course at a ranch in Utah for drug rehabilitation for teenagers. The kids there are not free to leave, but the course is imaginative and innovative. It appeals to me with its back-to-basics, elemental nature. The students spend the first two months in a totally primitive environment in the woods where they have only cloth and tools and have to build themselves a shelter to live in, sew together some kind of clothing to wear, and get only survival rations. Bulk food items are delivered to them: flour, fat, salt, large hunks of meat and raw vegetables—the kids have to deal with it and cook for themselves. After two months of this they move on for another month to the "eighteenth century" where they stay in cabins, have well-water and some rudimentary tools, and are assigned various building projects to be done jointly. Finally a "modern" era involves an intensive craft and construction project using modern tools. They have to take care of animals throughout during the process, each looking after his or her own horse. A no-drug, no-smoking environment is strictly enforced.

We get permission from Luke's probation officer to postpone the trial hearing since he will be going to this rehabilitation ranch. The courts seem ready to bend over backwards in the direction of any creative fix, especially for a juvenile, to avoid the harsher grinding of the gears of justice that might not serve rehabilitation.

The cost is high and there's no way we can do this without our health insurance program. They say they need more info on the Utah program, but they think it looks good, they can probably cover the major part. Luke is again game to go, no foot dragging. Why is he willing to enter these tough, demanding programs? Is it because he really wants to be able to get rid of drugs? His quick return to pot would seem to belie that. Or maybe they are a form of adventure and excitement. Or just something to do in a life that is otherwise laden with boredom. Maybe he likes *being* something different—or maybe it just simply beats other options.

So in October we pack Luke up once again and head out. On the way I have to give a talk in Monterey where we're put up at the fancy Pebble Beach resort, the touch of ostentatious luxury that Luke always relishes. It seems to fit his image of himself, the kind of place he wants to be associated with, even vicariously. I notice Luke is building up his mental Rolodex of fancy spots, intriguing experiences. He collects match-covers and calling cards from all of these places. Pebble Beach offers lots of little branded freebies he can pick up to take along with him. And after Monterey it's on to Utah, east via Reno, Nevada.

For the fun of it we stop off in the early evening in Reno to see the lights, even play the slots for an hour. Luke as a minor can accompany us in, but not play. Would Be Free accuse me of providing a bad role model here? Maybe Luke shouldn't be exposed to the enticing glitter of sin city. Worse, maybe he shouldn't note that even his parents think it fun on this occasion to drop a little money in the slots in this glitzy Disneyland Babylon. Reno's lure also includes fancy steak and lobster dinners for pennies, part of the illusory manna to draw the unsuspecting into the lair. Luke has the prime rib, surely his last white-suit-waitered meal before he finds himself having to rip hunks of semi-raw ox-meat off a bone with his teeth in front of some mountain campfire. Let him enjoy Reno for a few hours before the wilderness shrinks do their number on him.

We've had some fun in Reno, made a few bucks on the slots, and had a nice dinner. Now there's a long seven-hour drive ahead of us out across the desert to Utah and we need to make time. As we break out into the night desert of Nevada, Luke is in the backseat, geared up for talking, now spinning his perfect scheme for playing the slots that is fail-safed at each stage. "Get this, Ba. You start with let's say a hundred dollars, OK? Then you divide that into five twenty-dollar envelopes and start playing the one dollar slots with the first envelope. If you lose all that you take the second envelope and play the fifty-cent slots. Anytime you win more than what's in the envelope you put that back up into the higher envelope. See, that way you're bound to hit some jackpot." OK, whatever. It's surefire, just like all his life plans. But actually I'm impressed that he's thinking all this out in rational terms, imposing some kind of mental and procedural discipline and plan. Luke has always been intrigued at trying to figure the angles.

The freeway is virtually deserted, a thin straight line of concrete and asphalt scratched out east through the barren desert to the horizon. We drive ever deeper into the night, our headlight beams on high, probing the distant dark in pursuit of a new unknown enterprise, an exploit, a venture into creative ways. The sky is a black vault above us, punctuated by reassuring stars. The road is long, quiet, empty—motion towards an uncertain destination.

I must be doing about ninety miles an hour without really noticing when out of nowhere flashing red and blue lights pop up into my rear view mirror; shit, some goddam police car pulling me over. Give me a break. No towns, few exits, no traffic on the empty freeway; speeding at two-thirty am? This is a bad omen. I hear his loudspeaker—Get out of the car, sir, hands away from your body!—I suddenly now feel the hour, psychologically wearied, vulnerable, lost in the desert, seeking water and safety at the end of the road.

And in the dim, empty nightscape of reflective thinking I wonder, what am I doing here? Is this Luke's trip, or is this *my* trip? Am I on some kind of a huge mind-fuck as my imagination is seized with elaborate projects to save my son? Am I just flying around like some horsefly inside the house on a summer night, banging into walls, angrily bouncing off windows and ceilings in search of the elusive way out of the room I somehow stumbled into? Is this "creativity," or am I just stupid, on some will-o-the-wisp quest, tripping off on some romantic spillway out of reality in search of a world for Luke I'll never find, that may not exist? What in hell am I doing explaining myself to this inflexible trooper in a darkened desert in the middle of nowhere in the glare of his headlights in the middle of the night three hours out of Reno's fantasyland?

*       *       *

Late next day we finally get to the ranch admissions office in Provo, Utah. I'm beat after the drive, despite a good nap on the road. As we get out of the car I ask Luke if he would run down the street to the 7-Eleven and grab me a diet coke—I need a caffeine fix as I head into the office. Prue and I go in to start the paperwork. "Where's your son at?" they ask. "Down the street, getting me a coke." "Jesus Christ, out there on his own? You better get out there fast and get him!" "Look," I say, "Don't worry. He'll be back in a minute." "You sure about that, Mr. Fuller? It's our policy not to let these boys out loose and unaccompanied, ever. They might take off." "No," I snap, "Relax, he's not going to take off. He'll be back in a few minutes."

Bad vibes. Luke has his problems, but "loose and unaccompanied?" What kind of kids are they dealing with here anyway? Well, we can always pull him out if it's not right. We sign Luke in. I explain that the paperwork on the insurance is about to come through. The ranch will call them to confirm. Luke comes into the office now, carrying his duffel bag and my coke. The guy at the desk lowers the level of his security alert. Prue and I embrace Luke as we say goodbye, a now familiar ritual on the eve of his multiplying adventures. I try to think of more things to say, but I've already said it all, many times over. We won't be able to come out this far for a visit very often, but Luke sets off in good spirits, as he usually does. We tell the ranch we'll check back in to finalize the paperwork in a few days when the insurance comes in; in the meantime Prue and I will take a day or two to explore the mysteries of Bryce Canyon around us.

Two days later we get back to the ranch to finish off the paperwork. The same guy is at the desk, looking anxious. "I'm sorry, Mr. Fuller, but there's been a problem with the insurance company, they say they won't cover the costs."

Shit, what are we going to do now? "Give me the phone, let me call the insurance people myself," I grumble. It takes me a while to get a real person on the line. "Mr. Fuller, I'm sorry, but this is in accordance with our clear guidelines. We have looked into the ranch and we find that it is not qualified for our coverage; the chief administrator is not a licensed psychologist and lacks the kind of educational degrees that are a pre-requisite for this kind of facility. We simply can't cover your son."

"Look," I argue. "We've traveled a long way out here to bring him to the program. You had indicated earlier that you thought you could cover it. We have heard positive things about the program from other people in drug rehab programs. You're really letting us down at a crucial point in his treatment."

"I'm sorry, but that is our policy, we can't cover this program's cost."

I slam down the phone. We've been warned at Be Free that insurance companies are really leery about drug rehab programs and are endlessly creative in finding ways to get off the hook. "Look," I turn to the ranch administrator, "I'm sorry, we just can't afford this by ourselves without insurance coverage. We'll have to take him out of the program."

Another balloon of hope shot down in flames into the desert. We drive the fifty miles to the site where Luke is actually beginning his program to pick him up. Will he be relieved to be sprung? To our surprise, his face falls. "Damn, Ba, that sucks. I would have liked this program. The kids seemed cool and what we were going to do is interesting." "I'm sorry Luke, we wanted it too, but it's way too expensive without the insurance. We'll have to find some other kind of Outward Bound program." We stow Luke's duffel bag back into the car, with all its familiar emotional baggage, and head back west on the long drive back home to California.

The Utah national parks are wild creations of God and Nature; huge rock castles reaching up into the sky from the red desert floor. In simpler days they were the beacons, guideposts for those certain of their knowledge of God and of their earthly mission, to negotiate the wilderness on the way to the Promised Land. Today these sublime red towers are guideposts only to the spirit. Their promised land has long since been found and paved over, but the glowing red monuments still beckon, as if to show a safe way out of the endless featureless plains of the drifting mind.

## *November 1991, Thanksgiving - Joshua Tree, California*

We're back home in Thousand Oaks again, but for us the clock is ticking. We don't want Luke hanging around in this environment. I'm worried that all the gains of Outward Bound will quickly be dissipated while I'm hunting for something new. We find that Outward Bound has a two-week rock-climbing program starting soon at nearby Joshua Tree National Park, outside of Palm Springs, California. This is a normal Outward Bound program for young adults, not part of any Bad Boy program like Maine. Luke is a bit young for it, but they're willing to take him based on the recommendation of Maine. So Luke has upgraded his reputation within Outward Bound, a great sign. We haul him off on the three-hour drive to Palm Springs where he'll be over the Thanksgiving period and drop him off at the gateway to another zone of challenge.

Two weeks later we drive down again to pick him up at Joshua Tree. Luke is enthused. "Guess what, Ba, I was the youngest in the whole group and the instructor said I would have been a good leader for the class. I really liked the people in the class—they were all in their twenties. We did some really cool rock climbing! We should go down there again sometime and let me show you!" We meet a few of his fellow climbers. One of his friends is a young businessman from New York, a slightly hip and self-assured guy; he's on his way now to meet his girlfriend in LA, but wants to invite Luke to come up and visit them in New York some time. I'm always amazed at how Luke makes these connections with serious people: when they tell us about him, he's not the same Luke. He's talkative, mature, filled with stories. He tells us how Luke always won a game as they sat around the campfire at night, called Three Truths and a Lie. You tell three true things about yourself and one lie; people have to guess which it is. One of Luke's many winning entries, by his account: I have been blessed by an elephant, shaken hands with the chief of CIA, surfed in a storm in Maui, been in a military coup in the Middle East. The lie: I've surfed in Maui. Gets 'em every time.

Melissa and her fiancé Jim are home over Thanksgiving. Melissa is working on her PhD at UCLA; her dissertation will be on political violence in Mexico and India. She has been spending some time in San Cristóbal, Mexico, doing research among the Zapatista revolutionaries in Chiapas State. Thank God she's financially on her own now, given all the costs we have with Luke. Actually we're spending Luke's college education money right here and now. And in the mysterious ways that children often help shape one's destiny, Melissa's research plans will lead us deeper into Mexico's less traveled and impoverished south and towards San Cristóbal. I am increasingly inclined to think of Mexico as a next possibility, maybe a unique environment for trying to create a more mature, seasoned Luke.

*   *   *

But the Law must still be placated. Even as we are still on a high from Luke's success in the Outward Bound programs we get another dose of cold water—a letter from the local court system in Ventura county. Luke's community service penalty for marijuana possession last year is "unsuccessfully terminated." The court informs Luke:

*We are closing your case as uncooperative because you received a grade of 'poor' on over half of the community hours you worked. According to John, the supervisor, your attitude was that the work assignment was a waste of time and you had a problem staying on the tasks given to you. The unsuccessful closing of this citation will be negatively taken into consideration if you are cited or arrested in the future. Further, if you request that your juvenile record be sealed, this information will be considered by the court.*

This is no help to our case with the courts on the golf course case in trying to demonstrate that Luke is shaping up his act, or in our request for leniency and flexibility. But *we* see a Luke making progress and Luke's public defender presents a better case to the court.

"Mr. and Mrs. Fuller do not believe that the minor will benefit as much from a penal setting as he will from performing volunteer work for two years in Third World countries. The sanctions imposed by the parents exceed the sanctions that would normally be imposed by Juvenile Court. Therefore the minor is released on probation back home to the custody of his parents with an order to pay $2,000 restitution. He will be under the supervision of the probation officer and must follow specific terms and conditions of probation as attached to the probation report."

Luke has been lucky. He has escaped a felony conviction, a potential mark of Cain on his young life, has stayed out of jail, and shares a relatively modest demand for restitution for items destroyed, much reduced due to the insurance coverage of the golf club. I'm willing to pay the fine for now, just to keep his program moving ahead. "But Luke, this is one fine that I solemnly warn you about: you owe us; this golf course fine is your burden forever. It's your crime, it's your penalty, and you're going to pay it, however long it takes down the road."

Meanwhile we decide to go with our winning suit: another Outward Bound experience. This time it's a two-month program starting in winter 1992. This one will be no candy-ass sojourn in a beautiful setting. He will spend one month outdoors in northern Minnesota on the Canadian border—in January. The participants will live outside the whole time, make igloos, work on dogsledding and cross country skiing, have to sleep burrowed down deep in a snow drift a few nights during solo to stay warm. The second month of the course then moves far south to Big Bend National Park in Texas on the Rio Grande.

How I would have loved to have done these things! Prue and I derive great vicarious pleasure in taking Luke off to the Mountain Equipment Co-op where we buy him the required thermal-lined boots, long johns, winter parkas, snow goggles, and other arctic accoutrements. Luke is ready to go in all senses of the word.

*       *       *

To Luke, I'm "Ba." I like it that way. The act of naming is actually an ancient and powerful ritual. Only modern cultures take naming casually. In many ancient societies, knowledge of someone's name gives you power over them; their name is their essence; in many primitive cultures one's name must be concealed from outsiders and from dark forces that could exploit the name to harm or kill its bearer. Chinese often give their newborns derogatory names so as not to tempt the gods into jealousy; only when the child has survived one full year does he or she get a permanent name. In many Native American cultures the name changes as one's age and life status changes. Even in our culture, the way we call a person says a lot about our relationship, where we fit in its hierarchy, how intimate we are with them. Even with our parents.

Our own kids were encouraged from the start to call Prue "Mommy" in classic American fashion, but in England it's pronounced "Mummy" and quite quickly that name took over with Prue's accent. Luke as the third child inherited that same designation for Prue. And I was supposed to be Daddy for Samantha, but she was born in the Middle East where the near universal word for "Daddy"—from North Africa across to India and into China—is "Baba." The name was first regularly used by our maid who came periodically to our house in Beirut and we picked it up happily. Samantha and Melissa from an early age have continued to call me Baba down to this day and they passed the term on to Luke upon his arrival too.

But it's apparently a well-known phenomenon that as boys move into adolescence many change the name they use for their parents. In fact it symbolizes their development of a new and more independent relationship with their parents; the parents are no longer quite the same kind of revered authority figures, and this evolving relationship must be expressed by a new name, reflecting the new reality. Prue's older brother in the UK had always called his father "Daddy" but in his early teenage years took to calling him "Pa," an antiquated frontier-sounding name that was partly in affectionate fun. Soon the other kids including Prue picked it up and "Pa" stuck. Prue's mother similarly was dubbed "Ma." Prue's nephew as a teenager started irreverently addressing his father William as "Willie" and it stuck.

As Luke grew into adolescence one day he started to call Prue by the rather formal term "Mother." Perhaps "Mommy" was too babyfied for use in front of friends. Maybe he wanted to establish some new distance here, to indicate awareness that his relationship to her wasn't quite comfy-biological. And then he started to frequently call me "Father" which I didn't especially care for; I retaliated by starting to refer to Luke as "Son," although that is a much warmer term in my thinking than the more austere "Father." Luke clearly felt some need to formalize these names for us for a certain period.

Then, some months later, not fully at home with "Father" either, Luke returned to the previous name "Baba" but soon shortened it down to "Ba": he had now redefined our relationship by a name of his own creation. I liked "Ba" just fine. Prue then turned into "Ma," a name on which he held no patent, but it paralleled mine.

Luke didn't escape from name changes himself. I had run through a series of names for Luke as well. His cousin Elijah when he was little couldn't pronounce Luke's name, and called him "Wuke," a name that I picked up and used occasionally at home as the mood struck me. In Hong Kong I discovered that many Chinese had the name "Wucius"—an anglicized form of a more common Chinese given name—so that occasionally alternated with the use of Wuke. When Luke began to study Spanish, his teacher gave him the Spanish name Lucas which I then also occasionally used with him. And when he was quite young I had periodically referred to him as "Seyroka"—dating from the time when I was working on Japanese conversational dialogs prior to a trip to Japan—where St. Luke's Hospital in Tokyo had come into the lesson dialog. "Seyroka" is the Japanese form of St. Luke—not that he was, but what the hell, at least it was something to aspire to.

So who knows, maybe part of his troubles could be traced back to "name-instability"; maybe an adopted kid needs more certitude in his life.

### January 1992 - Minnesota-Canadian Border

A bright day! We get a rare letter from Luke, from Minnesota Outward Bound.

*Dear Mother and Father and Sister,*

119

*Hey, What's up? Today is 12 Feb 1992. Tomorrow our brigade is off on our final expedition of 15 days. We should have left today, but Jeff, one of my counselors has a bad back so we are waiting till tomorrow for the news if he is going to be able to continue. The other counselor is Amy, both of them are really cool. And I like them a lot. There are four other people, Pam, 27, Toby 22, Mike 20, and Todd 20, all of them are cool and we get along just fine. A week ago we came to base to stay, known as the crafts phase where we make a sled and moccasins and partake in some community work. Our sled we named "Asavati" meaning "hunter" in the Inuit language. My moccasins weren't done, but I'll finish them when I get home.*

*The second day of the week we helped out in a cross country marathon as a pit stop for skiers, that was cool, then we worked on our sled. Then later we went to a ski resort to go telemarking meaning skiing downhill in cross country skis, that was fun. Then a school of sixth graders came one day so we had to entertain them, they were going into seventh grade so we were supposed to let them get to know each other before school starts. We had some dog sledding, tobogganing runs and some snow shoe games for them and then ended the day with a Bar BQ of hot dogs. They had lots of fun, so did we. Yesterday we finished the sled, so here's a kind of a picture of it.* (Hand-drawn sketch is attached, complete with reins.)

*We are all excited to be back on trail because it got pretty boring here and people were getting antsy. Today is basically a really cold day, it got down to -30 F so I guess you got some of your money's worth* [personal in-joke I had with Luke about no-pain no-gain] *and yesterday it was in the -15, -10, so that was cold too.*

*So how's the Olympics doing? Have you seen the Mexican Bob Sledding Team yet? Big joke out here.*

*Mother, how is your hip doing? I hope you're recovering fast and feeling better since I talked to you last on the phone. I had fun with the Younts when I stayed there* [in Duluth on the way]. *They have a nice house on Lake Superior and we went out to dinner and went to the finish line of the John Beargrease dog sled race. Some dude named Swigley won the race setting a big record in history for the fastest time. So that was cool.*

*I hope things at home are going smooth. Also I'm now <u>eighteen</u> but I don't feel different. Also three other people, Jeff, Toby and me and John all had our birthdays in February, pretty strange.*

*For our expedition we're taking out 5 dogs, Pepe, Pogo, Radar, Pronto, and Banjo. Pepe and Pronto are known as the Heel dogs closest to the sled then comes Radar and Pogo as Helpers and then comes Banjo as lead dog who sets the direction. It takes two people to handle the sled who are called mushers—marchè in French-Canadian means "to go" then got turned into "mush" and musher got derived from it.*

*Tonite we all got to go into the sauna which was great and so we'll be refreshed for tomorrow. So I'm off to bed, love you all and always thinking of Barney and sometimes Nicholas* [Melissa's Sheltie]*, so give them a pat for me.*

*Love, Luke*

*Baba/Mummy, PS. Also I ran out of money here. U are wondering how I spent it and I used it for the bus ride to the LA airport and eating dinner at the Ski resort and I was wondering if it would be possible if you could send some money to me to buy some items in the Outward Bound store and the way back home. Many thanks, and Happy Valentines.*

Classic Luke post-script—having fun, send money—but I read it as the letter of a happy, busy kid. I'm almost like a vampire here with a constant craving for the blood of more information and deeper insight into Luke; I try to follow up on every lead. I am quick to get back to Amy, his councilor in Minnesota that he refers to. I call her up, tell her we're eager for additional feedback and ask for her candid opinions. Amy is willing to talk a little about it, but she also reminds me that Luke is now eighteen and has certain rights as an adult; his parents don't automatically get to know all the details of his life. But she understands our purpose.

"I'm happy to tell you, Mr. Fuller, that I think Luke has a lot of wisdom for his age. It's really to his credit that he was in with an older group but he was fully accepted by them. He was always entertaining to have around. He has an interesting command of English and can be quite articulate. I actually found his self-appraisal to be at a high level for his age, maybe that's as a result of his earlier drug program that he told me about. Also I found that he was often perceptive about other people or in group interaction. He was always outspoken, and never afraid to address touchy issues. He was able to address his feelings to others.

"At times Luke could be a little rebellious when things weren't going his way, but he also understood the need to show respect for others. I recall he did have conflicts with one of the group members, a twenty-five-year-old woman and was not always diplomatic with her, but he understood her complaints and was eventually responsive to them.

"I could count on Luke to offer perspectives on the group. He talked with me a lot about himself and his problems. I trusted him on not smoking. He said he learned from his councilor's advice. I noticed that Luke is impressed by the attitudes of others. His lifestyle is daring, but that's appropriate to his age.

"I'd rate Luke as having good technical skills relating to climbing, camping and other physical activities. In my opinion, he definitely has what it would take to become a good instructor for Outward Bound in the future if he wanted to."

Again, what an exciting dramatic contrast to the customary Luke we know! This has got to be more than just some kind of a snow job he's pulling, councilors are bound to be savvy about people. Or is this just one of Luke's Janus faces?

### March 1992 - Big Bend, Texas

Luke is home for a week between the Minnesota and Texas stints at Outward Bound. He and I head up over the weekend to Big Bear ski resort in the San Bernardino Mountains just east of LA. He's a bolder and better skier than I am, but he's attentive and considerate with my slower capabilities. We laugh, enjoy each other's company. Again, Luke is always much more talkative about things around him when he's out of his usual environment—and when I don't have to parent watchdog full-time over him.

It's nice to be in another mode. At home I sometimes feel like I'm drifting into some recorded airport security warning mode, the kind that airs every fifteen minutes—recognizable as soon as the voice comes on, predictable from the first words, annoying the listener for hours with its repetitions, until finally you just tune it out altogether.

At the end of the week he flies off to El Paso and Big Bend National Park, on the Rio Grande. He's got mountains, canyons, rock climbing, canoeing, kayaking, canyoneering and backpacking. In addition, he gets a lot of contact with the Native American kids in the area with whom he'll work on some social programs. The participants also study Indian lore, learn about making Indian handicrafts, and learn the tales of the people to be told around the campfire.

New clue: Coyote as a facet of Luke. During the program he becomes fascinated with the character of Coyote, a central figure in Plains and Southwest Indian culture. Coyote is a positive force overall, but he's also clever, a trickster, a bit of a rake, sort of like Raven in Northwest Indian culture. He loves to trick and deceive, even while providing for the overall welfare of the people. Luke asks for a book about Coyote when he gets home. Luke asking for a book? That's great. I think Luke identifies with Coyote.

Then I'm surprised one day some months later when he suddenly mentions the photographs of Ansel Adams. I ask where he's heard about Ansel Adams. "Oh, we talked about him a lot and saw his photos at Outward

Bound." Luke may also like the idea that Ansel Adams quit school at age twelve to educate himself. Luke has a great capacity for picking up and remembering diverse pieces of information on the run, impressive at times. He may not like books for information too much, but he keeps his ears open when he's out on his own.

Insights like these give us hope. OK, we know now he isn't your average kid, but maybe he is plotting his own erratic course. I know he's not remotely out of the woods, but maybe, through all the thorns, failures and shortcomings, we can perceive the making of someone who could put his own life's struggle to useful purpose one day in guiding others. I'm encouraged to plow on ahead with our do-it-yourself, seat-of-the-pants, improvised mission of creative salvation—in which the raw material is our son's life. The penalty of failure could be high.

# CHAPTER ELEVEN

# LATIN DAYS AND NIGHTS

## *April 1992 - San Cristóbal de Las Casas, Mexico*

ruel and unusual punishment. That's what I've now determined to inflict upon him. Luke, you're eighteen, and we're going to abolish entirely your teen world. We're going to tear you away from it and make it hard for you ever to go back. We're going to hijack you into the adult world via the back door. Get ready for it.

We're talking *physical* removal from this American world, off to another culture. We want a society that is more direct, blunter, that comfortably and routinely mixes its generations. Where there's more to life than TV and the mall. Our family has spent a lot of time living in the Third World. For you, Luke, this is going to be healthier, more integral, more "real" and natural than this American teenage environment around you that seems to suck your soul, lead you astray like a willing lamb to an enticing slaughter house. You need an environment that offers you place, and *purpose*.

So Mexico it's going to be. We have registered Luke with the Instituto de Idiomas in San Cristóbal de Las Casas, a beautiful Spanish colonial town and art center in the southern state of Chiapas, deep in Mayan territory. Melissa had scouted out this town in the course of running around with the Zapatista rebel movement for her PhD research in the previous year and it sounds just right. I've been in touch with the director, Dr. Carlos Guzmán, to arrange for Luke's tuition and courses. He has arranged for Luke to live with a Mexican family in the town: the father is a lawyer; the family has a teenage daughter and an eleven-year old son. It will be part of Luke's Spanish immersion.

My own vicarious enthusiasms well up again. I can imagine myself undertaking such an adventure, going off to the heart of Mexico, the challenge and the excitement of living in a totally different world, learning the language and culture trying to integrate myself into its society. I wish I were going.

But does that mean it's good for Luke too? I think so. Luke, as nearly always, is positive about it—he likes action—he wants things to *happen*. His Spanish is really lousy, he consistently got Cs and Ds in high school, but he never worked at it either. I know because I tutored him, at least managing to keep him from failing outright. At that time he said he didn't like Spanish, but my own language instincts tell me that this kid definitely does have language ability, just no motivation. Now we're going to provide the motivation—outside the classroom.

And so we get into the car for the trip to LAX, to put Luke on a plane again, but this time out of the country, and all by himself. For Mexico City. These airport farewells are almost a ritual by now, but never routine. And we never fail to feel deeply emotional as we embrace Luke at the gate, and then watch our son saunter off alone, street-savvy and utterly naïve, confident and vulnerable, cocky and unsure of himself, into the bowels of Security and Immigration and on to foreign lands where the hope of a new life beckons. Luke is always soft, wistful and affectionate at parting, but happy to go. We're pretty confident he knows we love him and are rooting for him. We're conducting a kind of moon launch here: suiting Luke up and firing him off into space where he'll be incommunicado for much of the early phase of liftoff, breaking out of the gravitational pull of his American life; we watch the monitors hoping we'll eventually reestablish radio communication and see him in successful orbit. But this launch has to be his—it's no good if we ride herd. Luke turns back to give us one last smiling, hesitant wave before he vanishes into the departure lounge.

He's supposed to switch planes in Mexico City and fly on south to the provincial town of Tuxtla Gutiérrez, where he is to take a bus from the airport for the one-hour ride on up to San Cristóbal de Las Casas in the highlands. This is instant Spanish immersion with a vengeance; he's probably never spoken two words outside of a classroom in all his three years of desultory Spanish classes. But Luke's plane to Tuxtla is delayed, and the bus station in Tuxtla confuses him when he arrives late at night. Mexican busses are excellent. But you need to get on the right one.

First contact: we get a phone call from Luke the next day from Mexico with a story of things gone awry. He somehow got on the wrong bus, then maybe drifted off to sleep, or wasn't paying full attention, or didn't fully get the word until an hour later when they pulled into another town on another road. The driver suggested Luke get out and take a taxi some hundred kilometers to San Cristóbal. Struggling to communicate, he got in to San Cristóbal very late, spent a lot of time in the cab trying to find the home where he's supposed to stay. He didn't have enough money for the unexpected taxi ride between cities, maybe he got overcharged, maybe didn't understand. Anyway, his hosts were routed out of bed in the wee hours of the morning, had to help him out with money for the taxi on the spot. Already a reprise on the leitmotif: having fun, send money.

Luke finds it really rough sledding in the first few days. He can't yet say much in Spanish, doesn't understand much. I call his house mother to see how he's doing. She is very warm, but she says Luke is spending a lot of time sleeping, Luke's classical first line of defense. But gradually they coax him out of his shell, get him more integrated into the family routine. He starts attending classes, begins to lose his nervousness at speaking and starts to communicate. He has classes all morning, with one or two other students, then an hour one on one.

I'm as sympathetic as anyone to his plight. I've run the same language gauntlet many times. Controlled classroom situations are one thing, but using the language for real while abroad is quite another. You get this feeling of suddenly being reduced to a child, trying to wrap your mouth around the embarrassing new noises of the new language, struggling to say basic things, not fully understanding what is said, nodding stupidly rather than admitting after the fourth time that you don't really understand. And even when you start to communicate a little after a while, it's hard not to be cowed by the new culture—all those myriad patterns of subtle signals convey a world of missed meaning. It's like a human surrounded by bats—we don't pick up on the vital messages they are transmitting around us at high frequency. And all the while Luke is also struggling to learn the very language of life, how to live as an adult.

It's a six-month course. Prue and I are eager to take advantage of Luke's presence there to go down and see him do his thing on the spot. No, he isn't quite yet "my son the doctor," but I'm proud, at least he's my-son-the-budding-Spanish-speaker-trying-to-make-a-life. So several months into his course we eagerly arrange to fly down to Mexico and see him on his home ground, how he's coping. San Cristóbal is a lovely town, high up in the mountains, cool, picturesque—old colonial buildings brimming with artisan shops, colorful and charming little restaurants, cobblestone streets, delightful plazas. Few Americans get this far south, and it's far from the gringoized beach haunts of Acapulco or Cancún. We follow Luke's footsteps, this path he's leading us on, the same bus journey, only we make it onto the right bus. We check into an attractive little hotel with big courtyard, fountains, simple hacienda-type architecture, modest rustic rooms, local food. San Cristóbal totally grabs me at once.

Far beyond the outrageously colored dwellings on the steep green hillsides and over into the jungle is the Zapatista revolutionary movement, a symbol of rebellion against the poor conditions of the native local Mayan population. This is a movement more given to flamboyant rhetoric of liberation and empowerment under the charismatic and mysterious figure of *Comandante* Marcos than it is to fighting or bloodshed. The savage sweep of Chiapas history, dominated by fabled and rapacious *conquistadores*, provides the darker historical backdrop; it infuses the superficial charms of daily life for the tourist with a deeper sense of tragedy and struggle for Mayan identity, life and dignity behind it. Rebellion appeals to some elements in my own soul, but rebellion isn't what Luke needs right now; attaining his own identity and dignity is a far more important task.

Luke bounds into the hotel to greet us. "Hey Ba, hey Ma, it's great to see you guys here!" He embraces us with genuine warmth and pleasure; it's wonderful to see him, tanned, relaxed, looking happy as we show up on his own turf. We have supper in a traditional local restaurant, he shows off his new language facility in a long exchange with the waiter. He also orders a beer, and then another, but we're way beyond all that now, and then he's off for a late evening date, but we'll meet him the next morning at the Instituto. "I'll give you the guided tour to all the hot spots in town," he promises.

We walk down the sun-drenched cobblestone streets about twenty minutes in the morning cool to the Instituto de Idiomas. Luke, beaming and proud, introduces us around to a number of his teachers who are warm, welcoming and seem genuinely happy to meet us. I've been trying to pull my own Spanish into some shape—I've never studied it formally—but they speak English to me, despite my efforts. Luke smiles indulgently—in fluency he's already much surpassed me, his former emergency tutor. Most of the teachers are older women, who cast a maternal gaze over "Lucas" and hug him affectionately. They clearly have taken him under their wing. "Lucas is a very good boy, but not much studying," Encarnación offers. He comes to class to chat in Spanish with his teachers, but he doesn't want to work much through formal grammar lessons. But everyone is beaming. "Most of his Spanish he's learned at the pub across the street," they laugh. "That's his classroom!"

And in truth Luke has learned a lot. We hear him rattle off his conversations with teachers, doormen, barkeeps, passersby on the street. He seems to know a lot of people on the streets. He's comfortable here, he likes Mexicans. The family he's staying with is obviously very fond of Luke. Their teenage daughter has her own life, and is older than Luke—no budding romance here, but their eleven-year old son seems to adore Luke and Luke is teaching him tae kwon do moves. As I sit back on the bench in the town square and survey the whole scene I feel emotionally moved. The experience has been great, human exchanges across generations in a very different cultural setting, just what we had hoped for him. He's also very friendly with an

American girl at the Instituto, possibly something going there, but otherwise it seems to be all Mexican.

Luke is always smiling, gregarious, glad-handing around the Institute. We pay a call on the director, Dr. Carlos Guzmán, who gently chides Luke for his unorthodox and anarchic learning style, all said in clear affection; he seems to enjoy Luke's company. He says he's taken Luke around town to a few of the night spots on occasion.

We get the picture, the flow and texture of Luke's life here. He seems to have grown up a lot, able to move comfortably through the company of adults. Everyone likes his smile, his warmth, his camaraderie; you can't not like him, even when he fails to do what he is supposed to be doing. His charm seems to rescue him from sterner reckonings. It has been an emotionally rewarding trip for me, and I feel heartened, empowered. We head back home cheered by the thought that we seem to have done the right thing.

### July 1992 - Monteverde, Costa Rica

But it can't be student life perpetually. Soon it's time for Luke to move on to a more "real life" of using his Spanish in some productive capacity. We dig around and find a resource listing various options available for volunteer work in Latin America. There is an interesting program in Costa Rica, to work as a volunteer in a special nature preserve high up in the mountains in Monteverde. It comes much recommended.

Monteverde is a very special place, about four–and-a-half-thousand feet high up in the center of a Cloud Forest (*El Bosque de Nubes*), a kind of jungle in the mountains with six distinct ecological zones. It is a remarkable natural environment, a rare wild animal refuge and home to dozens of rare species of flora and fauna, unique in all the Americas. The reserve is always looking for volunteers to help work in the forest, to manage its paths and walkways, tend to the plants and animals. And so Monteverde will be the next stage of Luke's quest. He will be working without any salary, but his room and board will be supplied; it's considered a privilege to work in such a unique environment with other interesting people. The nearest working town to the Forest is Santa Elena, a little place that caters to eco-tourists.

Luke is assigned to an inexpensive rooming house in Santa Elena. We agree to help out if there are some costs over and above basics. Luke calls up and gives us a report that we are always so hungry for. His landlady Mama Josefina sounds like a maternal type who will watch over Luke's wellbeing, help feed him, do his laundry. We try to call when we can, eager for details, picturing in our minds his experiences and adventures. Luke is out on the trails, doing a lot of hard physical work every day, much of it with local workmen. But after a month Luke calls up to report further. "Hey Ba, I don't like this setup. The work is really hard, digging all day, planting things, making paths, dragging wheelbarrows long distances." "Well, this is paying for your room and board there." "Yeah, but the workmen get paid real money, and I get paid nothing. This is way boring. I don't want to do this anymore." "Hang in for a while, Luke, you signed up for it." But he doesn't hang in long. After a while he isn't showing up for work. The office in charge of the volunteers complains back to the referring outfit in the US through whom we had applied, and the director of the program there calls me up: Luke isn't living up to the terms of the agreement, he's let us down. So they cut off his room and board stipend and officially end the association.

We call Luke again at Mama Josefina's to find out what is going on. "I've changed jobs, Ba. I'm now working part-time at the Cantina here, helping cook food. And check it out, I've also started helping out with an excursion company here that takes tourists on horseback trips around the forest and over to Arenál. That's the local volcano. It's really cool, it's still a live volcano, and erupts a lot. It's amazing to see the lava at night." Luke wants to stay on in the town of Santa Elena and make his own way. Typically, he reports expenses higher than what we had anticipated. Every month we send him a modest money order to cover extra expenses above his modest earnings. I figure this is still a good experience; he's on his own, making his own way in an interesting environment, that's what this is all about. To get his monthly money order from us he has to take the four-hour bus ride down into the capital, San José, to pick it up. One day he calls and says that he's been stupid, he left the money he got from the money order in the top flap of the back pack, and after sitting in a pub in San José he discovered that the top was open and the money gone. Come on Luke, is this for real? Yet it sounds plausible. Should we say tough shit, be smarter next time? Or send a replacement money order? In the end we opt for half the amount. Luke claims his income from odd jobs makes it hard to keep going. He also is proud to tell us that he now has a local girlfriend, Luisa.

We don't know anything about her, but we hope she's sensible and could be a stabilizing influence on him. "That's great news about Luisa, Luke, we'd love to meet her. But just remember, I warned you before you left, be careful. We know you're charming, but there may be a lot of girls who like you for more than just your charming personality. Your passport may hold some charm as well."

I hate saying that, it sounds cynical and unromantic, and just the thing that would have infuriated me if my parents had said it to me, but that's the real world. This kid is eighteen, often a babe in the woods, an innocent in many respects, even as he thinks he's in control as he sometimes drifts into the seamier side of life.

Prue and I want to visit Luke in Costa Rica as well. This is one of the great rewards of having kids in exotic places; earlier on we'd visited Melissa in India and Samantha in Kyrgyzstan. We'd also like to have the opportunity of seeing this remarkable Cloud Forest through Luke's eyes and his local knowledge— and to gauge his progress. He encourages us to come down. I've got lots of frequent flyer miles so in early December that year we take off for eight days; Luke is to meet us at the airport in San José. After retrieving our baggage and clearing customs we come out to the waiting area and wait. And wait. After two hours I dig out Luke's telephone number and give a call up to Santa Elena. Luke's not here, no, we don't know where he is, maybe he's gone to San José. We sit on our bags another hour, and just when we're negotiating about a bus to go into San José to find connections up to Santa Elena, Luke shows up with a girl alongside him. He's beaming, apologetic. "Bus was way late, Ba, they're never reliable. And Luisa," he adds in Spanish, "this is my mom and dad." She is short, pretty, tanned face, black hair and eyes, a hint of Indian blood, a touch on the plump side, dressed in a white blouse with native embroidery, a kind of loose scarf, and blue jeans; she seems to be a nice, warm, straightforward, direct girl. Her English is rudimentary.

So we bus back in to the capital San José, have lunch there. While in the city we note Luke is walking directly behind Prue the whole time. "I just want to make sure nobody tries to snatch your purse, Ma. The city can be bad." He's increasingly solicitous of Prue's wellbeing. We then get in a much smaller bus, what Prue and I call a "chicken bus," natives carrying trussed live chickens with them, for the long four-hour haul up to Santa Elena and Monteverde, gears grinding, black smoke exhaust, chickens and dogs scattering as we wind our way up through the hills and into the mountains.

The bus finally lurches to a halt and we clamber out. This is Santa Elena. It's a small place, unpretentious, essentially a mountain town atmosphere, but also funky. A smell of cooking smoke, big tropical trees all around, a village really. It seems to cater to the backpacking crowd, lots of vegetarian restaurants, native cantinas and granola bars. It's a real throwback to the sixties with scattered little houses and shacks under the trees serving good basic food, local character, a great place to kick back, all the time in the world, mostly simple lodgings but a few slightly better places to stay. The air is wonderful and cool at this altitude after the steamy coast. The main street isn't even paved, not many cars, lazy dust-covered dogs lying along the side of the road, sleepy rhythm, backpackers, everybody knows everybody, time to chat with people in all the eating establishments and shops. Despite its many visitors, it still feels unspoiled.

We put up in the little motel where Luke stays. Mama Josefina hugs us like old friends, takes us in. She beams about Luke, "a good boy, but he's sometimes lazy," and she worries about his *malos amigos* with whom he sometimes hangs around. She's got that right. Luke's more questionable friends have always been a key bone of contention with us. From this day on Prue and I triage all of Luke's friends into basic categories of *buenos* or *malos amigos*; his good and bad friends even become the subject of regular banter with him: he will proudly introduce us to the friends he identifies openly as being in the *buenos* class. Over the passage I time I sense that we are launched into some protean struggle to prevent the weight of the *malos* from systematically outweighing the *buenos* in the Manichean clash for Luke's soul.

Mama Josefina has been looking after him well, but with his loss of his work stipend his quarters are no longer in the regular motel rooms; where he's living now is more like a glorified utility room, rough wooden floors, no interior finishings, clean but rudimentary, and at rock-bottom cost. Luke does various chores for her, helps out in the kitchen periodically cooking food. But she later takes us aside and says that she needs to settle up with us because Luke is behind even in his very modest rent. I ask Luke about this. He looks down hangdog and says that he hasn't always had the money to pay, that he has a pretty limited income and has worked off some of his bill with Mama Josefina. So I'm beginning to feel a little conned here again. Despite the money we have been sending, the bills haven't been paid, there are local "loans" he's gotten as well that haven't all been paid off. Luke's finances are classically impenetrable, rivaling at the personal level the Ponzi debt-packaging schemes of Wall Street's finest. I scarcely have the energy to investigate it all. Every story and statement leads to other tales and spins and side-stories and explanations—I can't sort out what is true anymore. I feel a bit like Daddy Big-Bucks who has arrived in the village and everyone crowds around, seeing a chance to settle up Luke's scattered minor debts he's left all around town.

But I still feel strongly that the best use of Luke's education fund is to secure the environment for him that helps him mature and gain a sense of realism, living life in an adult community. Santa Elena feels very wholesome compared to all kinds of other options I could think of. Everyone seems good natured and welcoming, the social life seems integrated; Luke seems to know everybody and engages in exchanges with nearly everyone we meet, regardless of age. We pay off his rent bill with Mama Josefina but I warn him that from now on we are going to be stricter about how much we send, it's up to him to earn what extra he needs. No more bailouts.

But in the end, who am I trying to warn, Luke, or myself?

Next day we go out to a main midday meal with Luke at a great little rustic place with a fine view down the mountains from the rough tables on the wooden porch, with a beautiful garden undulating with exotic flowers and vines crawling up the sides in this verdant setting. The food is hearty. We sample some of the traditional local dishes popular among *Ticos*, the local word for Costa Ricans. The national dish is *Gallo Pinto*, speckled rooster, basically a local variation on ageless rice and beans, two common ingredients that amazingly combine into full protein in the stomach—the *indígenas* of Mexico and Central America have been subsisting on it for thousands of years. Ageless or not, beans and rice do need some jazzing up, as it is here with onions or peppers, sometimes cilantro, eggs, or a little meat.

Prue and I each have a margarita in keeping with the spirit of the locale; Luke goes straight for a vodka *con limón*. A bit later he asks the waiter for a second. Still later in the meal he tells the waiter to bring him a third. This is our second day with Luke, I'm not looking to stir up issues. Still, trying for a lighter touch I ask, "Luke, after three vodkas are you still going to be able to take us around town?" "Nah, Ba, no worry, it's a special occasion, a little celebration." Yeah, it is a special occasion, but I wonder if this is an everyday special occasion for him. I know perfectly well that his drinking habits are totally beyond my control now; do I really want to draw an ineffectual line in the sand over our nice lunch for one day?

It's wonderful to be sitting with him in this place. Luke is especially voluble, genuinely happy to have us with him, telling us all about the area, the Cloud Forest, the village, the local characters, and his adventures. He and a number of friends often head out for parties in the hills, or sometimes down into San José on the weekends—probably best not inquired into too deeply. There is a lot of action for a small town, and Luke strikes up friendships with tourists passing through as well, and serves as an impromptu guide to the tourist spots.

Next morning we have another hearty Latino breakfast before Luke and I head off for a hike in the Cloud Forest. Prue is still recovering from her hip replacement operation; she can walk around a good bit now, but is not fully back into regular hiking yet. Luke and I enter the precincts of the Bosque. I step onto a well-tended trail winding through a great green cathedral dominated by huge liana trees; they are laden with these massive dripping vines that over time meld into the very trunk itself at the base, giving it huge sinews down and out the sides, almost like a ten- or twelve-pointed star all around the base of the tree, beyond the arm span of ten people. Massive leaves wave in profusion on trees like lazy flags—everywhere things that I've never seen before. Although we're in a tropical jungle, the air is cool. A periodic light mist blows through the trees creating shafts of sunlight piercing to the forest floor. The clouds graze the forest tops, the canopy under which we walk. Exotic butterflies and insects buzz about. We are on special lookout for the famed multi-colored *quetzál* bird, a kind of bird of paradise that has given its name to the currency of Guatemala; among the Maya, the brilliant *quetzál* feathers once served as currency. The Bosque is suffused with a special enchanted atmosphere, far removed from the dirt and roar of the capital city way below. It's bound to be therapeutic for Luke.

One hour into the forest I hear a tremendous growl or roar, like a lion or other fierce animal in the bushes not far off. Sensing my uncertainty, he smiles. "That's a howler monkey, Ba. It's really a way small tree monkey, but it's got like this big sac in its throat that it can fill with air and make that noise." But the sound isn't a howl at all, it's truly a deep roar, fearsome to hear, and coming from this small creature. The fierce roars of the jungle are never far from Luke's daily existence.

He's again in an expansive mood. He loves being in Monteverde and Santa Elena; he says he really likes Luisa. We're pleased he has this relationship with a girl and we like her; she seems a genuinely nice person, balanced and straightforward—definitely falls into the *buenos amigos* category. She lives with her family in Santa Elena with her five brothers and sisters. Luke often hangs out at her house. She works at a local hostelry.

The next day Luke takes Prue and me off on a horseback trip down the mountain, past some waterfalls to a little artisan village. He has a friend who rents us the horses, and who accompanies us. He looks disreputable, I spot him right off as one of the *malos*; he and Luke have some slightly furtive conversations; the guy has little to say to me. But the ride down the side of the mountain is breathtaking, the vistas superb, the rushing brooks and waterfalls a great site for our picnic. Luke is in high spirits, seemingly in his element. He's again solicitous towards Prue's welfare and comfort on her horse after her operation. The surly guy charges us more money than we had agreed on. Luke shrugs, "What can I say, Ba?"

What really grabs me is Arenál, the dark, brooding, rumbling volcano some twenty miles away that periodically puts on a free *son et lumière* show at night, ready or not. Sometimes during the day you can hear a belch, a bang, or some otherworldly geological expletive issuing from the bowels of the earth, coughing up the contents of the earth's core and delivering it to this exit point in little Costa Rica—the sub-surface inchoate that can at any point break forth into Luke's sunnier days here.

Luke often takes tourists on horseback to the Arenál overview point about ten kilometers out of Santa Elena, but we've already done the horse thing. We rent a car and make a broader swing through the highland towns, including Arenál. Luisa comes along with us; she's a warm spirit, seems very fond of Luke and they cuddle a lot in the back seat; Luke teases her good-naturedly. She also seems to know Luke's ways pretty well and demonstrates on occasion a touch of almost maternal common sense in handling him.

Luke directs us up a back road towards Arenál where we meet a sign that tells us to go no closer to the volcano. But other adventuresome *Ticos* are driving up much closer to the base of the cone and parking there. Luke and I favor moving in closer as well since the mountain seems quiet, although Luke warns about climbing up along the cone on foot where it is possible to break through the crust and land your feet in lava. We get out and walk up slowly towards the base of the great cone that rises perhaps a thousand feet or more above us. Then a rumble shakes the ground beneath us. A huge thunder clap cracks out across the valley from the cone in whose shadow we stand. Clearly we have angered Arenál. Ten seconds after the sharp report we suddenly see gravel spewing up, out and down from inside the cone, raining pyroclastic hailstones. We bend down to cover our head and run back about a hundred yards to the car, pelted by these gravel-like stones. Mercifully they're not molten. They haven't touched the car, but we and all the other visitors lose no time in driving quickly away out of range, back past the sign that forbids closer entry. My respect for Third World signage grows.

One night Luke asks to borrow the car to go with Luisa to visit her aunt in the next village some ten kilometers away. Reluctantly I hand over the keys, remind him that the car is rented. The next morning Luke doesn't show up with the car to meet us, and we walk down to Mama Josefina's to find him. The car is there, there is a dent in the bumper. He's sound asleep in his blankets on the floor in his room. I check the speedometer, he has done over a hundred kilometers last night, going God knows where. We roust Luke out of bed; he seems hung over, mumbles something about going with some friends down towards San José, and somebody dented the car in the parking lot. Goddammit Luke, you've ripped me off on this, you know damn well that you weren't planning to visit Luisa's aunt ten kilometers away. I can't trust you on these things. And I'll have to pay through the nose for the dent to this rental car. I'm pissed. Silent sheep-facedness. Gullible me, again.

Our time is closing out in Costa Rica and Luke wants to take us to the famous Manuel Antonio National Reserve Park on the sea. We all pile into the car along with Luisa and drive down the mountains back to the coast where we get two rooms at a motel. Luke and Luisa are happy to spend some time together in privacy away from the conservative prying eyes of her home town. We continue to like her more and more as we see her. She's a warm, decent and thoughtful girl interested in more than just a "good time." We can see she's a good influence on Luke, and I suspect Luke knows it.

Driving to the Park the next day we have trouble finding a place to park. In the end we have to settle for a "watched park" run by some teenage kids. Luke says the locals pay when they leave, to avoid hassles about whether they have paid up or not; he tells the kid we'll pay on the way out. But the kid comes up to me and demands that I pay now, he won't listen to Luke. He mutters, *Los Chinos no pagan*, "Chinese don't pay up." That really touches Luke's hot button, and he gets in the kid's face and says in Spanish, "I'm not Chinese, you jerk, I'm American and we'll pay just like all the rest." This is a small part of the mini-racism that Luke encounters here and there that we don't usually hear about. It's not all negative however. He tells us that when he travels by air he's often asked by passengers if he's Michael Chang, the popular Asian-American pro tennis player whom he somewhat resembles. In Turkey it was Bruce Lee. There are some good Asian role models for him.

We cross barefoot from the beach across a shallow rivulet where the sea separates the park's island from the mainland. We stroll all around the island that is filled with wild life, sea animals, colorful birds, pounding surf and a great tropical atmosphere.

In our photo we see Luke from behind, sitting contentedly on a large rock with his arm around Luisa looking out over the rolling waves of the Pacific—facing the direction of his origins.

Another picnic in tropical paradise. Hours later we walk back. What was once a rivulet has now been transformed by the tide into a significant gap of some fifty yards of fast running sea current. We either swim across or wait another twelve hours. We strip down to our undershorts and, doing our best to carry our clothes, camera, wallet and all above the water, walk/float across the divide back to the mainland. It lends a sense of wild isolation to the park, still pristine in its ecological areas.

It's time for us to head back to San José and fly home. Bye, Luke and Luisa, we had a great time, take it easy, Luke, try to be sensible, take care of yourselves, we love you. We watch them get on the bus holding hands to go back up to Santa Elena.

I feel good. In another month Luke will be flying back to LA to join the family for Christmas holidays. Luke's no longer operating in the adolescent world of California, he's learning to make his way as an adult, slowly, painfully. This is the right place for him ... isn't it?

# CHAPTER TWELVE

# GOODBYE SANTA ELENA

*Christmas 1992 - Los Angeles*

In great spirits Prue and I go down to LAX to meet his afternoon plane in from Costa Rica. We wait outside the gates where passengers emerge from customs. I note from the arrivals board that his plane landed over an hour ago, but still no Luke. Did he manage to miss the plane? "Mr. Fuller?" a uniformed officer inquires of me. "Your son Luke is inside, he's been detained. Please follow me."

I did not think that the warm vibes, the gratifying memories and the hints of optimism from Santa Elena just one month ago could be so quickly reversed. Luke's infirmity cannot long be kept at bay. For God's sake, Luke, surely you can't be that damned stupid to get in trouble here already. We are escorted in to see the authorities. A thin, pleasant-looking officer approaches me. "I'm sorry Mr. Fuller, but we've had to detain your son for possession of marijuana. Luckily for him it was only half a gram. That falls into the category of personal use. But it's still illegal and we are imposing a fine of five-hundred dollars. We can't release him until it is paid." Dammit, there goes Luke again, his police file swelling out like the body of a binge eater. We look at him, slumped in the chair, downcast eyes, spiritless. No hint of the boy who greeted us enthusiastically in Costa Rica a month ago. And wouldn't you know it, the damn kid is dressed in raggedy jeans, knobby knees showing through the large rip-holes, long stringy black hair below his shoulders, sandals, backpack, penniless, hippy written all over him, the kind of figure who makes the day of a computer profiler, sashaying into LAX in total naiveté.

It's Christmas. What else am I going to do, leave him to the narcs at the airport? Of course I pay up. "Dammit, Luke," I storm, as we leave the airport. "This five-hundred bucks is going to go right onto your bloody account of money you owe us. I'm willing to support all kinds of programs to help you get your feet on the ground, to grow up. But I'll be damned if I'm going to pay your fines to the law. This five hundred goes on top of the two-thousand bucks you owe us from your golf course spree. And by God you're going to pay it if I have to wait to the end of my days." Luke slumps, chastened, in the backseat of the car, seemingly angry at himself, the situation, and the lecture. We don't have much exchange in the car on the way back.

Luke arrives home to be greeted with unqualified joyfulness only by Barney, barking and squealing and jumping up and down—the only one in the family not to become immediately aware of the latest LAX caper. The magic of Monteverde and the Bosque and Santa Elena and Luisa and Arenál and Manuel Antonio has evaporated; back in the American reality of our home in Thousand Oaks nothing seems to have changed. Luke still has a past that can't be wiped away; no holidays, no rain forests, no charming little mountain cantinas can divert Luke's moth-like attraction to the flame of reckoning.

My father has flown out from North Carolina for the holidays, and Samantha and Melissa have arrived as well. It should be a nice family reunion, but the situation has already placed constraints on the warmth and ease of welcome. Our daughters see in the LAX scene only deepened confirmation of Luke's waywardness. My father really doesn't know what to say to Luke anymore, except to be courteous and pleasant.

It's like Luke is back in a different world now. Most of the time he sticks to himself; Luke seems to feel himself an outcast, sensing his parents' unhappiness, disappointment, dissatisfaction, the disapprobation of his sisters. He has little to say to my father other than a few polite remarks. Each day we ask, "Are you going to be here for dinner tonight Luke?" And as often as not he says he doesn't think so. "I'll probably be out with friends," is the answer. And when he comes back in to the house at night we often spot the telltale red eyes of pot, along with some of the irritability that goes with coming down off it. He'll just greet us in a perfunctory way and head off to his room. On the few times he does eat with all of us, the shadow of his problems seems to fall across the dinner table despite efforts to gloss it over with family good feeling. After getting up late each day he usually cooks himself a fairly elaborate breakfast, always including rice and soy sauce and eggs, various other Asian or Latino creative concoctions from leftovers. He's best in the morning, most congenial, good humored, more accessible. We banter sometimes in the morning about Mexico, Santa Elena.

But I remind him: "Luke, since you're going to be back here for about four weeks or so, we think you should go down to your old Taco Bell job and get on their shift schedule. You've got the time, you need to earn pocket money. And I want you to start repaying the money you owe on your five-hundred-dollar airport fine." Luke sighs, "OK, Ba." He does start working some shifts there, but the paycheck won't be in for a minimum of two weeks anyway.

On Christmas Eve and Christmas day he does make an effort to spend time with us, but he's fairly quiet. He brought some modest presents for all of us, Costa Rican handicrafts. He seems embarrassed at getting gifts from his sisters, like he feels he doesn't deserve them, but he thanks everyone. He works hard to be on his best behavior. I don't know what else to do to try to integrate him more into family holiday activities. Cooking things together is the best. I sense that Luke has something more on his mind, but it hasn't come out yet.

*      *      *

Heading out the door one day, I pick up my wallet from the top of my bureau where I usually leave it. I check the amount of cash, it should be about eighty dollars—but there's only forty in the wallet. I'm sure that at least two twenty-dollar bills are missing. But I'm not one hundred percent positive. I walk into Luke's room. "Money is missing from my wallet, Luke, maybe forty dollars. I'm suspicious about what happened to it." "I didn't take anything," he says defensively. "Well, I hope you didn't, but I'm not sure I believe you. You better be aware, I'm watching carefully." And over the next few days I keep close mental tally of the sum in the wallet. I still leave it out in my room as a test case, and now I am sure that Luke is periodically pilfering smaller amounts from the overall amount there. I then place a piece of paper in the wallet with the exact sum written out—handwritten so he can't alter it. And sure enough, over the next few days up to half the amount is missing again.

"Luke, you're a goddam thief!" I go charging into his room one morning while he is still asleep. "I know you've taken money, thirty-five bucks, from my wallet today, I wrote down exactly how much I had in it." "What?" he mumbles out. "I don't know anything about it." "You damn well do," I say, "nobody else in the house would take it." Luke mumbles something, clearly on the defensive. "This is intolerable," I go on. "We can't have you in the house victimizing us. If this goes on much longer we're simply not going to be able to allow you to stay here. You're on Christmas vacation, this is a family time. This really sucks—ripping off your own family." Luke will be going back to Costa Rica in a few weeks, so I can't take drastic action now about moving him out. But I'm mad that we have to be on high alert. And Prue now has to watch her purse closely. Worse, I have to warn Samantha and Melissa as well to guard their things. I can feel their disapproval and anger swelling; some of it is tacitly directed at me as well for allowing this to happen. Well, what in hell's name am I supposed to do about it?

One day Prue comes and says that she can't find her nice cashmere sweater, one that Luke had given her a year ago. We ask Luke, he says he doesn't know anything about it. Then I search around his room and in his luggage. There is the sweater. "Luke, what are you doing with this sweater? You said you didn't know anything about it." Luke hangs his head. "I wanted to take it as a Christmas present for Luisa after I get back." "Look, we understand you want to give her a present, but what kind of thing is this to be stealing something you gave to your own mother a year ago? How can we trust you around the house?" Some distress, a shamefaced look.

And with Luke's return home, the strange phone calls start. Louts calling up at late hours, sullen, uncommunicative voices. "Luke?" "No, this isn't Luke. Who's calling?" "Just a friend." "You want to leave a message?" "No," click. Or, "Just tell him to call Marty right away." Often Luke takes a call and then heads out the door, says a friend is coming by. Luke is acting surreptitiously, I'm sure deals are going down. "I warn you Luke, I'm going to start listening in on your calls if I think you're getting involved in drug deals here." Luke scowls, as if I'm improperly intruding upon his affairs. And I do start listening in on some of the calls he gets, but Luke is generally aware, he clearly interrupts the caller and just says, "Let's not talk on the phone, I'll meet you in half an hour."

One night when I can't sleep I get up around three-thirty and look out the window and see that the car is gone from the driveway. I check Luke's room, he's not there. I sit up and wait until I see the car pulling in, about an hour later; he walks into the kitchen where I'm sitting. "Luke, where the hell have you been with the car?" I bellow. He's taken aback, he didn't expect that I would be up. "Nowhere, I just went to see a friend," he mumbles. "You know you're not allowed to drive, you don't even have a goddam license. Where did you get the key?"

Silence. "Let me see the key," I demand. He hands over a single key, not the standard bunch of Dodge logo-keys that come with the car. "Where did you get this key?" "I made a copy," he mumbles. It's clear he's swiped the key from Prue or me at some point and had a copy made. "Luke, this is a damn outrage. You don't even have a driver's license—and you know why we won't let you get one. We don't even have any insurance coverage on you driving it either. What if you'd had an accident? Do you realize that I would be liable for damages out of my own pocket? Maybe hundreds of thousands of dollars if you killed someone? And you're breaking the goddam law." "I needed to go see some friends." "At three o'clock in the morning? What kind of friends are they? Seems clear as hell to me you've been out on some drug run." Silence, shamefacedness. Luke's usual non-belligerent passive—not even aggressive—approach; hunker down and ride out the anger. I confiscate the keys, and make sure the master keys are kept under close control.

And now I'm forced to start keeping mileage records—an odometer log each night. And yet twice more I find the car has been taken out, not for huge distances, but pretty surely taken out. But I'm less than zealous about keeping every odometer log-in or wallet tally up to date. I threaten Luke, warn him. But I also know that the tools—or weapons—at my command are pretty limited. I'm not going to throw him out of the house this late during this vacation period. I'm not going to call the police. I'm not giving him any allowance now anyway, so I have almost no financial controls. He's getting too old to ground.

We have some friends over for dinner one night and I notice that a big bottle of Stolichnaya is missing. I don't have a detailed memory for what I keep in the liquor closet, but I remember buying the vodka quite recently. It's got to be Luke. I accuse him of taking it. He denies it, only halfheartedly, but I know his style, it's as good as a confession. I can't be sure whether he has been raiding some of the other bottles as well.

He's also quick to get out to the mailbox before we do every day, he obviously wants to grab his paycheck before I do, or to claim it hasn't arrived yet. In fact, despite my riding herd on him, I have yet to recover any serious portion of his five-hundred-dollar debt, not to mention the two thousand from the golf course fine. "Luke, I'm angry with you about your failure to pay us anything back. Where is your paycheck from Taco Bell?" "I owed some friends some money," he lamely offers. "Yeah, and you owe me some money as well. A lot more."

The curtain drops. He pauses, raises his eyes and now looks at me intensely. "If I don't pay them off I'll be in serious trouble with them," he says quietly. "So this has to do with money for drugs?" Luke sighs, weary with me at the necessity of having to spell out the obvious. He knows I know. Even when he says nothing, his glazed eyes on occasion when he comes back from work in the evenings say it all. "Luke, is it just pot?" I ask. He nods. "And coke too?" "Sometimes." "Anything else?" He shakes his head. But I'm not sure I believe him. "Luke, you're ruining your life with all this shit, it's going to kill you one way or another," I say. "I know, Ba," he says, wearily. *I don't need to be told.*

And even before Luke goes back, in comes a credit card bill that clearly indicates Luke has "borrowed" Prue's credit card on at least two occasions, surprisingly only for lunch at some sushi place, apparently with a friend. He seems to get away with forging Prue's signature without challenge from these institutions. This use of our card under false pretenses of course has potential criminal consequences, depending on how we handle it.

Samantha and Melissa are filled with indignation as they eventually find out about these goings on. Worse, I'm almost in collusion with Luke now in trying to keep them from finding out all the latest sordid details, from having to justify all of this to them. "Baba, how can you let Luke get away with all this," they cry. "So what should I do?" I reply. "You should punish him," they say. I look up at them angrily. I'm getting it from both ends here. "Like what? Take off my belt and whip him? Take away his allowance, when he doesn't have one? Ground him at home when he should be out working? Take away his car privileges when he doesn't have a car and we won't let him get a license? Send him back to Costa Rica to get rid of him? Refuse to send him back to Costa Rica as punishment when that seems to be the best thing for him?" "OK, but why did you have to take him skiing up in Big Bear last time he was here, does he deserve that?" "Look," I say, "you may think this is a reward for bad behavior, but I'm just trying to get through to this kid, to communicate with him on a lot of problems. If going to Big Bear will help then I'm going to Big Bear. It has nothing to do with rewards."

"But his stealing your credit card, forging signatures, that's a crime!" "Yes, it is. You want me to call the police? Will that solve the problem? I'll testify against him in court? Jail is the magic answer?" "Well, you have to do something so he doesn't keep on getting away with these things." "Yes," I respond wearily, "yes, I have to do something."

Something. I feel isolated, surrounded. I am angry at Luke, angry at my daughters, angry at Prue. They are angry with me. Prue feels the tension. She silently hugs me from time to time. We don't say anything. We know what we are feeling. It spreads like a contagion.

Days before Luke leaves, I go to turn on my stereo and I find the speakers are dead. When Luke gets home in the evening, I demand an answer. "OK, Ba, look, I'm sorry, Mark came over today and me and Mark took the speakers out to the pool so we could play music out there. I guess we turned them up too loud or something, because they just popped." "Goddam it, Luke, that was irresponsible. You should at least have had the guts to tell me yourself. I want you to stay the hell away from my property, all of my property; that means my wallet, our car, our credit cards, my speakers, anything! Got it? *Entendido?*" Just one more item to put on Luke's great big tab up in the sky. No, this wasn't malicious, but, as usual, it was totally irresponsible, unthinking.

The clock keeps ticking out the time to the end of his stay. Prue and I and Luke go down to Chinatown for dinner on his last night home with us, to smooth over some of these rough edges with Asian food—a reliable lubricant. I want to engage in some serious exchange on our concerns. We're sitting in a booth where there's no escape. The drink is tea, which Luke pours into our little cups; we're fiddling with our chopsticks, picking up peanuts with them from a little dish in a little game as we wait for our order. It's nice to be together, but we all know we're just fending off for a few minutes a more serious summing up. "Luke, you know this hasn't been a very happy Christmas for us this time, and maybe not for you either." "I know, I'm sorry. It's just that things aren't working out so good." "Well, it's clear you seem tense a lot, and you've been high on pot or other things for a lot of the time." "It's just that I feel a lot of pressure, Ba. I don't want to do these things, but … I don't know, it's just things aren't working out." He trails off into silence. As always, he doesn't want confrontation, he seems acquiescent with us. "What things?" "I don't know, just jobs and shit in Santa Elena."

"But Luke, what bothered you so much at home with us this time? I notice that you avoided spending much time with any of us, or your sisters or my father while you were here." "Yeah, well it is sometimes a strain. I mean you guys always are talking and talking all the time, and it's not about stuff that interests me, and you're always asking me questions and stuff. I feel like I'm under a spotlight. I just like to be with my own friends sometimes. Kick back … I mean you guys are good to me and all, and always try to help me and look out for me and stuff—I know that. I know you love me. I don't like it when I make you feel sad, but I can't help it sometimes." Tears come to his eyes. "It's just me. I need time to work out a lot of shit for myself."

"Luke, you don't need to feel guilty about being uncomfortable hanging out with us all the time, or doing your own thing. I know we can be sort of overwhelming as a family sometimes. We're all different people in some ways, but that doesn't keep us from caring about each other. But you seem to be tuning out on drugs. They're getting a grip on you." Luke averts his eyes. "No, it's OK, Ba, I can control it. I'm going to try to quit soon, after I get back to Costa Rica and get a job."

The waiter puts down a dish of fiery Szechuan tofu and meat.

"OK, but this time things feel different. You barely even communicate with us. Like, I waited a long time over the holidays in the hopes that you might want to go skiing with me again, or fishing, or something over Christmas. But you never asked like you used to. It was just pot, some shifts at Taco Bell, more pot, staring at TV screens while you were here. We could have done some stuff together." Luke picks at a piece of tofu with his chopsticks, eyes averted, and looks pained.

"But you know what worries me most, Luke? I'm afraid you're into drugs big time now—as a user and a seller. Think about it, Luke, you know from Be Free meetings where this can head. To theft and crime to support the habit. If that's your problem you'd better count on spending a lot of time with AA when you get back here—or else some serious prison time."

"I'm not going to go to prison, Ba," Luke says with quiet determination, "I'm going to stay out of trouble." "Well, I hope so, but prison is at the end of the road you're on right now." Silence. "I know," he says quietly. "So how do you think you can help turn this around if you're not in a program like Be Free?" "I don't know. I think if I can just get a decent job in Santa Elena and be with Luisa I can get my act together." "You know we like Luisa, we think she's a good influence. But you're going to have to refocus on where you're going, not just drift." He turns, plaintively, to look right at me, tears in the corners of his eyes. "But where can I go, Ba?" he whispers. "What do you think I should do?"

I feel deep pain. Where do I go with this? "Luke, you know we think you have a lot of good qualities, talents." I try to speak softly. "You could do a lot of different things. You have a good mind—even if you've got lousy judgment right now. You have a nice personality and people like you. You have a good sense of humor. We enjoy being with you a lot of the time, like our trips across the country, or running around Costa Rica with you. I would love to do more with you like skiing or fishing or traveling. You have a lot of talent for mechanical things. You cook well, you could be a good chef. You have abilities for languages. You have some good business instincts. But you know what? Honesty too, is essential in business if you aren't going to destroy your reputation early on." We pause to let things settle, get a second wind. His defenses are down and we're a deeper level in.

"I know, but ... see, I just can't get organized, I don't know what to do," he says slowly. "I just don't know if I have enough willpower to do all these things I'm supposed to ... it's tiring to have to keep it all up."

"How do you know you don't have willpower, Luke? You're still young, you don't have to decide yet exactly what it is you want to do with your life. Most kids in college don't know. Samantha is still thinking about it even after college. It may take you quite a few years to decide."

"OK, Ba, but how do I decide? I don't know what I want ... or where I belong."

"Is that partly because of being adopted?"

"Yeah, partly … I mean, no, I don't think about it that much. Just sometimes. People ask me about what it feels like to be adopted and shit."

Wow. This is the first time the adoption issue has come up seriously with us. "Look, I can only imagine what it's like to be adopted. I can see how you can feel upset about having been abandoned, having to be adopted—by anybody. And wanting to find out about your birth mother and your past. That's normal. But there are also worse things in life than being adopted. It certainly doesn't make us feel bad if you want to know more about your background. If you're interested, we are totally willing to help you try to look into your past, to see if anything more can be learned about it."

Luke glances up. "Yeah, I might want to do that. I mean, maybe I should go to Korea for a visit."

"Luke, we're absolutely ready to let you go to Korea to poke around if that would be useful. Holt has some young adults program for adoptees, or you could go on your own. We'd even be happy to go with you if you'd like."

"Thanks, Ba, I'll think it over. Or maybe I should think about joining the Marines or something."

"Yeah, that could work too, Luke, I remember you kind of liked Army and Navy. But it's the same old tune, if you can't get off drugs, they won't take you, or they can throw your ass into military prison if you violate the law as a soldier."

The adoption issue. Does it really sit on his mind, some lurking sense that our bonds with him are fragile, legal, based on kindness but not on family ties? Are my threats of action, of tossing him out of the house raising deep anxieties about yet another chapter of abandonment? That scares me, breaks my heart.

"I just want to say one more thing here, Luke. Obviously we are upset about where your life has been going, but that doesn't mean we're going to wash our hands of you. We are never, never going to do that. I want you to know that. Whatever happens we're not going to abandon you. Even if you go to prison, we won't abandon you, we will stay in close touch and visit you and work to help you. So you can always count on us as long as we're alive. But I don't think that jail visits is what either of us wants either."

"No, I don't want that. I appreciate you guys' support … Even if it doesn't look like I do," he says.

"But I'm going to have to lay it on the line with you now, Luke. When you eventually come back from Costa Rica you're going to have to find some shared apartment somewhere. We're not going to take you by the hand and organize your life on a daily basis. It really bugs us to have to nag you. When you're back here with us you just regress back to being more immature, like a child again—and then we start treating you more like a child. We hate that, and it's not healthy, for either of us."

Luke listens in silence, no objections.

"And you need to finish high school or somehow get your General Education Degree. That's vital, unless you want to flip burgers for a living."

I feel like a broken record. And the dishes come and go, and fiery beef gives way to chicken and cashews. It's not all just hard-core parent-to-kid talk. We ask all about what's going on in Santa Elena and with all the various characters we met there. We talk about music, what he likes, what I like. "How is it, Luke, that you generally know what kind of rock bands I'm going to like? I'm impressed, you're pretty good at guessing right." "It's not hard, I know you don't like all that techno-shit and stuff, but I like some of the older rock classics too that you have."

"Luke, did you hear that Brandon Lee, Bruce's son, was killed a few weeks ago while making that kung fu movie, *The Crow*?" "Really?" "Yeah, incredibly someone had put—or left—one live bullet in the guns they were using that were loaded with blanks and shooting at each other. They don't know if it was an accident or what." "Wow, that's really weird shit, Ba, I read about how there is a curse on that family that somebody in Hong Kong had prophesied." And we talk about the latest mystery related to Bruce Lee. And we talk about past trips, news from some of our friends whom Luke knows, some of the trips we've taken. I feel good, we're connecting over the meal, it doesn't feel forced. But this is not the setting, or norm of everyday communication.

"I haven't had a chance to tell you yet, Luke, but you know, we've been thinking things over, we're probably going to move back to Maryland early next year. I can work in the RAND office in Washington, and it's a lot better for me to be working in DC for all this foreign policy stuff I do. But what would you do, Luke, if we leave California?"

He looks worried. "Jeez, I don't know, Ba. Hard to say … Right now I think I'd like to stay on in Santa Elena, I know I can find odd jobs around there. I want to be with Luisa and have some time to think things over." "Would you want to stay on in California by yourself if we go back?" Real pause. Pregnant question. "Gee, I'm not sure, if you guys go back to Maryland, hmm … I guess I wouldn't want to stay on here by myself." "You don't think you have enough connections here in California, enough of a life to be on your own?" Luke shifts around on his seat. "No … I don't think so, Ba," he says quietly.

This is a moment of truth, for both of us. He's *not* growing up, he doesn't seem to crave independence, even to want to break away from his parents like most kids get itchy to do. He's anxious about himself in the real world. And I think we're talking about more here than just a roof over his head. He doesn't feel he's ready for the world.

"OK, look, we'll talk about the move more a few months down the road. In the meantime, you're heading back to Costa Rica. But you're on notice, this time you're going to be on a strict budget, no exceptions, or bailouts from us anymore. *Entendido?*" "Yeah, Ba, *entendido.*"

And the next day we put Luke back on the plane to Costa Rica, my heart again churning with mixed emotions. He doesn't head off with quite the same spirit. When he is clean I enjoy his company, I want to try to share his life, share his problems, be a good father, assist him, protect him. But my heart is fearful now and I feel teary.

That night as we're preparing for bed I tell Prue. "You know what makes me really feel worst of all? I recognize that deep in my heart I wasn't unhappy to see Luke leave again. I feel really guilty about that." "I know," Prue says, "I felt the same way when I saw him go, and I don't want to feel that way. But I'm just tired of having to be suspicious, mistrustful, locking our stuff up all the time, waiting for what he's going to do next." I sigh. "You're right. When he's away it's his responsibility, we don't have to ride herd on him all the time." "But we still worry," adds Prue.

But even as he wings off for Central America, the story is not over, the slate is not wiped clean. A backlog of shit from his month's stay with us continues to flow in, raising my ire. A few weeks later, I fire off a letter to him, I want it all down on paper in front of his eyes so he can read it, so he can't just tune it out.

*March 1993*

*Dear Luke,*

*You're now nineteen! How did you celebrate your birthday?*

*We still spend a lot of time thinking about you and how you are coming along in Santa Elena in the hard struggle to grow up and gain maturity. We love you and we care very much about how your life is progressing. We are pleased that you're settling down in Costa Rica with your new job as a cook.*

*I wish we could have had a happier Christmas. But you know what made me saddest of all? That I felt some relief in seeing you go. We both cried after we saw you off. We love you very much, but we feel that we are losing you to drugs; they're destroying any moral principles you might have towards us or anybody else.*

*You should think carefully about the impact of everything that happened in the short time you were here, when you were probably in a cloud of pot-smoke much of the time. Your theft of money from my wallet, your mother's purse, taking our car illegally. Use of drugs and evidence of selling them. We simply can't live like this anymore. We consider you have abused us, abused our confidence, and our trust, in our own home—your own home. We can't live in a constant atmosphere of distrust and suspicion; it makes our lives miserable.*

*Frankly, the shit still just keeps piling up. Since you left we've gotten a number more credit card charges that you forged. That is a criminal offense. Worse, it's a pretty lousy way to treat us.*

*We think of you often as we see you in our mind's eye—wandering around Monteverde in the clouds. We are really happy we visited you there. It was a great visit, and it brings us closer to you to know what your exotic world is like there. Samantha and Melissa ask regularly about news from you. They may be angry with your behavior now—and they have a right to be—but they care a lot for you, and are concerned about your welfare. Other family members also ask about you and tell us to pass along their love and best wishes. You have a lot of people who care about you and want to help, but you have to help yourself first.*

*We're off to Santa Barbara tonight to go to a jazz club. Barney misses you too. We're having to clean the house up, paint it before putting out a For Sale sign. You're lucky you're not here for all the chaos.*

*We will always love you and care for you and be in touch, wherever you are and whatever the problems may be. We can work together on helping turn your life in meaningful directions. But things must change.*

*Love, Ba*

*In extremis* I have turned again to words, written words, my strong suit, my perpetual vehicle to get through to him. Will he even read the letter through? Or just blow it off? Or will he be pained by it, shaken, chastened? Or just remain paralyzed, stuck in a groove, unable to break out, regardless?

Or maybe I just should have beaten the shit out of him and thrown him out of the house. That's a statement too.

*　　　　　*　　　　　*

And then, a break! Luke has gotten a message from a Canadian adventure tours company in Toronto. We get the fax from them to forward on to Luke by phone.

*Dear Luke,*

*My partner at Travel Adventures just returned from spending a week in Costa Rica and suggested that I contact you. He really enjoyed meeting you and recommended that I should book a horseback riding excursion with you from Monteverde to Arenál Volcano for my group coming through this spring. If you could just confirm that, either by faxing me in Canada through your father, or we can just wait until I get there.*

*I look forward to meeting you soon.*

*Best regards ...*

We call Luke and pass along the message. He is happy. He tells us that he had hit it off with this Canadian guy who really liked the horseback trip Luke took him on. He says that the guy wants to talk to him about a possible year-long job as a guide in the region for the company. I send back Luke's response. We get back another note from the company for forwarding to Luke.

*Dear Luke,*

*Thank you for your quick confirmation for my group. I am including more information regarding tour leading for our Adventure Tourism so that you can be more familiar with what we are looking for in a leader. We do have an opening coming up in December for a guide in Belize and Guatemala that you may want to think about. I will talk further to you about it when I am in Costa Rica. Looking forward to meeting you and exploring all this.*

Luke has won another ally, an impressed traveler who might hire him as a representative and agent of their company in Central America. This is exactly what Luke loves doing, taking people around, showing local knowledge. His Spanish is good, he's very gregarious. This contact has genuine promise, linked with a serious international travel organization. I think it's hand-tailored for him. In our phone calls to Luke we ensure that the date and the task are clear for his meeting with the company rep. We're excited at the prospect and look forward to his report back on how it all went.

Could Luke fuck this one up?

He could. He does. Inexplicably he fails to show up on the date, even for the horse ride. He totally let them down, not to mention blowing off the option of interviewing for possible further employment. Where in hell was this kid after these arrangements had been made? Stoned somewhere? Some kind of a mind disconnect? Or did he shrink back from a potential serious commitment that he feared he couldn't handle?

It turns out that the job description was fairly rigorous; it involved making schedules and logistical arrangements for each group of tourists coming through, "managing the expenses and troubleshooting unexpected glitches." Prue and I know already that there is no way Luke could summon up the necessary discipline and responsibility to handle such commitments. Luke himself is the unexpected glitch. Other people's money in his hands would most likely be quickly invested in a line of credit for pot, or harder stuff. And he can't even manage his own life, much less others'. The wonderful and personable impression he makes vaporizes in the face of real world personal commitments, even in the funkier world of adventure tourism with the backpack crowd.

I call him up to try to get the story: "Luke, this is what you love doing. Where in hell were you? This looked like a fantastic opportunity." He has no answer. "I don't know, it's just … I completely forgot." But my questions are becoming increasingly rhetorical; do I really need to ask any more? Forgot? I think subliminally he knew he wasn't up to it. Now he'll go on working as cook at one of the cantinas, at least until something better—or worse—comes along.

Later in the spring Luke calls us up, it's after midnight. I tense at what the story could be at this unpropitious hour. "Ba, I've got a bad medical problem. One of my balls has gotten really infected, it's all swollen up, and it hurts like hell. I've been to the doctor down in San José. He says he needs to do some surgery on it quickly, but I don't have the money for it." His testicles? Then the fleeting thought: Is this yet another ruse for money?

"How did you get this, Luke?" "I don't know, I just woke up the other morning and it was really sore and it has been swelling more and more. It hurts me just to walk now." "OK, look Luke, I don't want you going to some unknown doctor there, we can't know if he's any good or not. Especially I don't want you to have surgery on your balls. God knows if you really do need surgery, or what might happen to you. Let me check around and get some advice." I check with our local doctor. "No operation! You'd better bring your son back here where he can get reliable medical treatment, but bring him back fast, you don't want to fool around with something like that," he warns. We arrange a flight back the next day. It's got to be for real, Luke says he is in terrible pain.

We line up a doctor to see him immediately at LAX as soon as he arrives. The doctor says the testicle is indeed badly infected and very swollen, he'll give it heavy antibiotics. He is not even sure that the testicle will survive, but if worse comes to worst Luke's other testicle is still untouched by infection. The doctor says a variety of things could have caused it, including physical damage, an accidental twist of the testicle cords, or it might be sexually transmitted. Luke, unpersuasively, says he doesn't know where it came from. He's hobbling around and will stay with us in LA until it gets better. We do get him HIV-tested, and heave a sigh of relief when it comes back negative. It's been an expensive visit back and he's due to go back shortly. Or so I thought.

After a few days convalescence the infection seems under control. I ask Luke one morning when he's cooking his breakfast about his plans. Hesitation. "Actually Ba, I'm thinking about if I should go back." "What, why wouldn't you?" "It's just that it's getting harder to find a job in Santa Elena, and I'm getting into a hassle with some people there about regular work. There's some people that don't like me there either." Obviously there is something more going on. "Why don't they like you, Luke?" "See, well, I bought some pot from some of these guys some time back and they claim I owe them money even though I paid them. They're just goons and they're trying to squeeze money out of me."

"Luke, this doesn't sound good at all. We're going to have to clear this thing up pretty quick. I don't want to send you back there just for a short time. This is too much money. If you're not going back you're going to need to make some firm plans for here. We're not going to have you lounging around here at home with just part-time Taco Bell work. We talked about this earlier."

The next day the story sharpens. I get a call from Mama Josefina, his landlady. "I'm sorry to tell you this, Señor Fuller, but Luke is in trouble with the police here in Santa Elena." "What kind of trouble?" "I don't know, but it's not good, they've come around and searched his room here, it's over some drug thing. They think Luke has stolen some money. The police want to talk to him when he gets back." Mama Josefina strongly recommends that Luke not come back if he wants to avoid further trouble with the police. And she claims Luke owes her two months rent. I confront Luke with the story. "I'm sorry Ba, I didn't want this to happen, but I got into some drug trading there because I needed money. I just didn't have enough to live on when I couldn't find a regular job." He looks despondent, helpless. "I don't want to go back now, Ba," he says softly, "it won't be good."

In August Luke gets a letter in Spanish from Luisa that I find lying around among his possessions months later. It provides still more clarification—and touches me deeply.

*2 August 1993*

*Hi Dear Luke!*

*Right now I'm in my room thinking a lot about you. It's sort of late, around 1130pm, but I'm not sleepy; I'm just sad and very worried about you because Alex's father told me that you had stolen 14,000 colones from some guy and he said that you are a bad person. I don't know what's going to happen now, but my brothers and sisters were very surprised about this theft and say it is the worst thing a person can do. But only you can know if this theft is true or not.*

151

*My parents don't know anything about this, and I think that's for the best, but they will find out soon enough and then they will start driving me crazy again asking me questions about you. I don't know what I am going to do, every day I'm feeling more disappointed by you. There are a lot of things going on with you, and you know very well what kind of things. I think if things keep going this way with you, even if I don't want to, I'll have to break off with you …*

*Luke, please think about our love, think how much I love you. I don't understand why you don't do something to become a more sincere person, more responsible, honorable, and clean of heart. Luke, please think, if you don't try to change your wrong way of life, then you won't have any friends in the future, or anybody to love you and have trust in you. Remember that there is still time to lead a better life, to change and not have more problems.*

*Remember, and realize that the problems are not with me, but with yourself. Still, in spite of everything, I love you and can help you make a free person out of yourself, a good person, although here in Monteverde now your reputation is gone. So for that reason I want to go somewhere far away with you as soon as possible. I know that God will help me be an example to you. Remember that God loves you even if you don't believe in him and he wants to help you because he loves you even more than I do. Just ask God to help you and open your heart to him.*

*I'm rereading your letter again and you say that you love me but that you need help. I want to help, but I don't know in what way, please tell me what I can do. Please think carefully about all of this, that's why I'm writing you this letter. I don't want to argue about it or fight about it; forgive me if I have done anything bad to you.*

*I love you a lot and don't ever want to break off with you, but you need to think that if you really love me then you must change. I will be your love for your whole life.*

*Luisa*

# CHAPTER THIRTEEN

# DEALING WITH THE HOMELAND

## *Summer 1993 - Thousand Oaks, California*

I'm surrounded by a jungle of Monteverde vines growing up around me on all sides, monstrous weeds, fertilized by drugs and shit. I can't find ways to penetrate through the thickets. I feel a tightening claustrophobia from my own impotence in the face of this situation—not just Luke's lack of options, *my* lack of options. What lies at the heart of Luke's anguish, his self-destructive spiral downwards? Is it "just" drugs? "Yes," say Prue and Melissa, "you've got to realize that if Luke has a drug problem it doesn't make any difference where you send him, he takes the problem with him." "Of course there are drugs," I reply, "but there's probably something deeper going on with Luke here. Is this just 'plain' addiction? We've got to know if he's ever to break out of this."

Have I really been naïve in my hopes for some kind of Third World therapy? Maybe this has been some heroic, foolish, maybe even arrogant intervention to kidnap Luke and exfiltrate him out of the meaningless American teen environment around him. It was maybe a romantic faith in redemption through immersion in the greater simplicity of life in a simpler society, a place where a nineteen-year-old Luke could face the coming of age in a simpler world. I recall Sergeant O'Brian at Army and Navy school: "Luke's past don't matter very much to us, ma'am, we just want to get on with where he needs to go."

In the middle of sleepless nights I lacerate myself in debates within my own head. *Face it, in all this fancy sociology about distant environments you've just been rationalizing your own incapacities in handling Luke. There is no Third World cultural nanny to magically cure Luke of his adolescent torments, his withdrawals from reality, his fatal flaws.*

OK, then, where in hell do we go from here? I'm plumb out of creative schemes. I'm tired. And Luke is not now in the relaxed Third World, he is here in America facing a computerized world that keeps precise tabs, chapter and verse, on every single one of his mistakes, crimes, and past legal tangles. How can I save my son from the workings of the Law?

153

Or is that the answer? Maybe I should just let things take their course. What was that first admonition of Be Free? "We recognize that our usual resources are powerless to free our families from the abuse of these chemicals and that our old solutions are not working to resolve our new problem."

*        *        *

Luke is back now to getting these damn phone calls all the time. Hello, is Luke there? Yeah, who's calling? Nobody, a friend. Can I have your name? Click. Hello, is Luke there? No, he's out. Do you want to leave a message? No, click. Hello? Just tell him Joey called. Click. Hello? I know Luke is there, you better tell him to answer his goddam phone.

This is obviously bad business, big-time *malos amigos*. I tell Luke I'm not going to answer any calls for him or take any messages. (This was still in the days when we just had our one home landline with multiple extensions.) I know from occasional eavesdropping that money is discussed with veiled references. Sometimes Luke takes off to meet a friend who comes by right after a conversation.

I grow more devious. I go to a spy shop—*this is what my background has come to?*—and buy a small instrument that turns on a little tape recorder in my bedroom when Luke is on the phone. It's a clunky device that clicks and Luke pretty quickly catches on there's someone eavesdropping. But I learn enough to know clearly that deals are going down. I confront him with it; Luke looks weary, like, *do we still have to pretend about this anymore?*

### October 1993 - Barcelona

I'm invited to a conference in Barcelona. I've never been to Spain before. We decide we'll take Luke with us. Same old arguments: we won't have to worry about what he's up to; it especially relieves us of the fears about what he might do to rip us off in our absence. It takes him away from his drug transactions. It limits the amount of drugs or booze he can take without our knowing it. It helps us bond with him, free from the distractions of home. And believe it or not, we actually enjoy his company away from home. He is generally in a good mood on the road, there are lots of things to talk about, he's somewhat interested in the things we do, he likes to go to interesting restaurants and hear local music. It's good for his education. He makes no objection.

Objection!—Samantha and Melissa snort. You're rewarding him again for his bad behavior! (I would love to have taken them in an earlier era, but I wasn't traveling then.) I'm not sure why Luke alone with us is always in his best form. In point of fact, Luke hasn't shown much of a "typical" teenage embarrassment with his parents. He has rarely accused us of being prehistoric; he'll generally tell us in moments of thoughtfulness that we're "cool," and, better yet, we know he has told some other friends the same thing about us, who report it back. Shoe's on the other foot now: I sometimes feel almost like the eager puppy-dog, grateful for a few reassuring pats from my son periodically to know I still belong. But above all, with us he'll have less access to daily drugs.

Madrid-bound, Luke strikes up a conversation in the back of the plane with a Spanish soccer team. They take to him and promise to show him a good time in Madrid. We concede one night to Luke for this enterprise. Luke gets back to the hotel late, has obviously had quite a number of drinks, says it was a great time; he's still pretty coherent. I do a homeland security number on him and go through his stuff with no apologies, but don't find anything. We head off to Toledo the next day. Great medieval city, superb city walls and fine old buildings. Luke abandons his usual cool appraisal of things, he's actually impressed. What really grabs him though is when we pass the artisan workshop of a master sword maker.

Luke always liked D&D, Dungeons and Dragons. Samantha was actually his keen mentor for years in the game, training him up, bringing him along, playing a lot of games with him, creating their characters, testing their powers and ramping their ratings up with rising combat tests. This was part of a onetime close bond between them and Luke was responsive. He still has a bent for the medieval, gothic, role-playing.

This all seems to come flooding back at the sword maker's. He finds a magnificent sword looking like something out of Tolkien with a great dragon head worked around the handle and down part of the blade. He decides this is what he wants to spend his modest money on, income from his fast-food job. Should I confiscate those funds for myself, or is this a "worthy cause?" I am touched that he also wants to buy a smaller medieval-style sword for Samantha. The *espadas* are wrapped up in a long corrugated cardboard box. Every night at the hotel Luke attentively brings them up into the room from the car for safe-keeping, all across Spain. His *espada* is his grand prize.

We go on to spend a few days in Córdoba and Granada, country of Muslim heritage, and of course its Flamenco. One night we visit the caves high up in the hills above the town for an evening of Flamencan music and dancing by torchlight, the burnt, yearning, rough off-key voices of the singers along with the guitarists who rip the very soul out of the instrument. It is commanding, imperious, overwhelming. Luke too, is visibly impressed, he's never heard music like this before. He wants a Pepe Romero album. He is opening up as the trip progresses, now far less intent on preserving his cool, or shielding his identity, seemingly openly growing and expanding his interests. He's absorbing experiences by the bucketful. Yes, this is why we brought him along.

Our photo shows Luke sitting on the ramparts in Granada looking out over the city with a deeply serious look and furrowed brow, even as he has his Walkman plugged in. What is he thinking as he surveys the scene? Some summation of life and self? Or do I read too much into this? Maybe he's simply caught up in his music, empty mind far off.

We finally reach Barcelona a few days later. This city has special meaning for me: my uncle, who was an artist and a communist during the Depression, at age twenty-one joined the Abraham Lincoln Brigade and came to Spain as a volunteer to help fight against Franco's Fascists. He took a bullet in the head on the ramparts outside Barcelona six weeks after arrival. His gravesite is unknown. Luke is impressed by the story, especially when we're standing near where it happened. He asks a lot of questions about the Spanish Civil War and about my uncle, whom I never knew.

Prue and Luke wander this creative city on their own until my conference is over. Luke goes out one evening on his own. The kid's nineteen, I'm not going to dog his footsteps. He comes back around ten pm, however, seemingly shaken. He says he's been to a bar. One of the women there came up to him and took a seeming fancy to him; they had a long conversation in Spanish, Luke telling about his adventures in Latin America and she tells him of her troubles. All the while she asks Luke to buy her a few drinks. After two hours he decides to move on: they stick him with a bill that comes to over three-hundred dollars. Luke is aghast, has no more than about fifty on him. The manager tells him to pay up or he'll call the police, or have the bouncer deal with him outside. Luke has no option, finally gives up his camera and Walkman and what money he has and gets out. He's mad, hurt at being taken. The thought flickers through my mind that this could be an elaborate ruse, that he's simply pawned his camera and Walkman for some harder substances, but Luke seems legitimately angry, humiliated and upset. Could it be in all the fleshpots of Costa Rica and Mexico that he's never been through the buying-cognac-for-the-bar-girl routine before? Chalk it up to experience— but his, or mine? I'm not about to replace his lost items.

We finally take off north for the Pyrenees. We get higher and higher into beautiful river valleys in the mountains. In one valley-top we stop and have a picnic with a loaf of good bread, some local *jamón*, some hard goat cheese, and a local bottle of wine. Luke is entertaining in his speculations and often crazy ideas of what we've seen or experiencing. He's responding, he's not brain-dead. We get up to the snow line, and it's actually snowing.

Our photo shows Luke standing by the sign marking the Spanish-French border, shivering in his light jacket in the snowfall. We look out over the landscape near the end of the trip. Out of the blue: "Ba, I've decided I want to get my GED and then go into the Marines." I conceal my elation with a brief comment: "Sounds like a good idea, Luke." Maybe the trip has provided some kind of introspection after all.

And he follows up. Shortly after we get back to LA, Luke shows up at home with a thick red paperback, *How to Pass Your GED* (General Education Degree), the California high school equivalency test. And damned if Luke doesn't spend ten days lying on the floor, book and papers in front of him doing practice tests, rock music blaring all around him. I help him on a few things like critiquing his compositions, but I try to stay in the background. We've never seen such sustained concentration; we kind of tiptoe around the house lest the magic vanish. And in a few weeks he goes off to take the damn test—and passes! His high school diploma equivalency arrives in the mail a few weeks later. This now means he can apply for the Marines at something above droid level. *Sí, se puede.* Yes, we can! We go out to celebrate, Korean restaurant of course, with beer.

And, armed with his GED certificate at age nineteen, Luke goes off to see Sergeant Yazi at the Marine recruiting office whom he's talked to before. Yazi congratulates him, but reminds him that he's still got to get his felony record sealed up, and pass a urine test at some point. A camel passing through the eye of a needle?

*       *       *

Luisa writes to Luke in Spanish from Monteverde, a letter I come across long after.

*9 October 1993*

*Hello my dear little flea!*

*How are you? Today is Saturday and I'm alone in my room. My brothers and sisters are talking and dancing about in the hallway, my parents are watching television and I'm more bored than ever. You know I really miss you and I can't get used to so much time passing without seeing you. I feel very alone and sad. I'm thinking about the times we spent together, and even though I don't want to cry, I am crying because I want you to hug me fiercely and tell me that you love me, just like I love you. You know sometimes I think that I will never be able to forget you*

157

*and I keep dreaming about being with you in your country where nobody knows me or asks me anything about us.*

*My love, I hope that you are studying a lot so that in the end everything will turn out fine in your life and I also hope that soon we can be together again. Don't forget that I love you and want the best for you. Say hello to your parents for me.*

Luisa has made little drawings on the page, saying, *Smoking is bad for health! Do a kind act every day!*

*                  \*                  \*

There's insistent loud knocking on the door one afternoon. I open up, it's the cops. Is this the residence of Luke Fuller? Yes. Is he here? No. We've got a warrant to search your house. What's this about, officer? We want to search your son's room. I take the two cops back to Luke's room. A cop car sits outside in the driveway, red lights flashing, nosy neighbors peering by. The cops' aggressive search couldn't leave the room in any greater turmoil than it's already in. They pull apart his bed, examine the mattress, go through drawers, closets, books, piles of clothing. They turn up a bong, nothing new, some brown substance in a baggie, looks like a pretty small quantity, maybe hash. They ask to see the kitchen, garage but don't go through much there. They seem to size us up, don't make any request to look in our bedroom or the rest of the house. They won't share any speculations with me, but obviously they know he's dealing. Please tell your son when he gets back that he is to report to the police station right away.

Luke gets home around nine-thirty pm. "Luke, the cops have been here while you were out. They searched your room." He blanches. "What did they want?" he asks in a small voice. "What do you think they were looking for, *Playboy* magazines?" Luke goes in and surveys his room. "Jesus Christ, Ba, why did you let them do this shit to me?" "Luke, what in hell can I do about this? You brought it on yourself. I can't tell the cops to stay out. They had a warrant. They're obviously onto you for something. You know what kind of stuff you're into, I don't."

He knows the noose is tightening. We take him down to the station and they talk to him alone. Surprisingly no charges are pressed, for the moment. But I'm growing pretty weary of this, harassment from all sides: Luke, the cops, his shady cohorts. But we're going to be moving back shortly to the East Coast and it simply isn't worth it to try to work out some whole new arrangement for Luke.

One afternoon Luke comes in again, smelling of pot and I lose it. In a moment of bitterness, I let loose: "You know, maybe we shouldn't have sent you to Mexico and Costa Rica after all, Luke. I think it's just been a fucking waste of money and effort. I don't see anything that's better in your life, and a whole lot that's worse. And frankly it's worse for us too."

Luke takes it in. "No," he replies firmly, "I really did like being there. I think I learned a lot. There's more to do there, I get bored here."

"Bored?" The word really presses my hot button. "I'm tired of hearing that shit all the time, Luke. Bored by what? You know that if you were really a Mexican or Costa Rican teenager or a kid living in any other developing country, you would have been just as bored there. And drugs would have found you anywhere. You've been pretty damn lucky—and pampered in your life living here. You know what? If you'd grown up in one of those places, and stolen stuff or gotten into drug deals, they would have tossed you in jail and thrown away the key. And your teenage ass might have been butt-fucked in jail by hardened criminals. Or if you hung out with a local girl and were screwing her, her father might just have told you to marry her now or face a machete. Or get your balls cut off. Or if you were screwing around dealing in drugs, how long before some other drug pusher comes by and slits your throat? It might not have been so pretty if you really had grown up in some of those places either. It's a tough, real world out there. You're lucky that didn't happen. You're damn lucky you can still live here in safety." I'm over the top, but the moment had to come.

Luke frowns, rocks back on his heels, either from my spontaneous anger or a pot high. He just stands there, for a long time in silence, taking it in. "Yeah, I guess you're right, Ba," he whispers, as he heads off quietly to his room. No blowup back at me. "Dammit, I don't want to be right, Luke, I want to save you from all this," I yell after him. I turn to Prue, "I hate myself for saying these things."

"No," she says, "he needed to hear it."

*   *   *

As all this mess unfolds, much of it seems to devolve upon Prue. She's around in the daytime of course, when I'm usually not, so she has to assume more of the duties of riding daily herd on Luke. Also I'm out of town off and on. I worry how much my absence has direct impact on the situation. I don't really believe I'm just trying to avoid being around because I know I'm always happy to get back home from any trip and very much want to be hands-on every minute that I am at home. Luke has been absent himself a lot over the past few years while I've been developing my own new professional life and doing research projects. But now Luke's back and he's more high maintenance than ever. It's hard for me to cut back on a lot of these professional obligations and meetings around the country or overseas simply based on the likelihood of Luke being in residence or not. And I get to work a lot from home too, rather than having to go into my RAND office.

Still, I'm worried for the toll it takes on Prue. "Are you doing OK? Can you handle this? What would you like me to do? I'll try cutting back." "It's not so much that terrible things happen while you're away. What wears me down is just this need for constant vigilance. I hate having to maintain active suspicion about most things that Luke does." "I know," I reply. "Nothing is as it seems with him," Prue goes on. "He's just so adept at providing false stories now, he dishes them out often even when there is no need to do so." "I know. He seems to tell lies gratuitously, needlessly. It seems almost reflexive to him, to keep the surface waters calm with us ... until the shit hits the fan again."

We embrace, in silent sadness.

*       *       *

It's the day after New Year's, 1994. RAND has agreed to transfer me shortly to its Washington office. We both love California, but we'd talked it over; I had asked to go back to be closer to professional activities, foreign policy institutions, and the multiple visitors there from the Middle East. Prue doesn't mind going back to DC where we have a lot of friends. But I also have real qualms. I feel I have betrayed my heart, out of professional considerations; I feel my soul belongs more in the West Coast than the East. I will tendentiously wear my West Coast RAND outfit to work in Washington—blue jeans, jacket, shirt but no tie—until I'm shamed out of it by too many stares from the button-down East Coast establishment during visits to the Pentagon and State Department.

But what of Luke? Do we abandon him to his own devices in California at this point? *What* devices? The roadmap of Luke's downward trajectory begins to admit of less and less byways, diversions and detours capable of slowing the process. There is ever less chance of finding some new, previously undiscovered road—or silver bullet.

His life is on a rollercoaster: it plunges down from great heights into the depths, rising back up again in new hope. But each new descent sinks a bit lower each time, and the rise back up is a little less high, on a ride that must eventually grind to a halt at the bottom. And I'm a passenger on that same damn ride.

# CHAPTER FOURTEEN

# TRACY AND THE LITTLE HYUNDAI THAT COULD

*January 1994 - Thousand Oaks, California*

We're packing up for our move back to Washington DC. Luke is now nearly twenty—an ideal time for him to stay on in California on his own, to become an adult, to become master of his own destiny. But I'm not sure I believe this. If it's sink or swim for Luke, my gut warns me that it will be sink.

*I know my parents tell me I need to be on my own. It could be fun. But where can I find a job which will work for me? How can I get enough money to get a place to live? I don't think I can pull it off. Who will look out for me when I fall down?*

Luke may sense his own vulnerabilities more deeply than even we do: he seems actually to want to go back to the East, following his parents. Hardly the sign of a confident young man seeking independence. What associations in California might persuade him otherwise?

Enter Tracy. Unlike a number of other girls Luke has introduced us to, we don't really take to Tracy. He met her recently, who knows where, starts hanging out with her pretty seriously, something we haven't seen much before. She's no dumb-bunny, but she aspires to a flashy lifestyle, wears too much makeup; maybe pretty, but in a cheap way, verging on the trampy. She's a high-school dropout, but there's no doubt she knows what she wants, and knows how to work the angles. She's confident enough that she doesn't shrink from the "meeting the parents" as many kids do, but she clearly has little interest in talking to us apart from the basics. She's over at our house pretty regularly now; Luke cooks food for both of them before they retreat to his room for long periods. We're unenthusiastic, but stay cool with it so far; it may not last.

Within a few weeks Luke comes to me, looking hesitant. "Ba, listen, check it out … do you think it might be OK if Tracy could, like, move in with me?" "Me" of course means "us." "Luke, I'm not too keen about having her living here in the house. She can come over all she wants, but living here is a major deal."

"Look, Ba, I've never been able to actually live with a girl before, and I really want to," he says. "I'm almost twenty and I'm old enough to have that kind of relationship." We're unenthusiastic. Tracy doesn't seem to have the solid qualities, the sense of openness and honesty that Luisa has and I don't see any future to this but, who knows, she might bring some kind of stability into Luke's life. It might keep him from roving around outside with even more unpalatable company. "OK, Luke," I say, "you know we're only going to be around here a month or so more anyway ourselves. After that you're going to have to make some basic decisions for yourself." Luke is grateful. He then adds, "Tracy is going through some problems with drugs right now but she's working to get clean." That's just great.

Why do I somehow not really feel much confidence about this? Her parents are divorced, her mother lives in some nearby town and seems unengaged in Tracy's welfare or whereabouts, her father lives down in New Orleans and is not in touch with her. Well, we'll see what happens, we can be flexible for the little time we have left in California.

And so Tracy moves in—our first live-in girlfriend. In fact, Luke and Tracy are out much of the day now anyhow, so we don't see that much of them. She actually works fulltime at a restaurant and Luke now has a three-quarter-time job as a waiter at a local Mexican restaurant. I note that she seems to push him into getting his act together. And I have to say, Luke does in fact seem a bit more stable now, there is marked reduction in suspicious phone calls, Tracy is not unpleasant toward us and they don't present too much of a drag on our lives. This may be better than I expected.

Then one Sunday afternoon I suddenly hear a lot of screaming right outside the front door—like someone is being killed. It's Tracy. She's on the ground, rolling and keening, having some kind of fit, apparently totally zonked out on some shit, having hallucinations or bad acid trip, "Oh my God, Oh my God!" she cries. Luke's at her side, appalled by the circumstances, trying to help her up; apparently he's not on this particular trip with her. We want to get her into the house before neighbors call the police—whose visits are not unprecedented. Luke half drags Tracy in and works to calm her, gets some black coffee down her throat, gets her into a cold shower and then makes her lie down, sleep it off. He looks worried—no, he even says he's worried. He too is scared that something bad might happen to Tracy, or that the cops might show up. Not all bad, I coolly note to myself in the middle of this drama, maybe it's good that he's on the receiving end of the drug thing this time, it might put a little scare into him. Actually we've never seen Luke in anything remotely like Tracy's condition. If he has his bad-shit moments he has managed to spare us from witnessing them.

But there is no repetition of the event. Apart from the onetime freak-out at the doorstep, Tracy poses no special problems. Nonetheless she still is an outsider in the house whose style and manner is uncongenial to us and we don't have a lot of trust in her. I warn Luke that he's got a major decision to make about what to do once we depart.

On more than one night when I get up to go to the bathroom, I hear moans and cries of passion coming clearly through the wall from Luke's bedroom next to us. Sexuality across the generation divide is never fully comfortable, especially the early sexuality of one's children—just like parental sexuality is totally uncomfortable for their children at almost any age; it's in the don't-ask, don't-tell category. But, guiltily, I feel some erotic pangs at the sounds, a fleeting envy at the insatiability of youth, and also a guilt that I've even overheard it at all.

*        *        *

As our packing date draws close, Luke makes his non-decision. "Yeah, Ba, I've been thinking, maybe it would be good, like if I could go back to Maryland with you guys as well. I'm not really set up here in California." Potential loss of the umbilical seems to wins out hands down in his mind, no contest, even with Tracy here. Prue and I really feel ambivalent about this. "I don't really want to have Luke continuing to live with us indefinitely," Prue says, "but I'm even more nervous about leaving him on his own a continent away. He's barely managing as it is, and his residence in California may end up being the California prison system." Well, maybe it is better if he comes back to Maryland where we can keep an eye on him and intervene if things get badly offtrack. "So what about Tracy, Luke?" "See ... she says she'd like to go too, to get away from California and see the East." OK, but we warn Luke that he's got to find his own place in Maryland within a few weeks of getting back, they're not permanently living with us. "No problem."

Luke now has wheels. We'd finally relented on letting him get a driver's license just last year, at age nineteen; we gave him our old beat-up red Hyundai with its faded plastic parts to use for work and getting around. We're going to fly back to Maryland, but Luke plans to drive the Hyundai back east with Tracy, if it will make it. They plan to stop together in a few places along the way, including a visit to her dad in New Orleans. "It'll be a great experience for us," Luke says. Even better, they don't ask for any money for the trip—and I doubt we would have given it. "We've saved up enough money to cover the expenses ourselves," he says. Most likely Tracy is the "we". But this seems to be the beginning of some new financial independence for Luke since Tracy has arrived. There may be a few positives emerging here. Could Tracy be a "halfway house" to Luke's move to independence?

The van arrives to pack up the house in Thousand Oaks that I love; the movers erase the traces of our six years of life here item by item from the house. The last morning before Prue and I leave for the airport I wander emptily back through the stripped rooms, feeling highly conflicted, looking out over the pool, the fire pit and the California hills. This is where I really feel at home, far from eastern stodginess. Regrettably LA has been too professionally isolating for my line of work. In choosing to go back East, my intellect, my professional needs have triumphed over my heart. Self-betrayal.

### February 1994 - Rockville, Maryland

A few weeks after we arrive back in Maryland and to our old house, we get a collect call from Luke on the road. "We're in Texas, on our way to Tracy's dad in Louisiana for a week. But the Hyundai has broken down, Ba, and we need about five-hundred dollars to cover the repair bill." Luke offers to put us in touch with the garage to talk about it. It sounds legit; I know the car is not in great shape, so we forward the money. A week later Luke calls again. He's encountered southern gothic. "We've gotten to Louisiana and we've been staying with Tracy's dad for a few days. But things with her dad are really bad, Ba," he says. "We need to get out of here fast. Like, he's sitting around drinking all the time and cursing. He says he's a Vietnam vet, and he gets into like these kinds of dark moods and angry and turns this old evil eye on me. He's got all these guns around. Last night he looked at me kind of weird and quiet and told me how he's killed a number of gooks in his day. He told me he wasn't sure he could handle one fucking his daughter. I mean, this is really a bad scene down here, Ba, with all these rednecks around here, they don't like Asians. We've got to get back on the road, I'm scared about what this guy might do."

Next call comes about a week later from North Carolina. The Hyundai is having trouble again. The garage man tells Luke it's not worth fixing. It does have well over a hundred thousand on it by now. I tell him I'm not up for any more expensive repairs. Luke says he's abandoning it. "So what will you do for wheels then?" I ask. "OK, see, well … we didn't want to leave Tracy's car in LA either, so we actually brought both cars along." "What? You mean you two have been driving all along in separate cars?" "Uh, yeah. So we still have her car to get back to Maryland with." The story is beginning to sound like another one of Luke's half-ass maneuvers, and I wait for the financial hooker. But it doesn't come. He's not asking for any more money. "We'll be back in Maryland in a few days," he says.

Four days later they pull up in Tracy's old Chevy. Luke and Tracy take the downstairs bedroom until they sort things out. Actually, we're impressed: she proves her gumption by going out and getting a job as a waitress within a day. Luke gets himself another part-time fast-food job shortly thereafter, and he too seems to possess a little more discipline. Things are going smoothly and we're not pressing them yet to move out. But within a month Luke comes sidling up to me, a signature of one of his confidential moods. "Ba, I need to talk. Things aren't too good with Tracy. I'm getting unhappy about this situation. It's like she doesn't have any respect for me anymore. I'm pretty sure she's started to hang out with some other dude. She's all cold and won't give me any affection any more … I think we're going to break up." And a few days later Tracy announces that she is pregnant. Luke is aghast. "Luke, for Chrissakes," I say, "how could you be so dumb not to use condoms." "I have, Ba," he claims. "Well, they must've had holes in them," I say, "what are you going to do about this?" "I'm not even sure she's pregnant from me," Luke claims, "she's been seeing another guy." Total white trash soap opera.

Tracy wants an abortion. She makes an appointment herself in Rockville near where we live. Prue feels a strong obligation to accompany Tracy to the operation for moral support since Tracy's mother isn't anywhere around. "Luke, you're going to come along too for this," says Prue, "you're the one who got her into this, you're going to have to see the consequences of careless actions." "I don't think the baby is mine, Ma," he complains but he goes along with Tracy. They treat each other with distinct coolness now.

Prue also insists that Tracy call her mother in California and let her know what is going on. After the abortion Luke tells us that he has had it with Tracy, that she is definitely seeing other men and he wants her out of the house. Prue calls her mother again and tells her that Tracy can't stay with us anymore after the abortion. She reluctantly agrees to fly to DC and pick up her daughter. Luke by now can't wait to see her out the door—we've never seen him so disillusioned. I'm not quite sure I know what all the dynamics are, but we never felt she was right for Luke, despite the temporary stability of her practical feet-on-the-ground approach. She actually seems the bigger drug user of the two, but also the stronger and more in control. "She's trash, Ba," Luke sagely concludes.

Exit Tracy from our lives with no mention of thanks from mother or daughter.

*                              *                              *

You just can't keep the old red Hyundai down. It stages an unexpected rebirth, Lazarus-like, after its final reported demise in North Carolina. I get a phone call late one afternoon. "Mr. Fuller? LA Police Department here. Do you own a red '89 Hyundai? Well, we've got it impounded here. If you want it you'll have to come and pay impoundment charges of four-hundred dollars. We've had it in our possession for over a month trying to trace the owner." What, it's in LA? I tell the police we'll call them back about the car, but I'm livid. "Luke, what in hell is going on here with this car story? You told me you left it in North Carolina." Luke sidles into contrite mode, as if it was all just a big misunderstanding.

"See, Ba, look, I'm sorry, but see, I just didn't want to tell you. I know you gave me the Hyundai and all, but we needed money to get across the country and Tracy didn't have enough. So I sold the car to Rudy, you know, that kid down the street." "So then you did come in just one car across the country, and you lied when you called from Texas to get five-hundred bucks to fix it." He nods, eyes on the ground. "But see Ba, that's the thing, I don't know how the car got into the hands of the LA police."

Luke calls up Rudy in California to find out. It turns out Rudy drove the car around in LA for a few days, got picked up drunk and without registration, and the car got impounded. He abandoned it rather than pay stiff charges on the car. "Luke, you asshole, how dare you spin all this line of bullshit to us about the car? You're not a kid, you're twenty years old. This has been a pack of boldface lies and deceptions from the start—about the entire car saga and the drive back east with Tracy, phony garage mechanic stories and expenses, the lot. Can't I believe any damn thing you say any more?" Luke looks pained, crestfallen, as if this whole saga was a logical thing to do, only it just didn't work out. He's remorseful, apologizes, yada yada.

But the Hyundai won't stay down. Melissa, still at UCLA and finishing her PhD program, hears the car story from us, says she would be interested in having it as a second car since Jim, her fiancé, takes their own old Hyundai off to Claremont College every day. They could use a second cheap vehicle. For four-hundred bucks, be my guest. The Hyundai, astonishingly, now comes back into the Fuller family for another two years, the prodigal son, returning from its unsavory leave of absence for a period.

But what about this ongoing pattern of deception? We're almost inured to it by now, our standards have so bottomed out. Outrage exhaustion sets in. On the other hand, Luke seems pretty steady at work these days, even though the old glassy eyes still come and go. And while generally cheerful, he can turn sullen when he's coming down off something. Usually he just retreats to his bedroom to sleep it off. I still look for more permanent solutions. "How are the Marines looking these days, Luke?" "I'm definitely interested, Ba. I'm going to go see them as soon as my papers arrive here from the Marines in California," Luke says.

East Coast, new leaf?

# CHAPTER FIFTEEN

# EAST COAST SAME OLD

*1994 - Maryland*

The level of creeps and losers is rising around us like swamp-water. One really creepy type, Jerrdan, keeps coming by the house asking to see Luke after I've told him Luke's not home. He says Luke owes him money. When he calls, Luke refuses to take his calls. "He's just a loser, Ba," says Luke, the connoisseur. "I don't owe him money, he's just trying to make trouble." Jerrdan gets threatening at the door, says he knows damn well Luke is at home. Two days later I go out one morning and find all four tires on our car slashed. Never mind me, Luke seems genuinely furious, now that this affair has touched us; he says he's sure it's Jerrdan who did it and he's going to "get him" for it.

Whatever Luke's anger, I find a few lingering resources of outrage left in myself. "Luke, that is absolutely the last straw. We are simply not going to put up with this shit anymore, especially your running drug deals out of our house. You're leaving this house now, and not coming back until this drug pushing has stopped. I am accepting no more messages or calls for you unless it's a friend that I know personally. If after some time you clean up your act, we might consider talking about your coming back." Luke doesn't fight it. He never does. He sighs, moves in with a friend across the river in Virginia. After a month he calls and asks to come back; he says he's not going to deal in drugs anymore, "I'm trying to stay clean." OK, on a trial basis, but no phone privileges of any kind for a long period—as long as we're around to enforce it. And he's got to have a steady job. He comes back, and in fact any deal-making, at least over the phone, seems to have ended. He's now working in a grocery.

Meanwhile, Luke's made a Korean friend, a "real" Korean, Cho, whose father owns a Korean restaurant. Cho, of course, speaks Korean. Cho laughs at Luke for being a "banana"—yellow on the outside, white on the inside. But he often invites Luke over to their restaurant, and Luke tells us that he's learning to eat real Korean food. Our family has gone out for years to Korean restaurants in celebration of Luke's heritage and our own culinary interests, but we were never fully fearless in exploring every nook and cranny of this

168

cuisine; it has a heavy dose of uncertain sea creatures that none of us have a real taste for and can be fiery hot, so we've tended to stick to the many Korean dishes we do like, the delicious Korean barbecue, the bean sprout pancakes with soy sauce; Bi Bim Bop, a rice dish with grilled vegetables, a fried egg and a sweet, hot, thick sauce; and many others. Korean food rests on a basic and unbeatable combination of garlic, soy sauce, sugar and sesame oil—you can't go wrong. But Cho has brought Luke into the inner sanctum of real home-style Korean cooking with some highly fishy stuff and very hot sauces. Now Luke says he'll do the ordering when we go out to eat.

I'm pleased at this awakening of deeper interest in his own culture. Maybe it will help Luke on thinking about his identity—another kind of "cultural cure." African-American educators have experimented with teaching black kids about African history, African languages and traditions, in the hopes of strengthening the social and cultural solidarity of their community. Actually I've encouraged Luke for some time to learn some Korean. He'd never seemed especially seized with the thought before but now he says he's thinking about it. He actually finds out about a course at a local Korean church. We wait for a follow-up. As for Cho, mixed feelings. He's a few years older than Luke and seems a bit shifty, looks like he falls into the *malos amigos* category. But who knows, maybe something good might come of the Korean connection. As it turns out, that's not the case.

And now Luke gets a new job at a Chinese grocery store in Bethesda. He's always been interested in Asian food products and we regularly go with him to a huge local Asian supermarket. Luke knows his stuff. But a few weeks later I get a call from the grocer. "Where is Luke, he's supposed to be at work today." "No idea, I'll tell him when he gets in." Later that day I have one of those classic, utterly disconnected conversations with Luke.

"Weren't you supposed to be at work today?"

"No, I had the day off."

"Well, that's not what Mr. Chang said, he called asking where you were."

"Wait a second, today's Wednesday, isn't it?"

"No, it's Thursday."

"Well, I don't think I work on Thursday."

"Luke, just two days ago you told me you were working four days in a row, Thursday through Sunday."

"Oh well, see, I had to go somewhere today."

"Luke, where? You've got to show up when you're supposed to."

"I had to see some guy downtown this morning about something."

"Well then, how come you got up late and were with Cho here around noon?"

"Cho, well, see, he was the one who actually had to see somebody."

"But that was this afternoon, not this morning."

"Yeah, well, Cho said he needed me to go with him, I mean this morning, not this afternoon."

"I thought *you* had to see somebody."

"No, actually Cho did."

"But didn't you know you were supposed to show up at the grocery this morning?"

"Yeah, well, I couldn't make it, I told Chang I couldn't."

"He says he didn't know, you just didn't show ..."

The same old pattern, unreal, impenetrable conversations riddled with dissemblance, confusion, lying, all wrapped inextricably into one. Prue is constantly upset that she can't ever get a straight story out of Luke on anything, even the most trivial and inconsequential of issues.

Still weeks later, Mr. Chang calls again. "I'm firing your son, Mr. Fuller. He is not showing up at work when he is supposed to. And he owes me one-hundred-and-fifty dollars." "Why?" "Luke asked for an advance," he says, "and then never showed up to work it off before he got fired. So please, Mr. Fuller, you must pay me the debt." "Well, I'm sorry Mr. Chang, but Luke is twenty years old, I can't be responsible for his debts." "But he is a member of your family, he is bringing shame onto your family. He's your son, isn't he?" "Look, Mr. Chang, I'm sorry, but I'm not responsible for what Luke does. He's going through a bad period, problems with drugs, and he's been unreliable." "You're telling me, Mr. Fuller, that you let Luke get this job without telling me that he has a drug problem? That is dishonest. I am ashamed for your family." Hangs up. Yeah, well, I'm ashamed for my family too. But I'm not going to pay Luke's debts.

*             *             *

Another letter from Luisa in Spanish:

*Hi Dear Luke,*

*I got back five days ago from Tortuguero Park. It was a great trip and I had a lot of experiences that I'd never had before. It's really rich in flora and fauna with a huge diversity of trees and animals and amazing canals and huge beaches. That's why it's called National Tortoise Park. Every year thousands of tortoises come to lay their eggs. For me it's fascinating to see so many types of marine and land* animals. I feel very proud that in my country we have so many parks rich in vegetation and forest life.

My love, I missed your twentieth birthday. I wish that you could have been with me to share each moment of my life with you. You know there are times when I really feel alone and sad because so much time passes without seeing you. But when I feel that you may come back soon I feel very happy. So I'll always be here waiting for you and perhaps we won't have to separate any more. Perhaps I can go with you to your country. But then I'm afraid that sometimes I get tired of waiting and I think that if you love me like I do you then it's crazy to wait anymore, it just doesn't make sense. I think we have to be together, but you have to decide and I respect your decision whatever it is.

Enough for now, I'll say goodbye to the one I love. I'll always be thinking of you. Ciao, my little flea, and take care of yourself, I give you my kisses.

Your girlfriend, Luisa

*      *      *

After our years in our California house with its high-beamed ceiling in the living room, we really find our Maryland house boxy, low-ceilinged and dreary when we get back. We find a builder who offers us a very low price for building a small extension in the back that creates a high ceiling, split-level effect, and punches in a few more windows and skylights and takes out some internal walls. As the work proceeds the house is in utter chaos of course, workmen tromping all around the whole house most of the day, banging, sawing, dust, whirring saw blades, hammering, black plastic curtaining all around. And inevitably the work proceeds far more slowly than scheduled. One casualty is Luke's late sleeping hours, now incommoded.

Luke writes Luisa, in Spanish that summer. I find it later among Luke's papers, apparently never mailed.

Hola Luisa,

I'm in my bed now writing this letter to you. It's four o'clock in the morning. I drew these pictures for you when I was in California. One day when I was at the beach I saw dolphins, very beautiful. Now I am working in a restaurant in Maryland called Chichis, it's Mexican, I'm a waiter. I spoke with a friend there and she is from Costa Rica too, from Ala Juela.

I miss you very much, I've forgotten your kisses. Well, my love, I don't know when I'll be able go to Costa Rica but I want to go soon and see you.

My parents are re-building part of their house, expanding it. And the workers are here early in the morning so I can't sleep. What a bummer!

*Well, my love, I have to sleep, I can't write any more since I'm really tired. But that's OK. A clean life.*
*Love, Luke*

*            *            *

Samantha is now working for Price Waterhouse in Bishkek, Kyrgyzstan, part of a huge new US-sponsored privatization program. We want to visit her there. We have no choice but to leave Luke at home in the middle of all the builders, threaten him with the wrath of God if he rips us off, but we're unsure what will happen in our absence. As a precaution we buy a heavy metal box to put all our checkbooks and financial papers in, and close it with a heavy padlock.

We spend a week with Samantha in Kyrgyzstan in her Soviet-style housing—grungy concrete entryway, broken, irregular concrete steps up four flights, stairwell dark and smelling of piss. The apartment itself is better, quite airy and light, but Soviet unfunctional. Samantha is engaged to a young Chechen, Ruslan, with a BA in Law who also works as a local employee for Price Waterhouse. Ruslan is handsome, dashing, charming, polite, all the legendary social and hospitality skills of people of the Caucasus. He is living with Samantha, but with Muslim courtesy and sense of honor, he totally vacates the apartment while we are there.

When we get back home to Washington, the work on the house has transformed it. A day or two later Bill the builder takes me aside. "I'm sorry to trouble you with this, Mr. Fuller, but I'm afraid something embarrassing has come up. A few weeks ago while you were gone your son stole my checkbook out of the glove compartment of the pick-up. He wrote several checks made out to himself, forging my signature. I'm sorry to have to raise this with you." "No, Bill, no, that's all right, you should raise it with me, that is unacceptable behavior from Luke." "The total amount of three checks is five-hundred-and-thirty dollars." "I'm the one to apologize, Bill," I say, "I'll make good on it."

But that's not all. Luke has made a clumsy and unsuccessful attempt to pry open the heavy box with our checks and vital papers in it. Even so, Prue later finds among our canceled checks from the bank a series of forged checks from our own checkbook, apparently pre-dating the metal box that Luke must have stashed away. These checks bear Luke's poor imitation of Prue's distinctive signature, immediately evident at a glance compared with the real thing. "Luke, we've had it. We can't even go off on a trip without fear of being ripped off by you. You're out of here again, you're going to have to find some place to stay." Luke knows he's crossed a major red line. As usual, he has

172

nothing to say, he leaves meekly, without an argument. The drugs are talking louder.

I also go to the bank and complain about how they can let such patently forged signatures go through, without subjecting them to the most elementary signature scrutiny. We wait a few days to hear from the bank on whether they will make good on the forged checks. They will not. "I'm sorry, Mr. Fuller, but if you have a problem with this you're going to have to file a complaint with the bank, authorizing full criminal investigative authority."

Full criminal investigative authority? What in hell are we going to do? If we invoke a criminal investigation the outcome is not in doubt. Of course we know who forged the checks, that's not the issue. Luke will face a serious felony charge. He already has one such charge from California and we are trying to get that record sealed so that he does not have to carry around a crippling felony record. A second felony would doom him. It will result in an inability to seal the first offense, and will make him a two-time offender. As a twenty-year-old he is potentially looking at many years in jail. And the outlook for a handsome young male felon in prison is not a pretty one. Even worse, how would Luke possibly benefit from such a long stint?

A lawyer friend advises us that it is really worth considerable effort to spare Luke from a felony on his record, with serious long-term consequences that can have no positive affect. "Convicted felon is a losing tag," he says. Yes, we fully agree, we understand, but then what? What other actions can we take that we haven't already taken? Even the periodic expulsion from the house doesn't really carry great weight. He simply has very little money, can't hold a job long. I'm pretty sure he's now into cocaine, but I can't prove it. He can ill afford to be on his own. His drug demands will simply push him faster into riskier crime.

We try with some limited success to build security walls for ourselves, watching our money like a hawk. But this is an untenable situation when we cannot even be safe from theft in our own house.

*        *        *

And then another of these lovely, poignant and transcendent letters in Spanish from Luisa:

*Corrisal Alajuela*

*Hello my love, how are you?*

*Well, I'm in Corrisal de Alajuela since it's the time to bring in the coffee harvest and I need some money to buy some clothes and shoes and a bag, but picking coffee is really hard and tiring work. I'm living with the family of an aunt in a really small house here, so it's difficult.*

*I have to get up at five in the morning to make it to the coffee fields by six and I pick coffee all day long and don't get back until 5pm. It's a really cold place and I suffer a lot because the water is freezing and I have to take a shower every evening in it. So you can see I don't have any time during the day. But still, being on the coffee plantation is fun, very rustic, and I see a lot of people coming from different places in Costa Rica and Nicaragua to pick coffee. These people talk all day long and sometimes fight with their husbands, wives and children. Today was a little upsetting for me because I saw a man beating his wife and I got very angry. I'm not used to seeing such things.*

*I'll be here only fifteen days—I've already been here for ten—my skin is getting brown from the sun and my hands are in bad shape. I think this type of work is hard, but I need to learn to do both hard and easy work in order to learn how to live in any place I am. I'm thinking about going to Manuel Antonio Park after this to take a little vacation and rest my body and mind.*

*You know that after you left to go back home I'm almost never in Monteverde anymore. The people around there wound my heart with their comments about you. I have scars on my soul, and you know why.*

*OK, my little flea, I've got to get to sleep now because it's almost ten and I'm very tired. I hope you'll write to me soon and that we'll be together some day. I love you a lot. Take care.*

*Your crazy girl, Luisa*

This letter really touches me, the image of Luisa going off at dawn to pick the coffee crop by hand, seems like it's right off some Cuban socialist poster art. I wonder whether Luke wouldn't have been better off staying in Costa Rica, facing rougher social pressures and justice there, and learning to pick coffee for a while? Or would its justice system have been too rough?

*        *        *

Samantha meanwhile has gotten married in Kyrgyzstan. She has had a Muslim *niqah*, a strictly legal ceremony in front of family and the imam, followed by a small celebration with a few friends. A more serious celebration will be held off till later when she and Ruslan come back to the US. Samantha's job in Bishkek is coming to an end in December and she will return to live with us in Maryland while she looks for the next job. It will be great to have Samantha around again, but I worry about clashes with Luke, especially since he's in worse condition than when she left. I just don't dare think about a repetition of the kind of knife incident we had six years ago.

Luke is now back in touch with the local Marine Corps recruiter in Maryland, his file has been forwarded from California. He formally signs up, but on the basis of a deferred enlistment, pending clarification of his legal issues. We are pushing hard for the military option now, it could solve a lot of problems. But we point out to Luke that as great as the Marines might be, if he gets in trouble there, the military justice system is much less forgiving. He will be in far deeper trouble if he repeats any of these actions while in uniform.

And now, on a November afternoon in 1994, I look out the kitchen window and see a cop car pull up at our house—shit, not again. "Is Luke home? We have a warrant for his arrest." The statement ought to be shattering, but it has almost become routine. "What is this about, officer?" I wearily ask. "It's about theft of goods, you can come down to the station and get the details." "OK," I say, "he's sleeping, but I'll go wake him up." "No, I'm sorry, I can't let you do that, we'll have to go in to get him ourselves." They push into Luke's littered bedroom and Luke wakes up, startled, confused, shaken, gets out of bed, hungover. The cop takes the scene in, apologizes to me, "We're going to have to take Luke in," he says, "and I'm sorry, but I'm required to put him in handcuffs."

Nickel flashes, snaps, Luke's freedom and dignity are gone with a click. He's led out with his hands in front of him, head bowed, as if off to his own execution. He says nothing, but his spirit, or what is left of it, seems broken. He clearly doesn't want his parents to see him like this. I feel like I'm in some goddam TV cop show, only it isn't, and this is my own son being put into the back of the police car, hand on the back of the head pushing him down into the seat. Tears well into my eyes, it's all out of our hands now …

The next morning we get a call. If we are willing to vouch for him turning up in court, he can be released into our custody. Come down and pick him up. We drive to the police barracks; maybe the night in jail will have salutary effect, shake him up, bring home to him the disastrous nature of the course he is embarked on. The news is not good: Luke has been charged with burglary in the first degree. Worse, the victim is a family we know right on our own block—and their son Chris is a good friend of Luke's.

*26 Nov 1994, Statement of charges before district court of Maryland, Montgomery country.*

*Between the dates of 13 November 1994 and 14 November 1994, the residence of James Carson, XXXXX Whisperwood Lane, Rockville, was entered and a Denon stereo am/FM receiver, model DRA545a, serial # 2429879, having a value of $323, stolen. There were no signs of forced entry and a key to the house that had been hidden in a shed on the Carson's property could not be found.*

*ON Nov 17 1994, Luke BYUNGBAE FULLER pawned a Denon AM/FM stereo receiver with the same serial number at the Wheaton Trade Center for $55. Fuller used a California ID, with an address of 1278 La Jolla Drive, Thousand Oaks to complete the transaction. The pawn sheet described Fuller as an ASIAN MALE, 5-09, 160 lbs, having black hair and brown eyes. His date of birth is listed as 02-06-74.*

*ON 11-23-94 the reporting officer contacted Carson, the victim of the burglary, to advise him of the investigative leads and the discovery of his property. Carson advised the writer that his children had a friend by the name of LUKE FULLER who resided at XXXXX Whisperwood Lane. Fuller had been to the Carson house on many occasions. Carson described FULLER as an oriental male.*

*A record check revealed that LUKE Byungbae FULLER had a MD criminal history.*

*Based on the probable cause contained within this document, the writer requests that an arrest warrant be issued for LUKE BYUNGBAE FULLER CHARGING HIM WITH ONE COUNT OF BURGLARY IN THE FIRST DEGREE, Art 27 Sec 29 Code of Maryland, and one count of theft over $300.*

The Carson boys are really good kids, serious, mature, likeable, and they used to come by our house pretty regularly. What can I say to them? I call up the Carsons and ask if we can come by. As they let us into their home, it is hard to know who is more embarrassed by this painful mission.

"Jim, what can I say?" I begin. "We're just so pained at what has been happening with Luke, and now it has involved your family as well. I don't know if you knew, but Luke has been having growing problems with drugs, and now he has turned to theft to meet his needs." I tell it straight, and the Carsons share our pain and concern. "We like Luke and he is a good kid, we always welcomed him in our house," Jim says. "We had no idea Luke had done this when we reported it … I'm so sorry, we didn't mean to bring greater problems on you with this." The investigation has been swift and precise, and led the authorities straight to Luke.

The stereo receiver has been returned, there is no financial loss we need to make good on. But this is no longer just a neighborly affair anymore. A courteous, sympathetic, but no less palpable glass barrier has gone up. We're no longer talking about a kid breaking a neighbor's window or playing pranks, but formal felony that pushes us into a different realm. Chris is devastated, feels betrayed, and feels that Luke is slipping into a condition where maintaining the old friendship with him is no longer sustainable. The Carsons wish there was something they could do; if they had known it was Luke they would have been happy to settle it between families. Fortunately Chris is not there at the time of our visit, it would be even more painful for us as the parents of his close friend to see him after Luke had violated his friendship and their home.

The situation is now beyond one of outrage, yelling or remonstration. We simply have to cope, pick up the pieces as best we can. We're facing a serious court charge. We push Luke to go see the Carsons as well; he says he will, but he admits he can't face them yet. He knows that this incident has taken on a whole different character now; it's worse, dirtier, more shameful than a procedural legal issue with faceless and anonymous victims.

Luke is meanwhile wandering between friends, not even able to hold any job on any regular basis. He looks worse, he's not eating well. He has a constant bad cough. We fear for his health, along with his police record.

Prue and I decide that we have to keep closer tabs on Luke. We tell him that he can come home but must live in our attached garage/tool shed now, converted into a simple, closed-in living space. We put in a mattress, a simple dresser, amidst the workbenches and power tools. Luke will only have access to the main house when we are present, otherwise it is locked. We change all the locks on the house, and put on window locks—against our own damn kid.

*      *      *

A Christmas card from the alternate world, with just a simple note: *I love you, Luke, Take care, and love to your family. Merry Christmas, Luisa.* What might have been …

And a few days before Christmas, Samantha arrives back in DC from Kyrgyzstan, her contract in Bishkek over. Ruslan will join her in a month or two. She'll work in the Price Waterhouse office in DC for a while, living with us until she gets a place. She's really angry with Luke when she hears about the theft, and passes swift moral judgment. She's outraged on our behalf. It's simply wrong, decent people don't do such things, nobody is forcing these drugs on him. We should let him take the consequences. A wall of silence is developing between them, contracting the space around us. Tensions rise. I'm not being realistic, I'm not facing facts, I'm not taking action in what is open and shut, clear-cut right and wrong. Yes, you're right Samantha, this is unacceptable, but we have to live in the real world of what is feasible; I don't know what we can do without destroying Luke's life or pushing him over the edge.

I feel totally trapped: I now have to answer to Samantha as well, one more point of pressure on a shaped lens explosive. And I don't want to be put in the position of having to defend Luke against some of her charges that are dead on, even while she is insensitive to the grander dilemma. Prue backs her. "You are in denial on this, Baba," Samantha accuses. "This level of conduct is not acceptable." "Look, OK, I can see that myself." "Well then, you've got to take a harder line." "So what do you want me to do? Abandon him to the police entirely?" Samantha falls silent, aware there are few good options. But the house is crackling, enveloped by high-tension power lines. Prue and I sometimes share angry words ourselves, but more often just hug each other when things get depressing. These additional psychological walls in our house now immeasurably complicate our daily lives as we become referees on twenty-four-hour duty between Luke and Samantha. Fortunately their paths don't cross much since Samantha is at work all day and she's expecting to find her own apartment shortly.

But more and more other members of the family are witness to Luke's condition. It's Christmas day, 1994—the last Christmas of Luke's life. A lot of family is here. Melissa flies in from LA with Jim; my sister Faith, her partner Marita and Luke's cousin Erin come from San Francisco. The extra people bring cheer and warmth; everyone is caring with Luke, but deeply concerned. They try to engage him, and he can be warm and amusing but, as always on these big family occasions, looking to find relief from the intensity of it all by slipping out from time to time. I have the unpleasant duty of warning people to be mindful about not leaving purses and wallets lying around.

On the day after Christmas we're sitting around in the living room, quietly enjoying the post-Christmas glow. Several of us are playing Jack Straws on the floor. It's Luke's turn. He reaches out to touch a red jack-straw in a delicate position, but he can't—as his hand extends out he doesn't dare touch it, his hand is seriously trembling. He pulls it back in embarrassment and confusion and passes on the move. He then quietly withdraws from the game. A few minutes later Faith draws me aside: "Are you aware that this kind of trembling is a classic sign of cocaine addiction?" I am dismayed, but not surprised. I have suspected off and on for some time that cocaine might now be increasingly Luke's drug of choice. He had admitted once that he has "tried" cocaine, along with pot. This puts it into a far more serious realm of addiction. Worse, there is a high probability that it might be crack, one of the most addictive substances of all.

We've shared our concerns about Luke with Faith for quite some time. "You know," she says, "I think he might have a condition called ADHD—Attention Deficit Hyperactivity Disorder. Psychologists are becoming increasingly aware of this phenomenon, you might want to look into it and see if it relates to Luke. It might help in treating him."

I'm onto it fast. I immediately find a book on ADHD at the bookstore and plunge into it. ADHD is essentially not just a short attention span; it means a literal, physical momentary break in the train of electric brain impulses affecting thought sequences, often even preventing full understanding of what is going on in more complex sequential procedures. It impedes linking action with consequences. I'm astonished and really excited because I can now find some retroactive explanations for many, if not all, of Luke's behavioral symptoms.

One item really grabs my attention: on lying. We've long observed that Luke seems to lie a great deal of the time, sometimes as a defensive cover-up, but sometimes almost as a default reaction even on the most trivial or totally inconsequential of matters. Prue and I have often asked ourselves, why should he do this? The book notes that among people with ADHD lying is prevalent. With an inability to maintain sustained focus or to routinely follow trains of sequential thought or instructions, ADHD sufferers sometimes have to "fake it," avoid the social or work consequences of failing to get the message accurately. This ends up as a form of defensive or preemptive "lying" to mask the inability to understand. The condition can also quickly lower self-esteem. That precisely describes so many of my disjointed question sessions with Luke that wander all over the place.

Years later as I write this book I research further the ADHD question on the web and find some vivid comments, including one from an ADHD sufferer that beautifully captures the sense of Luke's dilemma. On the website *ADHDNews.com*, a woman shares her concerns:

*I believe that certain types of ADD* [Attention Deficit Disorder] *put people in the position of lying. For example, those times during a conversation when my mind "changes channels" and I miss pieces of the discussion. At the end of the conversation the boss asks, "Do you agree"? And I say "yes." That is a lie. The truth would be to tell my boss, "I'm sorry, I did not get all of what you said." If he or she were patient, they would tell me again. I would no doubt miss pieces of it again and if I were to be honest I would tell my boss "I'm sorry, I did not get all of that." I would most likely always miss something and if I were to be 100% honest, I would end every discussion and meeting by asking people to repeat themselves. I could not stay employed very long if I did this.*

*So I have to lie to stay employed. I have gone through my entire life "filling in the blanks" so to speak.*

This writer's painful self-acknowledgment hits me hard; this exactly captures the essence of so many countless conversations with Luke in which we could never get "the straight story," often on trivial matters in which the answer didn't matter, but he chose to "lie." Or maybe, more accurately, he felt it easier to fake it, to make something up, to finesse the issue at hand rather than find himself queried ever more deeply for more complicated answers when he has really missed the point. I feel immensely saddened, so long after these events, because I can imagine the feeling of frustration when one has to fake understanding when his mind has "changed channels" in the midst of a discussion or train of thought.

This woman's description hits the nail on the head. Those simple questions to Luke that often provoked a slightly quizzical look, a moment of hesitation, a sort of calculating, a what-is-really-happening kind of look.

*"Hi Luke, are you going to get the red shirt at the shop today, or the green one?"*

*"I'll get the green one."*

*Next day. "Which one did you buy?" "The green one," he says.*

*Next day. "Luke, I see you're wearing a red shirt. I thought you were going to get the green one."*

*"Well, I decided that I liked the red one better."*

*"That's cool. But how come you told me you got the green one when I asked you which one you bought?"*

*"Well, like see, I thought I was going to get that one."*

*"Yeah, but you didn't. It's no big deal, I'm just surprised that you told me you got the other one."*

*"Well, I was going to get the green one."*

A carbon copy of lots of short conversations with Luke about things that don't matter at all, but leaving me with the feeling, *just give me the straight damn story!*

A few days later I decide to address the issue head-on. "Luke, you know we've been concerned about you for a long time, your trouble in holding jobs and stuff. I want you to know I've recently been reading a book that Faith suggested about a kind of condition that some people have that I think may be affecting you. It's called Attention Deficit Hyperactivity Disorder. It basically means that people with this condition find that their brain sometimes has trouble processing information, that there can be a kind of disruption in the electrical process, in the thinking process that can make it hard to follow certain kinds of explanations."

He stares at me. "What are you telling me, Ba? Like, I'm retarded or something?"

"No, not at all, you know you're a smart kid, everyone thinks that. But it does mean you might have problems sometimes in processing information, in losing track of certain kinds of explanations, like it could be some kind of occasional circuit break."

He ponders. "So what am I supposed to do? You mean I can't have a job like other people, or be normal?"

"Luke, you know we've always thought you were 'normal'. You've got lots and lots of talents—we've always talked about that with you—music, mechanical things, working well with people, good insights into people and what makes them tick, providing leadership, a good sense of humor—all that. But if you have this ADHD condition, it can complicate your handling certain types of thinking tasks. Like school."

"So what's the matter with me? What can I do about it?"

"You're not alone in this. The book says maybe five percent of Americans has some form of this condition. It can be more serious or less, depending ... Does this make any sense to you? Do you feel like you sometimes miss stuff and then have to cover up for it?"

"Well, yeah, sometimes ... I mean it's like ... I dunno, I just forget things sometimes, maybe important things. I know that ..." His voice trails off.

"Hasn't that bothered you?"

Luke's lip trembles. "I've learned, I've noticed ..." his voice falls to a hush, "that I'm not like other people."

"What do you mean, Luke?" I lay my hand on his arm.

"I don't know, I just know I'm different, I don't think like other people."

"You *are* like other people in most ways. Everybody has some weakness or problem of some sort. It's just important to know what your particular problem is, so we can work with it ... You know what, Luke? I'm actually glad to have found out about this. I mean, not glad to know you have ADHD, but I'm happy to have some explanation for some of these problems now. Like getting a straight story sometimes. It makes it easier to deal with. I'm sure this condition has helped push you into drugs. And they're only making it all worse."

"But how come I have this, Ba?" Luke's eyes water up as he looks up at me. "How did I get it? I mean, could I have gotten it from my real mother?"

The fatal question. I instinctively fear going there, entering the dark jungle of biological determinacy, the poison pill, the bad gene, the evil piece of biology inside us over which we have no control, that we are victims of random fate.

"I just don't know, Luke, I wish I could tell you. People can have all kinds of conditions or health problems—there's no easy answer about where they come from. Yeah, it's possible that your mother or father had something like this. It can also sometimes come from alcohol or drug usage at a time when a woman is pregnant. But we'll never know."

I have now shifted the possible burden of responsibility onto his biological mother—aware that various forms of fetal alcohol syndrome can bring about conditions like ADHD, still not well understood. Should I have left his biological mother out of this, let her remain "pure" to him?

*My mother. She didn't take care of me when I was inside her, and she abandoned me afterwards. How could she have done all of this to me?*

Luke turns to me. I see no bravado, no confidence, only vulnerability. "So what am I supposed to do, Ba? I mean, how can I have a normal life, then?"

I hug him. "You can have a normal life. First, we're not totally sure that this is what you have. But other people who have ADHD do have normal lives. But you just have to be aware of some potential problems with certain kinds of mental processes. You may need to watch out for them. There are ways to work around it. We are not even fully sure about this, we can get some advice on it."

"Well, how come not one of all these fancy-ass psychiatrists ever told me anything about this? Now you're coming up with all this bullshit about something wrong in my brain."

"Luke, I don't know why this hasn't come up before. First, I guess that ADHD is something that people have only become aware of relatively recently. All I know is that you and I have been wrestling with this problem for a long time now. I've never had any good explanations for your problems. Like often lying about things that don't matter at all one way or the other. I won't accept that you're just some kind of bad kid. You're not, you know you're not. It's clear now there may be some very logical medical reasons for some of your problems that affect your behavior, maybe even push you to turn to drugs. Isn't it better to know this?"

"I don't know Ba ... I just don't know ..."

His sense of defeat is overwhelming to me. But I stumble on, putting the best face on it I can. "Well, we can talk to doctors about this, psychologists who specialize in brain chemistry. We need to get some better answers as to whether you have ADHD. I think there are some drugs that can help sharpen thinking in certain areas. We'll work with you on this. I'm sure that forgetting things can maybe make you feel like you're dumb or something. But you're not. Like your skills in working with other people, that's something that will never be taken away by ADHD. Or your musical abilities, or cooking, your personality that everybody likes."

Luke still seems more shaken than reassured. Does he take this as some kind of curse now hanging over his head? Damning his future? I hug him again. He's listened soberly, taking all this in. But I can see he is not necessarily relieved. But like me, Prue is relieved, she is gratified that there are some rational explanations to Luke's problems, his lying, his failure to follow through, why sometimes he just doesn't seem to get it. It helps us get past other dreaded thoughts.

*   *   *

The evening after Christmas we go down to a famous Bethesda pool hall with Luke, Melissa, Jim and Prue. Jim plays a mean game of pool, but Luke says he can "whip his ass." They play several intense games, Jim's really on the ropes, but he eventually wins. "Luke is really good," he says. "Yeah," I say, "the result of his post-grad work in the bars of Mexico and Costa Rica," Later Jim tells me that he valued this first chance to spend some time with Luke. "I'd only known him indirectly from the stories via Melissa of Luke's various disasters and misdeeds. Actually, I find him a really nice guy." I'm warmed by this comment; it parallels other outsiders who have known Luke at Outward Bound or other places outside the family. He *is* a good kid. He's not mean-spirited. But he's got a mess of problems.

Then, a few days after Christmas, Luke grants another member of the family an even more explicit glimpse into the dark side of his life. He takes his cousin Erin—they're the same age—off on a drive one afternoon. We only hear about the details much later from Erin. Luke drives to a really seedy ghetto neighborhood in Silver Spring. There he cruises around, pulls over to a rough bunch of guys in the street and negotiates a crack purchase, right there in the street and in front of Erin. No effort to hide it. Erin is appalled both at the risky and rough nature of the encounter, and the revelation that Luke is now doing crack cocaine. "It was like Luke wanted me to know," she says. Is this a cry for help? "I'm scared," she tells Luke, "you should quit all this shit." Luke only sighs, "You're right," he says, "I want to stop, I'm working on it." He's really crossed a fateful boundary here. But he *wanted* Erin to know. Sadly, I only hear this story too late. Faith had seen it that day in his trembling hands, reaching out, but unable to touch the Jack Straws. Unable to reach ...

Still hot on the ADHD trail, I call up a local doctor who treats children with it. The book mentions the drug Ritalin as sometimes being effective in helping restore "circuit gaps" in the brain that are broken, or to help remember follow-through. How many times have we simply yelled at him:

"Luke, *think!*" The doctor hears the symptoms, nods, but when I tell him that Luke is on drugs, he says he won't touch the case. "Mr. Fuller, I can't even give Luke a meaningful examination or provide an accurate diagnosis as long as he is on cocaine. He's got to be completely clear-headed in his responses. Only when Luke is clean could I begin to prescribe a drug like Ritalin." My emotions well up against this doctor who is unwilling to deal with our crisis, but I bite my tongue. Intellectually I understand his position, but the situation is too desperate for me to accept this cautious medical response. I find a second doctor who is willing to give us a brief trial prescription of Ritalin to see if it will help. A shot of hope, something untried, maybe the silver bullet we've been looking for. Luke takes it for a few days, but neither he nor we feel there is much difference.

One afternoon Luke looks really flushed. I grab his pulse, it's up to one-hundred-and-thirty while he's just sitting in front of the TV. That's a light jogging rate, no biggie to me as a jogger, but Luke isn't jogging and it's not good for the heart to maintain that sustained rate hour after hour. Luke swears he's not taking any coke at the time, but how can I believe him? Maybe it is due to the Ritalin.

I confer with the doctor; he definitely won't give a second prescription of Ritalin until Luke is clearly off drugs. He too mentions the danger of mixing Ritalin with cocaine. He mentions in passing that cocaine has similar qualities to Ritalin, it tends to help sharpen the mind, only it's a legal substance. Luke could be, in part, "self-medicating," not just for a high, but because cocaine actually helps sharpen concentration. I think back to reading Sherlock Holmes as a boy; Sherlock told his side-kick Dr. Watson that he takes cocaine as a recreational mind-sharpener—it's all right there in these stories from an earlier century.

We talk with Luke about rehab, but he doesn't want to hear about it. "I can manage, Ba," he says.

Manage? I find him increasingly, seriously paranoid now. He's taken to keeping an aluminum baseball bat beside his bed "to be safe." Late one night I'm reading in bed, Luke comes in. "Ba, I'm scared. I can hear people in the dark outside my room in the back of the house." I put on some clothes, Luke gets his baseball bat and is really tense. We push open the back door into the cold night; I shine a big flashlight all around and we walk around in the nearby trees. Nobody. But even paranoids can have enemies, especially when they welsh on drug payments. On several other occasions Luke comes and tells me he thinks someone is trying to break into the house, "Shhhh, just listen." He is trembling in his paranoia. Another classic symptom of cocaine usage.

And I can't keep the rest of the family safe from all of this. Predictable as the seasons, Samantha herself is now victimized by Luke again. He intercepted one of these free credit card offers sent to her in the mail, somehow managed to activate it, and ran up a bill of several hundred dollars. Worse, in these cases no one bothers even to look at the name on the card, or question what a male is doing signing a credit card slip as "Samantha." We hear that some of these big outlets have dishonest clerks who may accept dicey cards for a cut on the profit. Samantha is understandably enraged; she feels personally violated, and knows this has been going on a long time. We tell her in detail about Luke's problems, but she feels little sympathy for his condition. "He's weak," she says, "he could shape up if he wanted to. You could make him." For her Luke has now fatefully shifted beyond the pale … "I don't consider him my brother anymore."

# CHAPTER SIXTEEN

# THROUGH THE LOOKING GLASS OF REHAB

*1995 - Maryland*

Luke is now twenty-one, as of February 16—his non-birthday. Official adulthood—it may have big legal significance, but does it signal anything in Luke's actual life? We see scant signs of it over the next two months that are dominated by the same sad predictability. We consult with Luke's Montgomery County public defender, Mr. Parsons, on the theft from our neighbor's house; the charges don't look good, coupled with Luke's past record from California. And Luke is still wandering around in the minimum-wage wasteland of indistinguishable McJobs that rotate with a frequency I can't keep up with. He flips burgers, he works at a local gas station, he bags groceries, he works in a small grocery store, each for a few weeks, and then generally leaves or, more likely, gets fired for not showing, or possible pilferage.

Prue gets an idea and talks to Luke about enrolling in an art class at Montgomery College twice a week as some kind of recreational or art therapy. He responds very positively and she's delighted. He ends up going to his classes pretty faithfully and he likes it. We're impressed with his pen and ink drawings, usually gothic or fantasy—dragons, creatures, birds. The kid's got ability.

And then late one wintry afternoon as the setting sun fingers through the bare trees in an uncertain light Prue and I are down in the woods walking the dogs. Suddenly Barney takes off and runs way down the path ahead of us. Only then I spot a figure; it's Luke, stumbling towards us in the dusk. What in hell is he doing down here in the woods late in the day, he's supposed to be at work. He looks like shit warmed over, ill-dressed in a light hoodie, freezing cold, zonked. He sees me, and then lurches forward and collapses into my arms. "Ba, help me, I need help, I can't go on." He breaks down into tears. "Luke, for God's sake, you're in terrible shape! You can't survive like this! You know you've got to go to rehab, you've got to go." "OK," he whispers, "I know I do." "Is it crack?" He nods dumbly. And an hour later, after he's had a warm shower and gotten some food onto his stomach, Prue and I bundle him into the car and drive him down to Suburban Hospital in Bethesda where we register him in the rehab program. Yes! They'll take him in.

It's a sad mission, but also encouraging. This is the moment we have been waiting for, self-recognition of his crisis, self-admission. He needed to hit the wall; this may be the beginning of a glimpse of self-knowledge. The rehab unit says he must first spend two days and nights there under observation. Next day we get a call. Luke will be in the outpatient program—his condition does not merit compulsory inpatient residence. At least that much is good, his case could have been worse.

Prue now drives him down to the hospital every morning, picks him up at five in the evening. The course is pretty hard-core—long discussions of all the different types of drugs, what each one does to your brain, organs and nervous system, about the cycle of addiction, potential consequences of each stage, rates of recidivism, even statistics on how long people live after tangling with certain types of drugs. Discussions of the physiology and psychology of narcotics. Inspirational material—how to grab hold of your life and take control. Legal aspects. Stories by actual addicts who have recovered. Luke tells us about all this in a relaxed state each evening. He talks volubly, like he has had a lot of stuff on his chest he now wants to get out in the open. But he tends to talk about some of these drug problems in the abstract, we don't quite get much of the grim details of his own history.

Years later I come across Luke's notes from Suburban Hospital detox, notes on the PCPs, the benzos, sedatives, depressants, cannabis, hallucinogens, the uppers, the downers, the yellows, the reds, the blues, the time required for the brain to recover from each year of drug damage. On another page he has a list of people he's met in the program, teenage girls and boys, some adults, their phone numbers. I wonder how much they socialized—kind of like a certain bonded subworld as a result of this intense rehab experience.

Even after a week Luke looks much better, he's cheery, in good humor, almost seems to enjoy going off to his day's sessions. After about two weeks in the course, Luke seems almost cocky now when we pick him up. "No sweat, Ba," he says. "Things are under control" He feels he's got the whole thing mastered. "What about the withdrawal symptoms," I ask. "Isn't that supposed to be hell?" He pats my back reassuringly, he is in charge of himself now, don't worry Ba, don't worry Ma. It's cool. No problems. And there is no denying, he does look a whole lot better. Much later I come across a letter from Luke in Spanish to Luisa, clearly written in rehab, somehow never mailed, giving us lot more information long after the fact:

*Hi Luisa,*

*How are you? This is the first letter that I'm writing from this place. I'm now in a hospital in a drug program because I'm an addict. I've been using a lot of drugs for some time now. You know why? It's because I have a big problem, two weeks ago I was using and buying, spending two-hundred dollars a day for cocaine. It's really bad. And my life has been like in a circle, my schedule was get up in the morning, buy drugs, smoke drugs, then buy more and finally go to sleep. This is not the life that I want. That's why I wanted a drug program, like rehabilitation. I've been here for about two weeks. I have a week or so more to go. After that I think I'm going to a clean place ...*

In this sad letter Luke acknowledges, if only to Luisa, just how precarious his condition had become. We knew the drugs cost money, but *two-hundred dollars* a day? I wish he had been that forthcoming with us. I don't even know where he got all the money for this, not from us and surely not legally. And how evident here is his own awareness of his unhappy state. *After that I think I'm going to a clean place* ... a poignant yearning for the promised land.

A month later, the program comes to an end. Upon his release, it mandates that Luke take up residence in a halfway house in the area for continued supervised living. They are all inhabited by recovering addicts who manage the houses themselves, watch over each other, hold NA (Narcotics Anonymous) meetings on a regular basis in the houses. This would at last seem to offer the perfect venue for Luke to start assuming the adult responsibility of taking care of himself, and living in his own place. The NA meetings are mandatory and require twenty-four-hour advance written notice if you can't make it. Luke goes to Oxford House in the Rock Creek area.

He gets a local job at an A&P, now getting a regular and legal income again. Even this income isn't enough to cover all his room and board at the halfway house so we cover much of it, directly to the house itself—we know better than to give the money to Luke. His past hangs over him like a poised avalanche, calling for cautious action lest it all come tumbling down on top of him. This includes those few key symbolic debts to us that we will not forgive—his fine for the golf course spree, his marijuana possession charge at LAX, his debt to Samantha, even though we've made good on all of them temporarily.

We stay in close touch with Luke and encourage him to call anytime. We generally pick him up at his halfway house once or twice a week to take him out to dinner. As always it's where Luke is in his best form, most talkative and responsive. Korean restaurants are his venue of choice, and he works to expand our Korean culinary reach. He's warm, affectionate, happy to see us each time like he truly misses us; we embrace, have a good time, we laugh about his various doings, the details of the strange nature of life in the halfway house and the people around him. The progress he's making. Things are looking up.

Bullshit. A few weeks later we get a call from him. He's gotten kicked out of his halfway house. He admits he's "smoked a joint." You can't fool other addicts, their own lives are hanging from a string, they spot a druggie's moves in a flash, they're not going to jeopardize their own lives by tolerating any infractions. It's zero tolerance—the NA maxim. Luke's booted out. He registers in another halfway house, but under strict surveillance by the group members. He's also going to his regular in-house NA meetings. But over dinners Luke says he's burned out from NA meetings. "Man, it's always the same old shit, they're not that useful. Everybody lives in their own little world, everybody always repeats the same little phrases, 'one day at a time, man, just one day at a time,' and 'we'll always be there for you, man, hang in there, man.' And everybody's just looking for some other drug to take the place of the old—cigarettes, candy, food, whatever. Just look how fat a lot of these dudes are from overeating now, or else they smoke up a nicotine storm." "OK, Luke, we've heard this same talk too, at Be Free and other meetings. Yeah, it may be tiresome and repetitive and even bumper-sticker stuff, but that doesn't make it any less true." These people have looked over into the abyss, some have descended into its depths, and they don't want to go there again. It's some kind of death.

One of Luke's fellow members of the NA group, Walt, is a very nice guy, sharp, African-American, quite a bit older than Luke, he works at the big Johnston Motors dealership. He and Luke strike up a friendship. We take Walt out to dinner with us one time, along with Luke. Walt has a family. He tells us, in the now familiar confessional style of all AA/NA/Be Free meetings, of his own fall, the cost to him and his family, his rehabilitation, his determination to stay on the straight and narrow, his fierce desire to regain his life. He likes Luke, thinks he has style, he'll see about getting him a position at Johnston Motors. Walt also has a small extra room in his house, he's willing to let Luke live there for a modest fee. He wants to help him get back on his feet.

Luke goes by Johnston Motors, makes a good impression, and with the benefit of Walt's recommendation, he gets a job as a junior salesman-in-training. The pay is way better than the A&P, and more prestigious. We get Luke a decent suit, and drive him over to his job for his first day. After a week he announces to us proudly that if he does well in his training period, he'll get a company car to use to get to work. He's beaming like a little kid when he actually picks the car up the following Thursday. "Come on, Ba and Ma, check out my cool car! Come on, I'll take you for a ride." Nothing fancy, but it's a tangible, shiny, purring evidence of his new legal status and standing in the world. After work on Friday Luke tells us he's driving over to Virginia for the weekend to see a friend. Luke, for God's sake be careful and responsible. Sure, Ba, don't worry.

Monday afternoon the phone rings, it's Johnston Motors. Where is Luke? He hasn't shown up for work since last Thursday, he's disappeared with the car. "I'm sure he's somewhere in the area," I say, "I'm sure he'll show up." "If Luke's not in by Tuesday morning we're going to have to inform the police about the missing car," they say. Luke in fact does show up early the next day, with the car intact. But he's been AWOL and incommunicado with a vehicle that is not his own for several days. He was out with friends, he says, he lost track of the day. Wham, end of car, end of job.

Walt, his friend and sponsor, calls me up and he is angry. "I really put myself on the line for Luke at work," he says, "he's let me down, he's made me look bad. Luke is obviously using again. I can't have him anywhere near me, he's poison, my own life is at stake." Luke is booted out of Walt's house and told to stay away. The rehab sessions, the new confidence, the optimism and cheerfulness, all swirling away down the toilet.

And what is there left to say to Luke? That you blew it, big time? He knows it, he knows we know and we're all tired of the lecture. "The game is over, Luke, we're not taking you home; you can't live with us under these conditions. You've got to make it on your own now." So he goes over to Virginia again to stay with a friend there who was in rehab with him. He has no job right now. Maybe he'll find some fast-food something to stay afloat.

In a week or so, he calls up to say he has a job washing windows in people's homes, cleaning gutters on the roof. He wants to borrow our extension ladder to help on the job. I'm naïve, his request seems to make sense. He comes over with some friend in a pick-up truck. A week later Luke says he isn't going to do the roof jobs anymore, can't find enough work. "Where's the ladder, Luke?" "I'll get the ladder back next week," he says. Only it never comes back. And only then does the nickel drop. Almost surely the ladder has been used for breaking and entering. What did Luke say in his letter to Luisa? Two-hundred bucks a day in cocaine costs? He can't remotely earn that at any of the kind of jobs he's likely to get.

I feel hung out and exposed. I'm starting to cover up, I can barely even report all these twists and turns to Prue anymore, and certainly not to anyone else. I'm complicit in hiding the full extent of Luke's condition. Each mistake of his, each setback, each criminal run-in, each failure, each suspicion, each outrage—I won't pass it to my daughters anymore, or to my father when he asks me on the phone how Luke is doing. I can't hide most of it from Samantha's indignant and accusatory eye; she's been repeatedly victimized and had her stuff stolen and pawned. She's still staying in our house until she goes for an MBA in the fall in North Carolina. Melissa calls regularly from Minneapolis for updates. My default mode is simply not to volunteer, just to stick with guarded, but not very positive generalities. I feel like each setback is a personal recrimination upon me too. Now they talk about *your* son. To my sisters I impart slightly more—apart from being concerned aunts, they're both professional psychologists and often have useful insights. But even here, I can't, I don't call up with any regularity any more to pass all the depressing tales along. I'm alone, tired, isolated and depressed.

*　　　　*　　　　*

I have been urging Luke for some time to write Samantha a formal letter of apology for his theft of her credit card and pilfering of her funds. Very little has been said between them. Then one day Samantha shows us a letter:

*June-July 1995*

*Dear Samantha,*

*I know it's been a long time for me in coming around to writing this letter to you but in reality I first had to get into grips with myself. It's been taking a long time to get my life somewhat in order fighting my problems with drugs. When I took your credit cards I was thinking like a crazed crack addict not caring about anybody not even myself. Just thinking about getting high. And every time I got high I was happy but when I came down to reality I hated it and felt miserable. I was deteriorating from the inside out.*

*I needed help, I started selling my possessions and then pawned baba's camera and computer and without realizing I started to ruin the family. I don't know what told me to do so, but I decided to tell Baba and Mummy that I needed help.*

*I then checked into Suburban Hospital for rehab. When I left I felt good I began to go to narcotics anonymous meetings and hang out with sober people. But soon I felt the urge and I relapsed and smoked some crack. At the time I was living in an Oxford home which is for sober people but I soon left because they found out I started back into smoking crack again, but not at a heavy pace. Things started to return back as before. I then moved into a house with a friend and his family but later had to leave because he found out. I got hired to work for a car dealership but that soon fell through because I blew it. I then moved to another Oxford home in DC and this time I was working hard trying to stay sober but where I lived was in Adams Morgan and just two blocks away you could buy crack on the streets.*

*What really made me think and start being sober is that about three weeks ago I was in an area in Maryland where you could buy crack and I was with a friend and we were buying crack and the next thing I know is that two blacks ran at my friend and shot him. I got scared and ran. I don't know what has become of him but I want no part of it. So now I've moved to Virginia in Leesburg and am living with a friend I met in the hospital and staying sober. I have a job as a waiter and things are looking better. Different environment away from drugs and bad friends and I'm trying to start anew.*

*I'm sorry for stealing your credit card and your stereo but as soon as I make some money I will buy you a new stereo. I hope you will understand my problem and my disease and still be my sister. Please forgive me.*

*Love, Luke Fuller*

*            *            *

The next week we take Luke out again to dinner at the Korean restaurant. I tell him I'm pleased that he wrote the letter to Samantha. She does not accept the situation—who does?—but she is at least slightly mollified by Luke's acknowledgment of her pain and victimization in the situation. I get around to asking Luke about the incident with his friend Cho. Luke isn't hiding too much from us anymore.

"Well, me and Cho went down to Wheaton to get some drugs? It was a bad neighborhood, all-black ghetto, but that's where we go to get our stuff. We were in Cho's car. We get out and he, like, signals to this guy, like he knows him? The guy starts yelling at Cho, like, 'Where's my money man? You said you'd pay me for all that shit you picked up, you yellow bastard.' And Cho said, like, he didn't have the money right now. This black guy comes charging up and puts a gun to Cho's neck and tells him to pay right now. More blacks come over. They all start fighting and hitting each other, and I just took off, running down the sidewalk. Then I hear some gun shots and Cho screams. I was scared shitless. I look back and he's on the sidewalk, all bleeding. Some of the blacks starting running after me and I just took off again and ran down to where there was some park and a lot of woods. Then they came into the woods, charging around, but they couldn't find me in the dark and they gave up and went away. I stayed there all night man, it was cold but I wasn't going to go out on the streets there until it was morning. I finally got out the next morning and walked all the way home, I didn't have any money and it took me five hours. Cho's in the hospital, he's hurt bad but I guess he'll live."

We never hear about Cho again from Luke. A grim story, but not all bad if it's going to put the fear of God into this kid's brain.

*          *          *

Doing things together, the best form of communicating. Luke and I decide to make sushi together one day when he's over at the house. Luke was the first in the family to really start eating sushi, and always urged us to go out for it.

We go to one of our Asian recipe books and find the instructions for making sushi. We go to the Asian supermarket and roll our cart up and down the aisles. We buy the sticky white sushi rice, the yellow pickled *daikon* radish, the pungent pickled pink ginger slices and the *nori* seaweed in sheets. We buy some nice fresh tuna and some cucumber. We buy little bamboo mats to roll the sushi up in. We take it home and open up the recipe book. We boil the rice, we put in the salt and sugar, we stir in the sweet Japanese vinegar and we let it all sit, cool and firm up. We boil the Chinese dried mushrooms in soy sauce and sugar and then we slice them up. We shred the carrots. We slice the tuna filet, julienne the cucumber, roast the sesame seeds, and we set it all out on the table. We lay the damp sushi rice down the center of the *nori* sheet, one by one place the other components on top of the rice and then we begin rolling it all up inside the bamboo place mat, with just the right degree of firmness, sealing the *nori* sheet around the sushi roll so that it doesn't spill open. Luke has greater manual dexterity than I do. He patiently shows me how to improve on my too-fat roll; the ingredients are crudely spilling out of the end.

And what do you know, we end up with some pretty good sushi, Luke and I. We first share my one retarded, lop-sided roll together between us to test out the flavor, and then we beamingly offer the good ones to the rest of the family. A kind of peace offering given and received all around.

We've had a good time. We've said a lot … in the silence of our sushi-making.

*          *          *

In April 1985 Luke is out riding with some loser friend on the weekend, they're caught by the police speeding over the Chesapeake Bay Bridge. They were reportedly clocked at a hundred-and-five miles an hour. They had open liquor in the car, and worse, there was a bow and arrow in the trunk that the police treat as a concealed weapon. They are both arrested and taken to jail in Annapolis.

193

Luke has been on notice with us for a long time now on this—a strict policy of no bail. He's twenty-one, he did it, it's his predicament, he's got to work it out, pay the penalty, take the responsibility. At last I draw the line in the sand, and respond with the tough-mindedness that everybody has been yelling at me to demonstrate. We're not going to lift a finger this time. He knows all that well in advance. He's locked up in Annapolis jail pending a court hearing, the police say it's likely to be upward of three months. When he is allowed, we have a few brief telephone conversations with him, no visits. I've got to take off in a day or two for a trip to Turkey, a country on which I've developed some professional credentials. Luke's cousin Dylan, Meredith's oldest son, some five years older than Luke, visits DC and wants to go visit Luke in jail. He reports back that Luke seemed very humiliated at being seen there. He thinks he saw some needle-tracks on Luke's arm. This is Luke's first experience with in-jail therapy.

Prue needs a real break and I suggest she come with me to the conference—Turkey's a country she loves as well. Luke's in jail, he can't get into any trouble while we're gone. After the conference in Ankara we rent a car and drive to some of our favorite historic towns in Turkey. We call back home to Samantha at some point to find out if there is any news on the Luke front, any court dates, etc. She reports that Luke has already been let out of jail, unexpectedly early, after only one month or so. He has broken into the house in the daytime while she was at work. He may have stolen a few things, she's not sure.

Christ, is there is no let-up to this? And Samantha and Luke are a potentially volatile pair together with Luke in a heavy pilfer mode.

We get back home shortly thereafter. Luke is indeed around. He says he was unexpectedly released, almost unceremoniously kicked out of jail from near Annapolis, and was given just five dollars. He says he had to walk and hitchhike home back to Bethesda; he says he slept along the roadside one night. He knew we were away in Turkey. Samantha is really angry at his breaking into the house, and is concerned about Luke ripping us or her off again.

A few days later, I talk with Luke about the jail experience. "What was the worst part of it, Luke?" I ask. He pauses. "The people," he says, "the people ..." It was a very rough place; he had to keep up a tough pose and exterior the whole time, fight some people off to protect his butt. They were afraid of his tae kwon do moves. Luke says he is determined not to end up in jail again. He's coming up for a court hearing later in the fall on the incident.

Still, the contagion of Luke's condition spreads more widely into the family, now touching my sister Meredith. She has been a godmother of sorts to Luke, from inspiring us originally to adopt, present at JFK at Luke's arrival into our world, helping preserve the link between Luke and Laura, her own adopted Korean daughter, and a wise source of advice on Luke's problems.

Laura and Luke have always had a special relationship. From a small age they have been told in much detail about the other, how each of them was adopted from Korea—evident indeed at one glance. But they share something deeper than just shared ethnicity and adoption into the same extended family. Whatever their characteristics, they also temperamentally differ from the Fuller family mold. The Fuller clan is endlessly talkative, analytical, argumentative, creative, restless, often tiresome, artistic, opinionated in one sense or another, highly individualistic, relishing the pleasures of debating ideas, always coming on too strong.

Indeed, these are perhaps the nicer adjectives to describe these characteristics; to those who are occasionally made uncomfortable or feeling left out of the spirit of family gatherings, other, less flattering adjectives might come to mind. Neither Luke nor Laura is as verbal and tiresomely analytic. They know they are loved, included, cherished, supported, valued, but they instinctively know they are not of us. Luke says as much, and we have sensed for many years a tendency of Luke to withdraw when the critical mass of an extended family gathering becomes too intense. Indeed, even for the in-laws who chose to marry into the family there is a sense of being "out-laws," as Meredith's husband Jim once semi-humorously put it, himself no mean practitioner of verbal and analytic skills, including in the scientific field.

In one of my favorite photos we see Luke and Laura sitting together in adjoining chairs in Thousand Oaks at Christmas, both sharing some joke between them. Both are comfortable, totally relaxed with each other, laughing out loud together at some mutually shared comment—maybe about the foibles of the rest of us—in full comfort and intimacy, both in the full glory of their youthful Asian handsomeness and spontaneity. The photo is precious, we don't often see either of them quite that relaxed and spontaneous at these gatherings. And Barney is sitting on Luke's lap, being patted, looking happy and feisty. This photo for me captures the shared special relationship and spontaneous communication between Luke and Laura and dog; this is a private joke between them, a moment of unguarded and shared pleasure; they have expressions of spontaneous open delight on their faces that we don't often see in their family interactions with us.

Meredith has been well aware of the ongoing problems we've been having with Luke, especially his growing theft to feed his drug habit. We've been periodically on the phone about these matters; her advice is always sympathetic, thoughtful and supportive.

Now Meredith's oldest son, Dylan, is about to get married, the first in their family, my first nephew to marry. Meredith calls us up about general arrangements, and then the bombshell drops. She's been thinking long and hard about issues surrounding Luke's presence at the wedding. There will be lots of guests there, many staying in the house, leaving purses and things around over several days. With the greatest of regret she has concluded that it's simply too problematic to have Luke at the wedding. He would inevitably be a source of constant worry about what guest or family member might get ripped off in his hunger for money. With great regret she asks if we would leave Luke home.

I understand Meredith's request, it's based on a sober reading of reality, reached only after much thought and evident concern and even pain in the asking. It is the rational thing to do. OK, I say tersely, I understand. But in my heart I feel enraged, betrayed. For me this is a body blow of major proportions. What perhaps upsets me most of all is that doors are now beginning to close in on us, even within the family itself. I choke on an overwhelming sense of claustrophobia. There may be only one dark road left for him; I have a vision of some long-term reality that is now inexorably closing in.

Keeping Luke locked into the bosom of a loving and caring larger family has always been essential to my strategy of trying to shepherd him through these tumultuous and dangerous rapids of life. We have endlessly repeated to him that we will never turn our backs on him come what may, that he is part of us all forever. He will not be abandoned. His greater family will always care for him. But now that solid place and firm identity I hoped to create for him within the family has been shaken, thrown in doubt; the rock-solid solidarity is giving way. What will Luke make of this? If Prue and I were to die tomorrow, is Luke really still a Fuller? Is there an extended family there to take care of him? In my mind, pretty surely yes, but can Luke be sure?

To take him to the wedding of course opens up prospects of petty, or even not so petty, theft. But now our options are being foreclosed, even by those family members who are most concerned over his welfare. My anger does not dissipate, it is multi-directional—at Luke for being what he is, at myself and my visceral reaction, my anger at the whole situation and being caught in the middle—but also at Meredith herself since she was the one who felt the painful need to blow this particular whistle at a key family gathering. "I'm not even fucking going to go to the wedding, I've had it, you all go!" I yell to Prue in a moment of venting, my psychological isolation and alienation complete. "Dylan is your only nephew," she says, "you have to go. You can't let this build up between yourself and Meredith." And the next day I turn right around and throw it all in Luke's face—"You see where you have gotten yourself, Luke? And gotten me? Don't you see where this is all going? You can't even be trusted by your own goddam family anymore!" Luke gets angry. He feels insulted, hurt, he has been disinvited by his own aunt and cousin from a major family affair. What did they think he was? *Of course* he wouldn't steal anything from guests at the wedding. Of course not.

And so, as our family, *sans* Luke, drive up to the Cape for the wedding a few days later I feel no warmth on this happy occasion. Wrenching emotion overcomes reason. My heart is constricted and dark and I even make a number of snide remarks on the side about the dinner party. And I make a direct plea to my two nephews Dylan and Elijah not to lose contact with Luke in these, his more troubled, times.

Indeed, this incident, whose practical explanation is rationally understood by all of us, evolves into an unspoken, dark presence in the corner; it has now come to shadow my relationship with Meredith. Only the pure tears of shared grief at his loss can later wash it away on all sides.

I'm sliding down the same path as Luke. He's driven by drugs, I'm obsessed with trying to keep control of this vehicle that is swerving all over the road, out of control and the road is getting more treacherous and winding in these mountains of irrationality. We're both equally addicted it seems, both increasingly shutting out the rest of the world around us in our different ways, squeezing out other relationships with my daughters, my extended family, even sometimes with Prue. And I'm struggling to preserve even a thin lifeline, literally, between Luke and myself.

When we get back home a few days later we find a note on the kitchen table from Luke.

*Dear Mother and Father,*

*I have gone on a little trip to think things out. I am NOT running away and I love you all very much but I need some time to think. I will be safe and I have gone with Qays. [An Iranian friend whom we like.] I will return on Monday. So we will talk. So I hope you will understand.*

*Love you always,*

*Your son, Luke Fuller*

*PS: Please don't worry about me. I will be safe.*

# CHAPTER SEVENTEEN

# CANADIAN SURRENDER

*September 1995 - Maryland*

How do you throw your own damn kid out of the house, with no clear place to go, clearly unable to fend for himself? He's no longer in halfway houses; he can't hold down any serious employment anymore. He can't survive like this. He's staying God knows where these days.

Prue and I come home from a three-day trip away visiting my father and find our fax and answering machine gone. Luke has obviously broken into the locked house in our absence. When he comes around a few days later we confront him. I demand to know where he pawned them so I can recover them. Classic mode: looking like a little kid caught with his hand in the candy jar, crestfallen, at a loss for words, pained, but without any response, a series of little emotions surging across his face like glass shattering, trying to figure what to say, a sense of helplessness, a little surprised that this is happening, a little surprised that we're surprised, as if by now we should know that this is the way he has to operate, as if this wasn't really his decision but some external force operating upon him, after all, it's the cocaine that's in charge—not him, and he's just the vehicle, regretful, yes, at where it's all going, demonstrably saddened, expressing a few heartfelt feelings that it oughtn't, won't, shouldn't happen again.

Even though Luke is no longer living in the house with us, I have no confidence in the security of our house when we're out. We're nervous if we're gone too long. One time when we get back from a long walk with the dogs, unlock the door and walk in, Barney gets very excited and rushes downstairs to the lower part of the house. Surely a sign that Luke is, or has been there. Is Luke still in the house? We investigate, and find the downstairs back door unlocked from which Luke has apparently fled. More investigation reveals that the skylight upstairs was open an inch. I crawl up on the roof and find the skylight has been jimmied open. Luke must have forced it open and then swung down into the living room, some eight-foot drop right by a banister that edges onto another eight-foot drop—any miscalculation could have been really damaging to him, especially in a druggy state of mind. But he's clearly crawled his way into the house. We feel violated. We're not afraid for our physical safety—we never have been with Luke—but the sanctity of the house has sure as hell been violated.

A week later I find that Luke has removed a small ground-level window in the basement laundry room, where the lint-blower was attached to the outside. He had squeezed in, combed the house and found more items to pawn. I go down into the laundry room and using a few two-by-fours fashion a set of barriers that I jam into the window frame and nail tightly to close off ground access into the house. Are we living in fucking South Bronx here? Worse is the horrific feeling that our own son is now periodically transformed into a temporary malevolent being when the need hits. The anxiety that one day even fear itself might interject itself into our relationship with him. What limits will conscience impose upon his urgent drives?

*            *            *

We hadn't seen much of Steve and Kathy Ching—from long ago our weekends on the junk with them in Hong Kong—and later visiting in California. They too now live in Maryland. We periodically kept them abreast of our ongoing problems with Luke. Steve takes the initiative to invite Luke out to lunch, just the two of them. Luke unwinds a good bit with Steve, admits many of his problems and his worries but offers no major revelations into the state of his own soul, at least not yet. Steve talks with him about the problems of making a way in both Asian as well as American culture. I have hopes that Steve might be in a position to mentor Luke in some way; who knows, he has a special relationship with him. Steve is off shortly to Korea on business; he asks Luke what he could bring back for him. Luke said he'd like something really Korean, maybe a flag. Steve says he'll see what he can find. I hope this cultural nexus can create a special channel to reality for Luke.

And it's September 1995 now, and Luke's employment *du jour* is working at a Dunkin' Donuts in the nearby mall. The weather in Washington is still mild, and Luke has now opted to live in some kind of lean-to, packing-crate type hovel down in the woods, built earlier on perhaps by some kids as a hide-out, camping place, or maybe by some itinerant homeless. It is well down below our house, deep into the woods and beyond a stream—part of an extensive parkland and off the beaten path of visibility. We are unhappy with the choice, but Luke says he likes it as long as the weather holds. It's also a twelve-minute walk to his donuts job. He comes by periodically for a shower, a decent meal and to wash his clothes under close supervision in the house, but we enjoy sitting down with him for a meal.

In the meantime Prue and I want to take another trip to Vancouver, British Columbia, a city that is increasingly exerting its hold upon us. Prue really needs a break from her twenty-four-seven guard duty of manning the fort—literally—especially when I'm away. But we can't go off all the way across the country and leave Luke in these precarious straits, our house ripe for plunder. And the thought of him huddled in his hovel down the hill, partially exposed to the elements in the middle of the woods in a county park in the fall is agonizing. He has a paycheck, enough to eat presumably, but how long can he stay in a packing crate? We simply can't tough this one out. Samantha is now off at her MBA program in Chapel Hill, so the house will be empty. If we do go, he'll surely break into the house, for shelter, a shower, and something more to pawn.

We yield once again: better to embrace Luke, take him with us than to leave him. This has been all rather last minute—we're leaving in two days. I scrabble around for an extra seat on the plane. But where is Luke? We can't find him, and he wasn't on the roster for work that day. Maybe he's off with a friend. There is now only one day before we depart. We leave word at the donut shop, not even sure he can get away for ten days if he wants to hold his job.

Last-gasp effort—we can only leave a note for him at the hovel and hope he gets it in time. It's early evening and the sun is dropping off the horizon. Prue and I descend down into the darkening woods below, pushing aside branches that scratch at our faces, stumbling over rocks and holes to locate this little hideaway. He is somewhere out in these woods, but can we find exactly where he is? We grope through bushes, we're far from trodden paths or known trails, stumbling in the deepening gloom. We come to the stream. I remember my mother's words from my boyhood: if you get lost in a forest, just follow a stream, it will eventually bring you back to civilization. Will it? The water is dark in the evening light, moving along languidly in some unknown direction, to ultimately merge with other streams we barely know about. Then, over there, we spy the scattered detritus of human presence—plastic bags, once functional, later cast aside and now wind-born, lifeless, captured by bushes; styrofoam boxes, plundered of their one-time fast-food grease-trips, now to linger for centuries before achieving dissolution and release into half-life in the earth; plastic bottles of sport drinks—sport types out here in hovels? One bottle with its telltale hole in the base, yeah, bong technology, we know all about that. An old denim jacket riddled with holes and serving as a lode for field mice and tree squirrels to pad their nests. Deeper into the bushes we perceive the shack, more a lean-to, over a cavity in the ground—the builders seemingly ignorant of the basic physics of drainage. There is a sleeping bag, and apparently a few items of clothing in a plastic bag, some water. A cooler with some food in it. A Turkish shirt that we know to be Luke's.

But no Luke. Where could he be? A few hours ago we were coolly assessing the pros and cons of taking him along or leaving him to his own devices. Now, having made the decision and groping our way down into his forest of isolation and confusion to contact him, I feel desperate to find him, to take him away from all this. I can't wait another minute to get him out of this degraded status; leaving him behind in it becomes emotionally and morally unbearable.

I pull out a note I had written earlier in the slim hope that Luke will come back tonight from whatever rendezvous his habits dictate. Time is short, we'll be off tomorrow afternoon and Luke will be stuck on the ground in a hovel for weeks. Ironically I realize that if we do go without him, we almost prefer his forced entry into the house, the only real refuge he has, the only other place we can leave word about where we've gone and how he might reach us.

*Dear Luke, we are flying to Vancouver tomorrow afternoon. We're very worried about leaving you for that long alone here and the weather is getting colder. Will you come with us? It might be fun. We've gotten you a ticket. You can ask for time off from work ... We'd love to have you come along. But we're leaving tomorrow, so please come by as soon as possible, even late tonite, and let us know. Love, Ba*

Anxious hours. At eleven o'clock at night, a tentative knock at the door. Barney runs over to it with a bark. Luke peers through the windowpane of the door. He comes in looking disheveled, sheepish, and I breathe a sigh of relief. "Yeah Ba, I would like to come. I've worked it out with my manager." We're grateful, our conscience salved that we have not abandoned him to the woods, to coming storms, to the unpredictable, to the unknown dark of his private world which stretches like galaxies.

At least for the next two weeks he will be under our nominally watchful eyes, our caring, saddened eyes. We put his sleeping bag in the closed-in carport again for the night where he has a mattress and some of his stuff; he has access to the house itself only while we're up and around to monitor. Luke makes no effort to hide his relief. No more posturing adolescent pretense of what a drag it is to spend time with the parents; this boy knows he's hurting and he accepts a few weeks liberated from immediate existential worries. At least he'll be getting three squares and a bed, and see someplace interesting. He's always liked the road, our whole family does ...

As we get ready for bed that night, I ask Prue how she feels about all this. "You know," she says quietly, "I think that in terms of maturity Luke is now actually regressing. The clock is starting to work backward, I think he's becoming more childlike." "Is that because we're still letting him be dependent on us?" I ask. "No," she says, "I think he's just less able to take care of himself now than maybe since he was sixteen. It's the drugs doing this. I think he's lost heart." I recognize the truth of this, his growing weakness, impotence, a desire to return to the simple and reliable comforts of childhood. No longer do the rules of home seem to imprison a teenage soul struggling to break free: this is a soul that now finds that freedom's just a word for nothing left to lose. It isn't all that it's cracked up to be out there, is it; his parents now seem to offer at least a welcome refuge, love is available, the minimal demands they put upon him are worth it in exchange for increased certainty, security, TLC.

Are we copping out in making things easy for him here, too easy, sparing him the need to face reality? Yes, I realize, the addict is *me*, craving to see him survive in better conditions even if he is reverting back to a thirteen-year-old boy in spirit and mentality. He has been regressing month by month into a more childish mode, a more simple kid, warm, pliable, offering no resistance—apart from periodic momentary flashes of cunning about when to seize an opening to score some stuff off of us. But the alternative of this is all too clear to me: the trajectory of this particular life right now is moving unambiguously, undeniably, inescapably in the wrong direction, away from mature and autonomous decision-making into the blind needs of a child: food, housing, love, certainty—and the soft embracing womb of drugs.

Yes, I plead guilty. I'm tired, I'm naïve, facilitating, ostrich-like, unrealistic, out of touch, self-deluding, refusing to face the facts, in a state of denial—whatever you say. But scooping him up with us and taking him along feels just right. Don't ask me to justify it to anybody anymore—to Be Free, psychologists, to our daughters, other family members, probation officers, the rehab program, anybody—all I know is I just want to have this kid with us now.

On the flight to Vancouver Luke sits in the back by himself in one of the few seats left on the flight. Turns out he's in among a bunch of basketball players from Vancouver—Luke is always running into guys who take to him. I'm sure he gets a first class briefing on places to score in the city, the home of BC Gold. But he'll be on a fairly tight leash with us.

In Vancouver we go to a midnight performance of a laser show at the planetarium—they're doing Pink Floyd, his favorite band, music that we like too. Pink Floyd, a laser show—all we need is a little LSD to make it perfect. It's *The Dark Side of the Moon*, especially for Luke.

He seems fine on the trip. We overlook his few little absences, his unerring ability to find some provider in a strange city in minutes, like a bee for honey when we're not looking. Local head shops are always a good source of info, where someone can tell him how to score. Luke is not in our face on any of this, it's all discreet; I'm not even sure where he's getting any money, because I'm in firm charge of my wallet. There's so much less to worry about than when we're home. He's basically pleasant, good company, often funny. It's hard to see any clear signs of drug usage, but it's like the unseen forms beneath the swirling waters of a trout stream—you know they're there in the black recesses around the rocks.

We drive from Vancouver up into the Rockies across into Alberta to Banff and Lake Louise. Next morning we all plan to hike up the magnificent trail that runs along the lake and up into the glaciers. Breathtaking blue water on the lake, snowcapped mountains soaring in the distance behind it; we're high in the Rockies, the air crisp in citified lungs. This is the kind of place I want to live. There are still some things right with the world. We go down by the side of the lake to take a picture where I snap an iconic tourist photo of Prue and Luke standing by the waters of Lake Louise with the mountains in the background; then a picture of Luke alone, hamming it up in the cold, breathing into his rolled fists. It's the last picture of him alive I'll ever take.

We clamber up the trail, not too difficult, most people managing the climb handily until it reaches the glacier area where it gets steeper, with a lot of loose scree and rocks. There is a kind of plateau with a frozen meandering stream about fifty feet below where you can scramble down and get a superb shot right up into the glacier field and the peak. We decide not to try the scramble. But there's a guy already down there; he's taken some pictures and is now trying to get back up. He gets ten feet up, then the loose stones give way and he slides back down. He tries again, gets about a quarter of the way up, then slips down on his back. We can't reach him. He seems to have no choice but a long hike back down the mountain until he meets the trail again. Luke thinks he can help. He suggests we tie our jacket sleeves together, all three of us, and throw the end down to the guy. Luke then picks his way down the rocks some ten feet, holding on and tosses the end. The guy crawls up a short way and catches the last sleeve, and Luke pulls him up to the pathway.

He's Québécois, Paul from Montreal, late thirties; he and his wife, or girlfriend, are really grateful. He insists on buying us a drink at the lodge. It's too early for a drink, for us anyway, we settle for coffee. Paul is a publisher, he talks to Luke, takes a shine to him and asks him what he's doing. Luke mentions he's now looking for work, he might want a change of venue. Paul asks why Luke doesn't consider coming up to Montreal, he could easily find him a job at the printing office. Luke looks interested, Paul gives him his card. We're happy for Luke, that he had the thought, gumption and generosity to help pull this guy back up onto the trail. Maybe in his fantasy, or ours, we imagine how it might work out, a new venue, a new country, new conditions, a new start. But we also know that treacherous feeling of encouragement and hope, we've been there before, too many times. If San Cristóbal or Monteverde couldn't do it, would Montreal? Still, we talk it up with Luke as if it were something real, urge him to think about it. Another one of life's chances, one even created by Luke's own spontaneous generosity of impulse, may yield no more than coffee in a chalet up in the mountains at Lake Louise. Still, the speculation warms the heart. We're happy with the moment. A moment of grace.

We've had some great day hikes around this incredible area, soaring mountains and glaciers, crystal lakes, sacred snowcapped mountains in the distance. The potential menace of grizzlies is understood, but in perspective a modest threat. We plan another hike around there in the morning. This time Luke begs off. We know what the likely drill for him will be, sussing out the local scene with the hotel busboys, score some stuff, but we're not going to sweat it, it's small stuff by now. We come back that night and Luke is in a good mood, apparently his needs met. He and I go down to play pool together—a game I wouldn't be playing except for him—and he whips my ass as he likes to say, but it's really a form of bonding, and I'm happy to lose to him, really, anytime.

While groping around under the pool table with my hand to find the billiard ball outlet, I slice my hand badly on some piece of sharp metal. It cuts a vein, there's a good bit of blood flowing that doesn't stop for quite a while, not really dangerous, but a lot of blood. Luke is highly solicitous of my welfare, runs around demanding some bandages and antiseptic from the hotel manager, rebukes them for leaving something menacing like that inside the table. He helps wrap up the bandage tight. I feel like he is seeking briefly to reverse roles, to show some concern on his side for his wounded father, maybe unconsciously aware that this may be a rare chance to return the favor, to reciprocate our concerns for him, to make up for them in some small way. Little moments like this are telling: his drugs have not yet sundered all the bonds; we enjoy the brief emotionality of caring communication.

Our last night in Vancouver, and it's laden. We go off to see the new Spike Lee film, *Clockers* with Harvey Keitel and Delroy Lindo; it's about young black drug runners and a concerned white cop. We're not there for the theme especially, we're just old Spike Lee fans. Luke comes along. There's a scene near the end of the film where a drug-running uncle in the ghetto recruits his teenage nephew to help with the distribution of crack on the streets. Looks like the kid may have tried some. The uncle explodes at his nephew in the car, "You mother-fuckin' idiot, I'll beat your sorry ass to a pulp if you ever touch this shit. Sell it, make money, but don't ever, ever touch it. Anyone takes crack, no two ways about it, they're dead." Devastating message, deadly darts fired right off into the darkness of the theater with our names on them. Did Luke squirm in his seat at this scene? I mention it casually after the film. Yeah, Luke says, seemingly sobered, pensive. Yeah, maybe Spike Lee has called it right.

But we've had some warm, unhurried, uncontentious, often silent time together enjoying each other's company. "You know, Luke, you can't even steal from us when we're together on the road." He laughs. I'll take this over the tough love of leaving the kid in the hovel in the woods.

As I look out from the window over the splendor of the Rockies on our flight back home I wonder. Haven't I just kicked the can of reckoning down the road a short way, nothing more? But then … so what? I'm just grateful for the time together. I'll worry about tomorrow tomorrow.

I don't even think I'm resisting any more. Maybe I too have yielded, now at one with the drug.

Just doing one day at a time myself.

# CHAPTER EIGHTEEN

# FALLING LEAVES

*November 1995*

Luke has come in from the cold now. Literally. And from the outside world which he's barely negotiating. We re-admit him back into our home with us—that spartan, enclosed carport that is now his space.

His mattress lies on the concrete floor, next to a hand-me-down college-worn generic honey-colored scratched-up laminated old bureau standing nearby. It's not even really his room, it's my workshop. Luke doesn't seem to have the will to impose himself on it, to make it his own space, even as Prue offers to make it homier. There are paint cans on a window shelf over his head, heavy hammers and sharp tools menacingly scattered across a long workbench. Electric saws and drills lying about, their threat thwarted as long as their cords remain disconnected. Disarray.

But it's just temporary, and the room is heated and it's a place to sleep, an asylum that's part of our home. Luke gets to come into the house proper only when we're there. We'll try to work something else out eventually. Prue puts up some material to drape across the outside windows for privacy. The carport has its own entrance out onto the driveway; only a few steps from his mattress there is another door with glass panes that opens into the kitchen and the house.

Except that door is locked. Against him.

*Why am I locked out? I know why, I steal things from my parents. But I am alone. How can I make any of this different?*

But nothing really is different. Luke goes back to his Dunkin' Donuts job, walking there each morning. Each night he gets to take home some leftover donuts and donut holes, fat pills. They're not even on my list of goodies anymore. But ever the entrepreneur, Luke meets up with some kids who work at Popeye's Fried Chicken around the corner from Dunkin' Donuts. They work out a swap deal for leftover chicken, so now when I swing by to pick Luke up in the evening he slips beaming into the car, "Check it out, Ba, got some spicy fried chicken for you, I swapped it for donuts." Cool, Luke. Although I'm not too much into crispy double-batter-deep-fried spicy Jamaican chicken these days, Luke shows a child-like pleasure in finding me these goodies and bringing them home. He's like a cat bringing home a mouse in its mouth as an offering of peace and reconciliation, food as a shared communion. It's a small act of symbolic triumph, the gift for someone who deserves the very best. Luke wants to make up for things, he wants to *feed* me.

I find Luke still asleep on his mattress one morning when he was supposed to be up at five to start up the donut production.

"Luke, wake up, weren't you supposed to get up early this morning and go to work?"

"Umm … no, not today."

"But you said you're on three times a week for the early shift, you haven't gotten up early once this week."

"Yeah, well, see, actually I'm not working there anymore."

"Whaddya mean you're not working there anymore?"

" I quit."

"Quit? But why, Luke, you said you liked Dunkin' Donuts. It was a good job."

"Yeah, but it was too much work."

"What was so hard?"

"I don't like getting up early. And anyway it was boring. "

"But you need to stick to something for a while, get some experience, you were only there a few months. And you need the money."

"Yeah, well, I found a better paying job in the same mall, at Radio Shack around the corner."

"Really? How come you didn't tell us all about this?"

"I don't know, I just hadn't mentioned it yet. It just happened a few days ago."

"What made you choose Radio Shack?"

"I dunno, it's more interesting stuff. It has more of a future."

Like Luke's ever thought about the future. Luke says the manager at Radio Shack liked his style—they always do—and hired him on as a trainee salesman. And now Luke comes home to show off the badge and blazer he's been given for the sales floor. No more smell of grease. But I wonder if he's now swapping electronics for fried chicken. Radio Shack has done what we surely never could have done—gotten Luke into a blazer and tie. His uniform is a sign of coming up in the world, he has a nice big engraved black plastic pin with LUKE on it, a modest statement of belonging somewhere.

*I am somebody. I am Luke.*

Just in case anybody wondered.

Over the next week over supper Luke takes pleasure in filling us in on developments. "The manager really likes me," he says, "He says I'm good with the customers. And I've learned all about the specs on the hi-fi systems. I get to advise customers about what kind of plugs do what, recommend various lines of hi-fi equipment." "That's great, Luke, we're sure you can work out well at a place like that. And you're right, if you play your cards right, you could move ahead over time—without all the grease." To show our support we drop by to see him at work in all his professional finery, he beams, introduces us to his manager. I don't know what is happening on the drug front, but he seems to be getting to work on time these days, on foot. We offer him the use of a bike, but he says not now, it's not that far. We drive him when the weather is bad. And in a few weeks he qualifies to go off to a three-day orientation and training session at Radio Shack's regional corporate headquarters in downtown Washington. Starting tomorrow in fact.

I try to shield in my cupped hands a delicate, flickering flame of hope, to protect and sustain. Don't they say that every day is the first day of the rest of your life?

Yes, but only one day is the last day of your life.

That's great Luke, goodnight Luke, remember Luke, you've got to be up early for your ride downtown to the training class in the morning. Good luck with it. Get a good night's sleep. OK, Ba, goodnite.

Next morning I check in on Luke at eight to make sure he's on his way. Shit, he's still sound asleep in bed. Dismayed we rush in to roust him out of bed to get him off to his training day, even though he'll be late. But the pretense is now over. This kid's in no condition to go anywhere. I try to drag him out of bed but he exercises passive resistance. His head is rolling, he's barely able to mumble responses to our questions. This time he's fried his mind out on something, big-time. I watch Radio Shack go down the tubes ... *Luke, it seems clear, you really didn't want to go to this training at all, did you? You feel you can't face it, can't hack it, is that what you're telling us, telling yourself? Is that what this is all about?*

And sure enough, the phone rings around eight thirty, it's Radio Shack; where is Luke, the van is leaving to go downtown right this minute to the training site. Hello, yes, this is Luke's father, I'm sorry, Luke can't come to the phone right now, he's zonked out of his fucking mind on crack. But if you'd like to leave a message ...

Is that what I say? Or how about I slip into the old facilitator mode, option B: Gee, I'm sorry, but Luke's got a bad case of flu today, but he probably should be OK by tomorrow. Or C: I don't know where Luke is right now, but we'll have him call as soon as he gets in. I end up opting for B, the flu, and I see myself as Facilitator Exhibit A in the Be Free mugbook.

Later in the morning, Luke seems a little steadier, he gets up to go outside for a while for a cigarette. I watch him out of the kitchen window, standing on the driveway, smoking, staring off into the distance with narrowed eyelids. He doesn't want to talk. But when we look in on him again in the afternoon, his condition is worse. He's obviously taken another hit of something. Somewhere outside. He's now utterly wasted, a condition we have never seen him in before, lying on his mattress, barely capable of speech or response. I realize now how much he has acted to protect us from seeing him in these wasted states over the years, staying away from the house until he was fit to be seen. We've seen the glassy eyes, the slightly slurred speech on occasion, but nothing like this wipeout. He no longer even has the energy to conceal it, to spare us.

He lies on his bare mattress, barely coherent. More. His wallet is out, driver's license in hand, along with some other ID cards which he is in the process of attempting to shred, with the meticulous focus of a drunkard in fumbling attempts to squeeze out every ounce of sobriety for the task at hand.

What is he doing? I should have grasped the symbolism at once: *Luke is shredding his identity*, his official personage in this world. He's flushed, mumbling nearly incomprehensible words in response to our urgent and upset queries. I take his pulse; it is over one-hundred-and-forty, the classic racing cocaine heart.

"We better take him to the hospital right now," Prue says. It's mid-afternoon. I pause. "No," I say, "maybe let's give him a few hours, let's see how he does first. We can monitor him, take him later if he doesn't get any better." Prue goes and gets him a glass of water. "Please try to drink this down, Luke," she says, mopping his sweating brow. "You've got to wash out this poison." He drinks. We offer him some soup as well, but he shakes his head mutely. We stand up, and look back at him on his bed. We urge him to sleep. We check back in on him every half hour or so as he dozes, drinks more water, heartbeat slows.

At about seven pm Luke reappears, comes into the house from the carport. To our relief, he is a good bit recovered. He can speak, but is still groggy. "Yeah, I feel a little better," he says. "I'll take Barney out, grab a cig, get some fresh air." He comes back about half an hour later. "Luke, don't you want to sit down with us for a bite. We're really worried about you. You're not in good shape." "No thanks, Ba, I'm not hungry. I think I'll just go back to my room and get some more sleep." "OK, Luke, we wish you good night, try to get some decent sleep. We'll check in on you later. I hope you'll feel better in the morning." "Thanks." "And Luke, we really need to sit down tomorrow and talk about all this, what we're going to do. This is getting very serious." "OK, Ba, sure ... good night."

Later that evening I check in on him, he's sleeping quietly, Barney at his side as always.

Next morning things are busy. Prue is flying off early to Minneapolis/St. Paul to spend a few days with Melissa and Jim. Before leaving for the airport I peer through the window into the carport briefly, see one leg sticking out from under the covers. Luke is still asleep and apparently still in no condition to even think about salvaging his position at Radio Shack. I run Prue down to National Airport. It's a bright crisp November morning, a good day for flying. When I get back, sometime around ten am, I check in on Luke again. He needs to get up and face the day.

I open the door into the carport. One glance does it, there is not the slightest doubt in my mind. I instantly grasp that Luke is dead. He is twisted up, limbs awry, head at a strange angle. Faithful Barney is lying on the bed next to him—but bizarrely, Barney growls at me on sight, instinctively expressing canine fear and trembling. This is no blanket-pulling game, Barney exerts fierce guardianship over Luke—something is very, very wrong, and even he knows it. But what does he know?

I lean down and touch Luke, but the touch only confirms the fear jagging through my now taut system—he is cold. Stone-cold. Futilely, instinctively, I search for his carotid in one last vain hope of finding a trace of life. Nothing. I too now grow icy cold, numb. There is no need now for shouting, for crying out, for hysteria, for frantic phone calls to 911. Time stands still. It is all over. He has been gone for many long hours.

What we had thought could happen, feared might happen, tried to keep from ever happening, has now happened. The game has run its course. We have all lost, irrevocably.

In icy control I go downstairs to Samantha's room; she's up and getting ready to drive up to Philadelphia for her interview at Wharton Business School. "Samantha," I blurt out, "it's a terrible thing, Luke is dead." She rushes upstairs with me, appalled at the sight, indeed, the first time she has ever seen anyone dead. We stand there, numbed, silent. In front of me, twisted on the mattress is the summation of twenty years of struggle with this boy. I mumble something about how he had seemed better last night, why I had opted not to take him to the hospital right away even when Prue suggested it. After minutes of unspoken mental reruns of where we were, where we are, where we're going with all this, as the mind struggles to take all this in, Samantha gently touches my arm and quietly suggests, "We've got to call 911 and report it." I weakly acknowledge. I'm not lucid enough to think forward to such an elementary first legal step, to translate personal grief into the realm of official action. If I couldn't manage Luke's life away from disaster, I have even less brief to handle his death.

But I go, I dial. "I wish to report the death of my son, he's almost surely OD'ed on something. His body is already cold." I somehow impart some other basic information they ask for. It's only a minute or so before we hear the sirens from afar, the police car and ambulance racing down Tuckerman Lane and turning up into our cul-de-sac on Whisperwood Lane. Medics jump out, followed by cops, they come rushing in, brushing me aside as I try to offer a few details. I know it's too late to save him, but they are on autopilot and I'm simply in the way. A few minutes later a medic confirms that he is gone and can't be resuscitated. Their task now loses its urgency and falls into the routine. Another routine death by drugs. They cut off his T-shirt and boxers, slide him into a white medical bag and move him onto a stretcher.

The medics give me a plastic ziplock bag with Luke's personal items that were on his body: a silver chain from around his neck, a bracelet of colored cords from his wrist, and a snake ring off his finger. The body—it's a body now, Luke no longer—is wheeled out to the ambulance. To all but the family he has now been reduced once again to identification by a number—just as he had been upon arrival at an orphanage a long time ago in a far-away place. It's surely not the same number. But there is nothing else now but a case number.

The medics depart with their cargo; officialdom this time extracts him permanently out of my life. The police now take over. "I'm sorry Mr. Fuller, I'm afraid we require a good bit of information about this case. I know it is difficult for you, but first of all we have to rule out any possibility of foul play." I nod weakly. "And we are required to take the body to the morgue to perform an autopsy. This is routine on any unnatural death outside of a hospital. Can you tell us what you believe took place?" I wearily offer them a thumb-nail account, all too familiar, of Luke's long struggle with drugs, well-documented in court and police records; I tell them about his condition in the last afternoon and evening of the last day of his life. I'm still wound tight like a drum, and although my voice cracks at the telling of much of it, tears don't come yet. Samantha stands by me as a quiet but strong, vital and supportive presence through these grimly procedural details, taking up the account when I flag and sparing me of some of the routine questioning. "And can you tell me why your son was staying here in this carport?" they ask as they poke and sniff through old cans of thickening paint substances. After one hour of courteous but persistent questioning, the most immediate veils of suspicion seem to lift. They leave me with a card that gives the name of the funeral home to where Luke will be eventually delivered in a few days after the autopsy.

The authorities depart out of our lives. Taking Luke. Their system has finally prevailed over mine.

∗          ∗          ∗

What is the sequence of passing on crushing news? Samantha takes on a particular gentleness with me as I struggle to think about next steps. She immediately calls Wharton to cancel and reschedule her interview there. My first step is to call Melissa in Minnesota. Prue's plane won't even have arrived there yet. I can only say it bluntly, "Melissa, I've got some terrible news, Luke is dead." Melissa is too stunned to reply, then breaks down into tears. She asks briefly about the circumstances but clearly is not ready for a more detailed recounting. The news is shocking, but it is an eventuality that lay in all our hearts, unspoken, as a very real possibility over the past few years. "OK, she says, voice trembling, "I'll try to meet Mummy right at the gate as soon as she gets off the plane … My God, I don't know how to tell her."

I am relieved that this time at least, Prue was the one on the road while I am left to deal with Luke's crisis, his last. To carry the immediate burden for Prue who has otherwise borne the brunt of so many earlier incidents.

Next I telephone my father in Chapel Hill. "Oh Graham, I am so terribly, terribly sorry … I know how long you and Prue have struggled and tried to help Luke. This is a terrible thing … I want to come up and be with you both." He too cannot be totally surprised. He is aware of much, but far from the details of the long saga; he has always refrained from any criticism or second-guessing of us. I then call Meredith in Cape Cod who has been there from minute one of Luke's life with us; she is out so I call her husband Jim at work and leave a message for him. An hour later he gets back to me, shaken. He will pass the news to Meredith as soon as he locates her.

My sister Faith is not at home in San Francisco but I leave her a message as well. And I call my brother in London, also out. Within hours they all call me back, horrified, shocked; yet in so many ways it had to be one of the few likely outcomes of Luke's tortured trajectory. Meredith calls, deeply emotional, stunned, invariably supportive, our mutual unspoken awareness of the distance that had crept between us since Dylan's wedding, now melted away. The body of pain spreads out like fluid from a leaky bucket, inch by inch, acknowledged, shared, absorbed by others. I'm not quite the lonely iceberg anymore; it's OK to cry now.

That afternoon Samantha and I set out for a long walk in the woods in the fading November sun. I desperately need contact with the woods, trees, falling leaves, the eternal realities. The pungency of the leaves underfoot churn up in my mind an ancient Chinese proverb, *luo ye gui gen*: the falling leaf returns to its source. The words now bring more tears to my eyes as I recognize how this ancient phrase, so long a piece of abstract Asian wisdom for me, has suddenly become transformed, personalized; today it speaks to me, speaks of Luke, and somehow it is a comfort, an expression of the natural order of things.

We walk through the fall smells, crisp leaves underfoot, colors still drifting to ground around us, to the earth, plants beyond their season now fading and shrinking before the certain onset of winter; we blindly follow any path that presents itself as long as it leads away from the house. From where it happened. We share a lot of silence, exchange a lot in silence for a while. What is there to say? Nothing, and everything. Samantha at one point offers, "I'm sorry that you have lost your son." I don't know quite how to react to this pregnant and loaded remark. It is directed to me, it is *my* son in her words, not her brother; and, intentionally or not, it is a reflection on this whole project that has caused her more than a little pain as well. And "son" too, I feel is freighted: a frank and inadvertent acknowledgment that she was not that son, and that Luke had indeed received vastly more attention than our own biological daughters had over the last half of his life—one of the classic traps of any adoption that the Holt Adoption Agency had warned about in its first letters. I feel doubly guilty at her words. "Samantha," I say, "it's not that he was my son, it's that he's our child, and you are all equally loved." Samantha responds simply, "I wasn't implying anything more in what I said." Maybe not, but in my guilt I read into it volumes. My conscience is aquiver with mistakes made, things that might have been, and visitations of pain, even indirectly, upon other beloved family members all through this experience.

*         *         *

Melissa has meanwhile met Prue at Minneapolis airport. She has wondered about how and where to break the news, she has asked at airport information about where the airport chapel is, should they first go there before she breaks the news? In the end, Melissa can't long conceal her own emotions right in the arrival gate, she breaks down into tears and gives Prue the fateful news: "Mummy, Baba just called. Luke is dead." Prue takes a few moments to react, she is stunned into shock, but remembers the parlous condition in which she had left Luke the night before. They sit down and hold each other, grieve and cry together for long minutes in an empty gate area, timeless silent floating moments against a backdrop of heavy air traffic. Luke arriving at JFK. The airport bringeth and the airport taketh away. Slowly Prue fills Melissa in on the course of deteriorating events over the past two days. They agree they will take an afternoon flight back to DC that same day.

The bell has tolled; its fading halftones now spread and reverberate among all our family in its diverse places, summoning us to foregather, to draw an end to Luke's tale.

# CHAPTER NINETEEN

# THE VOYAGE

The family arrives; its mission of support is enfolding, releasing. Faith, with her particularly strong emotional intelligence, asks to spend some moments alone in the room in which Luke died. She sits on Luke's mattress in the carport and emerges some fifteen minutes later. She is relieved, she feels no aura of a violent struggle or special ugliness residual in the room.

And now the practical details of death are upon us. My father strongly urges that Luke be cremated. I had never even thought about such issues, burial versus cremation, but instinctively, on practical, philosophical, financial, ideological and esthetic grounds, we agree that cremation is the course we should take.

The autopsy has been swift and uneventful. It verifies death by cocaine intoxication. The next day the funeral parlor calls—Luke's body has been delivered. Meredith and my father accompany Prue and myself on the trip down to the parlor to discuss arrangements. We inform the funeral director that we will opt for cremation. In hushed tones the undertaker gently guides us through the array of coffins and other services available; he is the modern boatman on the Styx, guiding the living alongside the realm of Death and all its accoutrements, informing us of the physical requirements required for the journey into eternity. But I feel no respect for his task; I do not feel that our tour through these various cargo vessels for final passage is enlightened or enlightening. I know this is his professional mask, I am angered to think that I must share my grief with this merchant of bereavement. Raw, immature emotions surge from my primitive amygdalic brain and rise into my throat, partial transferal of unexpressed grief. I want to react harshly, strike out against his maudlin profession and all his works. But I hold back. Prue lays her hand on my arm, sensing the latent aggression in my voice, but it stays latent. It's not this poor bastard's fault I'm here. He's seen such transferred resentments before.

I tell the undertaker bluntly that we want only a plain, simple, corrugated cardboard coffin, vastly the cheapest thing they have available and not even on display. We're not interested in his elegant silk-lined caskets of fine wood and brass appointments to assuage sorrow and guilt; I can assuage my guilt in other ways that don't line the undertaker's pocket. We're talking here about no more than a vehicle for Luke's body for two short days before it is consigned to the flames. At this point I'm coiled tight like a rattlesnake, poised, waiting for the undertaker to dare suggest "something perhaps more worthy of our feelings towards the Loved One." But he doesn't follow the Evelyn Waugh script. He fully accepts our choice in correct, professional terms. He does inform us that some "special handling" is required since Luke had been subjected to a full autopsy. He says delicately that "the full autopsy process can slightly affect the face's appearance."

*The face's appearance.* Suddenly, I'm confronted with a decision I had not thought about. I find myself doing what I was sure I would never do, wanting an open coffin. I want to see Luke one last time, to view him, even in death, with a presence of mind I could not have when the urgency of 911 summoned officialdom into our space. All the old esthetic debates about open versus closed coffin are now no longer theoretical. This is our own child, his funeral. What do we want? "I don't favor an open coffin," Prue says. "For me the remains in the coffin are not Luke." But Melissa says she does want to see him, to bid farewell. Meredith and Faith acknowledge that seeing the body can facilitate closure if we're up to it. That's the way I feel. In the end we ask for an open coffin, requiring minimum cosmetic work. We decline the other services of the funeral home—music, minister, flowers—we will take care of that ourselves.

We will have no public funeral as such, only a family ceremony at the funeral home—two, in fact: a viewing on Thursday followed by our own family ceremony Friday morning at which point we escort Luke to the cremation room. Since none of us except my father belongs to any formal church, we do not ask for a minister. Still, the finality of death creates an unexpected craving for ritual and closure of some kind. We want to prepare our own statements and create our own rituals for the farewell ceremony. Yes, although we are not practicing Christians, we have strong spiritual feelings that require expression in various ways and through other traditions. My father volunteers to read some appropriate materials from his Book of Common Prayer; we all hungrily accept his offer of an element of formal timeless ritual.

\*　　　　　　　　\*　　　　　　　　\*

Thursday afternoon. We foregather at the funeral home, a plain brick building with a faux colonial façade, suggesting little of the emotional devastation that the building generates in those who must enter. Together we are only just Prue and myself, Samantha, Melissa, Meredith, Faith and my father. My brother and his family are in England, too far to come. We chose not to invite any friends. We step into the viewing room, a dark oak-paneled room, heavy curtains around the windows, thick carpets muffling footsteps and sounds—the whole place is suffused with deafening institutional hush. The air is heavy. And at the back of the room we discern the purpose of our call: a thick corrugated cardboard box, coffin-shaped, raised to chest level on a kind of high dolly that bears the vessel in which the body of our son lies. I compel myself to behold the harsh reality of death once again. Although I had been the first to find Luke dead, it is a shock now to see him. The precise ordering of his clothing, his posture in the box with his hands crossed in front of him, seems more unnatural than the twisted shape of his body on the mattress that I had last seen. But Prue is right—this is no more than a facsimile, a counterfeit of Luke. His face is somewhat waxen, not fully right, not quite exactly normal; there is some slight, almost imperceptible displacement of the features, a shape around the cheekbones, perhaps as a result of the autopsy, that, however slight, robs me of the illusion that this is still Luke. Nonetheless, I am comforted to see him. I reach for his hand; it is quite cold. I feel a need to hold it for a while, as if to inject some warmth into it. For Prue, Samantha and Melissa the experience is somewhat unnerving; it is the first time they have beheld anyone dead, much less a son and brother. But Melissa had wished to see him in death and she stands closer. Samantha seems to hang back. Prue finds no further gratification in the viewing; she too now retreats back from the body. She does acknowledge later that seeing the body, especially as an empty shell, did reinforce for her the feeling that he is gone. "But it was not Luke."

First we drape around all sides of his body a colorful piece of Indian cloth to give the coffin a warmer, more ceremonial, human look. We have all brought certain mementos to go into the coffin with Luke, readying a Pharaoh in his Funereal Boat for his voyage to the Sun. Luke is dressed in his blazer with his name tag from Radio Shack—something he was proud of, and the blazer lends appropriate formality. We place in his box a variety of simple personal items that characterize him to us: a package of instant Korean noodles to which he was so addicted, and some chopsticks. There is one of his Korean shirts that came with him when he arrived on the plane from Korea as a baby. We put in a fantasy novel that he especially liked, and a Pink Floyd album, *The Dark Side of the Moon*, that he loved. We bring a picture of Barney and his adopted cousin Laura, as well as a picture of the family together. They are all placed in the box around his body to go with him. And some flowers that we each put in. Hesitantly, I take a photo of him in his coffin, unsure of what its future viewing will hold for any of us. I may never want to look at it again, but I don't want to regret later on not having taken it. We spend about one hour, quietly sitting, sometimes exchanging a few words. Melissa asks to spend a few moments alone with Luke after we all leave the room. We tell the funeral home we will be back the next day for a one-hour family ceremony before the actual cremation process in the building.

Friday morning we are back early. Our ceremony will reflect our diverse and largely shared spiritual orientations, some Buddhist, some Christian, some more generic spiritual. We play on a boombox Pink Floyd's *Wish You Were Here*—also a song of loss; we recite some invocations, personal recollections, blessings; a ceremony to attend to the things we want and need.

Luke's box is now closed. We bring personal handwritten farewell notes to Luke, including from family members and relatives that could not be there. We tape them all to his box. I offer a few formal final personal words directed to Luke. And now all has been said that we can say. And almost nothing has been said of all that needs to be said. We inform the funeral director that we are ready. We owe it to Luke to accompany him now, to see him on his way, down to the last minutes of his material existence.

The box is on a wheeled dolly and we help maneuver it down several hallways with the precious empty cargo on board, moving towards the big elevator. Down we go, descending into the nether regions where Luke is to cross over. We exit the elevator into a larger room with a huge brick furnace. Obscenely, a visit thirty years ago to Auschwitz flashes through my mind. The room is practical, unembellished, utterly utilitarian; it is there to do no more than it is supposed to do. But it imparts absolute finality; like an execution scene in the gallows hall of a penitentiary, this is a one-way trip, there is no going back.

The director opens the cast iron door to the furnace—the maw of a dark brick tunnel looms open before us. "My God," gasps Melissa, overwhelmed as we all are with the finality of the scene, of this mechanism whose purpose is to obliterate every last recognizable feature of Luke. The director points out the button that ignites the process; "many people like to push it themselves," he confidentially assures us. Discomfited, I decline the invitation. Luke in his box is raised up by the trolley to the mouth of the oven, and the box slides in. The cast iron door clangs shut. At a loss for words, yet feeling impelled to say something, I find myself saying out loud, "Safe journey."

I'm not sure what I am trying to say. What are the theological underpinnings of such a statement? I don't know for sure, but years of

Buddhist lore stored inside me makes it somehow feel right. I don't know about the others, but I couldn't remain silent in the face of this powerful physical process that so swiftly reduces the body to only a few ashes and bones, telescoping years of natural decomposition to less than an hour. We all stand in awe, transformed, each taking away from this process what our souls require.

The button is pushed, initiating the action. A flash of yellow brilliance, like the sun, flashes behind a very small glass aperture in the iron door, followed by a loud whoosh heralding the destructive forces now irretrievably unleashed against the frail cardboard box from whose cargo we have not yet been emotionally released. We stand silently for a moment or two, in helpless awe, then slowly move back out of this nether world at the cusp of life and death, to take the elevator back up. And suddenly it is over. We are back out in the human world, out onto the sidewalk on a sunny, crisp, windy day. I take Prue's hand and we walk, immersed in silence, struggling to grasp all that has happened as we all proceed a few blocks down for a big brunch.

Melissa, much later, trying to make some sense in her own way of this process we have experienced, draws me aside to ask just what I meant by "Safe journey." I can't really answer. "I don't have any good words for it, Melissa. I just somehow think that ... something of Luke in some form abides, if only in our own collective timeless senses. That some kind of journey is occurring— for him or for us." I fall back on the old Buddhist analogy of the drop of water that distinguishes itself as a single entity as it plunges down in a long waterfall, on its own course, only at the bottom coming to merge with the river again and on into the sea. Or a falling leaf in its cycle back to the source. I know it helps me, at least, to make some sense of this moment of life and death and that is all that matters.

*        *        *

All burial ritual is designed to help the living godspeed the dead. But somehow industrial cremation moves too fast, is too mechanical. I wonder whether it is also too modern, too high-tech compared to the literal earthiness of the graveyard, the smell of the soil, and the lowering of the body into the bowels of the earth, our source. We will, of course, soon have Luke's ashes, and we know we will eventually hold another ceremony in which we take the tangible tactile elements of the earth and his ashes in our hands, transmitting them to a more permanent resting place for Luke. Where that spot will be, we don't even know.

We are to pick the ashes up from the funeral home in three days. All the rest of the family have now finally gone their separate ways, their mission of mercy—the sharing of the grief and the lending of moral support—has been fulfilled, and we are grateful.

Days later Prue and I drive yet again into the hateful parking lot of the funeral home. But it feels still part of the same religious ritual—to come to receive the ashes, the spiritual and physical remnants of our son. Yet the actual process of retrieving the ashes is utterly practical, bereft of ceremony. "Let's see, Fuller, Fuller, it's right here somewhere," says a custodian, peering around shelves as if searching for something little more meaningful than locating a distributor belt out of a Sears catalog. We sign on the dotted line. We sign for a life, or what once was a life, a matter-of-fact reduction of a life, or a precious relic of a life, or an irrelevant leftover from a physical process that is now history. It is contained in what this time is a much smaller plain cardboard box. The ashes are wrapped in a thick plastic bag inside. As I pick it up I note its weight. What is this heaviness? The very physicality of the box and its contents again challenge one's theological premises. What remnants of life or person are left here? How do they differ from the person we left in the much bigger cardboard box in the cremation room four days back? What does it mean to refine a physical existence down to its constituent parts of carbon and other basic elements? What is the relationship between this box, Luke, and his spirit, his soul? What do I invest these ashes with?

We walk out of the funeral home; they are done with Luke and we are done with them. I'm not eager to bring them more business anytime soon. But they can wait. And I can never drive by that establishment again without noting the dark black chimney jutting up from the squat addition behind the cheery colonial-facade of the formal entrance, through which much of Luke's essence evaporated into the air around us.

I open the car door, where do I put the ashes? I go to put them on the floor behind the driver's seat, but on the floor just doesn't feel right. So we put the ashes on the back seat, carefully placing the box so it won't tumble off onto the floor, desecrated. It's now carefully wedged in place as if it were in a child's car seat. Safely home, we need to decide where to put them for now, a question we had not earlier considered. The garage, the basement? Too dismissive, cold, utilitarian, uncaring. I want to put them in our bedroom closet, but Prue feels their presence would be too powerful. We end up to putting them on the shelf in the closet of a separate bedroom. My driving desire is that they need to be kept safe. But kept safe from what? For what? The tidal wave has, after all, already lumbered in and receded.

**April 1996**

Six months later the family gathers once again, this time in much greater numbers, and for a happy occasion: celebration of Samantha's wedding. Ruslan and Samantha have come back to the US for two years for further studies—he for advanced law, Samantha for an MBA, before probably heading out again to the wilds of Central Asia. Now that they're both back we want to hold a proper wedding ceremony—technically a blessing of an existing marriage—since none of us could make it to the steppes of Central Asia for the legal Islamic ceremony. Among them is Steve Ching from Hong Kong days, now in his naval uniform; he cuts the cake with his dress sword.

But we have sounded out Samantha and Ruslan on a delicate matter: since so much of the family from all over have foregathered for the wedding, might this not be a good time to have a farewell ceremony for Luke as well, for most family members who were not able to be at the funeral? We'll do it after an interval of several days after the wedding ceremony so as not to tinge her moment of happiness with any feelings of grief.

Samantha is discomfited, but ultimately poses no objection and two days later we hold a small ceremony in our yard. We have a few spades and will all take turns digging a deep hole in which we will plant a large Korean maple in Luke's memory. Once the hole has been dug—everyone taking a turn to help turn out the earth—we drag the huge round ball of maple roots and tree into its new home. We then bring out a small portion of Luke's ashes and each of us scatters by hand a bit of them among the tree roots. Like many satisfying ceremonies it involves a physical component, a sense of rebirth, a literal hands-on with Luke's gritty physical remains, mixed with dark earth, to be combined with a living tree. The physicality of it is comforting. Many of us then take turns offering words of recollection and reflection about Luke. Some tears are shed, embraces exchanged.

I offer a few thoughts of my own:

*We remember you Luke for your many lovely qualities. You were always a gentle person in an ungentle society. You were always generous with what you had—never grasping for accumulation of possessions. It makes us sad to realize that you left this world with hardly a possession left to your name. Yes, virtually all of your possessions and money went to the habit that eventually killed you, but you never seemed driven by passions of acquisition.*

*You also never wanted to compete with others, but to coexist—a lovely quality but something that makes it hard to function in a competitive society. You preserved an essential innocence and gentleness even during a hellish spiral into the dark world of narcotics.*

221

*The control that those drugs tragically began to exert over you in fact led to patterns of behavior that were so sadly destructive—and not just to yourself, but to your family, for we could never know what we should do to protect you. We fought among ourselves, all out of love for you, as to how to best save you from yourself— but also sadly as to how to protect ourselves from you. Some anger and bitterness emerged among us over this. I know you knew this too, were pained by it, yet you seemed basically helpless to prevent it.*

*But as your life in this existence has come to an end, we celebrate all of what you were. Life enriches, even in unanticipated ways. Intentionally or unintentionally, your uncertain life opened new dimensions for us, whether we wished for them or not—including an awareness of social problems that people like us—often too comfortably insulated from some of the rougher sides of less affluent life—needed to know. Our lives are the richer for it, and for you.*

*For me, Luke, I am grateful that you helped open up my own stiffness of style, to help shake up my personality rigidities. You were able to bring out a more playful side of my nature and a greater emotional compassion that is fulfilling.*

*We send you off with all our deepest love and prayers. We rejoice that so much of what we loved about your spirit will forever remain with us.*

*Farewell.*

The tree is now planted, enriched by Luke's ashes across its roots. It astonishes me to think that within a year some of Luke's bodily elements will actually be inside the tree, forming part of its physical and biological structure, investing it with very special meaning to the witting observer. Appropriately, we note later that his Korean maple happens to turn fiery red at just about precisely the anniversary of his death each year, a glowing reminder. "A falling leaf returns to its source."

And I am aware, in some slow uptake, that I have in a small way also hijacked a bit of Samantha's wedding through coupling this ceremony so closely with hers.

# CHAPTER TWENTY

# HOW COULD IT HAPPEN?

I have been over the sequence of the last twenty-four hours of his life like a tape-loop rerun of a film scene, over and over, straining to see if something appears down in the corner of the screen that I might not have noticed in earlier viewings, some explanatory signal otherwise missed. *He died accidentally from an overdose of drugs.* That was what it appeared. That was what we told our friends. That was what we told ourselves. But was that what actually happened?

Luke, was this truly an accident? We struggle to understand your mindset on that last day. Did you really just happen to have gotten some bad shit that time that overwhelmed you? Or were you really trying to close down your life on that last day? At the time you sounded like you were pleased to be attending the Radio Shack training course; it seemed to be a job that made you happy, a real step up from flipping burgers. You didn't seem morose. That wasn't your style. But then, on the actual morning of job training you were more zonked than we had ever seen you. I'm inclined to believe that you felt you couldn't face the rigors of the training course, that your ADHD would prove a humiliating barrier to grasping the course material.

And then that last afternoon of your life you must have gone outside and gotten a new hit of crack. Did you feel you had reached the end of the line by then? How else can I read your tortured, focused efforts to shred your ID cards in a stupor?

And yet you had sobered up a bit yet again, that very last evening of your life, after I had decided not to take you to the hospital. You came out of your room and said you were going outside with Barney for some air. You seemed somewhat clear-minded. We exchanged a few remarks about how you were feeling. But it's clear now that you went outside for yet one more hit, from some hidden stash. Did you just want to sink into ever deeper oblivion without regard for the consequences? Or was it a calculated drive to achieve fatal overdose?

A decision to simply end your life doesn't ring quite right with us. Nobody ever felt that you were suicidal—not in any of your sessions with psychologists, not your friends and certainly not your family. At least not in a conscious act. We would want to believe that if you really had chosen to die that night you might have said something, or given us a special hug goodnite, or told us that you loved us, or made some kind of lasting remark. Or perhaps left us a letter, a note of some kind. You had done so before when you vanished from the house for a few days. But it was just "Nite Ba, nite Ma," as usual. Nothing special. Did you expect to die that night? Or did you just keep on dosing up without caring how it would affect you? We will never know.

*        *        *

"We were terribly sorry to hear of your tragedy," so many friends say. Tragedy? Despite our grief at Luke's death, we find ourselves avoiding that word. In some way it seems excessive, even presumptuous as I think about colossal tragedies that befall so many around the world. Instead we tend to say, "Something very sad happened to our family last month, we lost our son at age twenty-one. It has been very painful." Yet how many people do we know who routinely refer to all deaths in anyone's family, at any age, as a tragedy? No, by any measure, Luke had been lucky in most respects: he led a fairly comfortable and protected life, in a family that loved him and tried to work with his problems and keep the law off his back. This is not a tragedy. But it is a sad tale of a struggle against inner demons—some perhaps built-in, some self-generated—that ultimately paralyzed and snuffed out his life.

But untimely death can still evoke anger: how could it possibly happen to us that we lost our son at age twenty-one?

But then, given our particular life experiences and views on life, that somehow wasn't the question we asked. On the contrary, why *shouldn't* we lose our son at age twenty-one? Others do. All the time. Life carries no guarantees. Our number—his number—simply came up.

Death in poorer and harsher societies is a familiar visitor, thrusting its way indiscriminately into daily life—in onslaughts of disease, neglect, civil strife, wars, barbarians, crimes, tsunamis, plagues, bandits and other timeless disasters. How long ago was it that even our grandparents in the Western world faced the likely loss of several children to the cruel imperatives of childhood disease? My own father in his infancy lost two brothers in one week to typhoid. Death has been a familiar, even if not welcome visitor. Watch Mexicans celebrate *El Día de Los Muertos*, the Day of the Dead, the family outings to sweep the graves and picnic upon them, to sing songs, eat candies made of little skulls and skeletons, display semi-humorous, semi-macabre pictures of skeletons performing the full range of daily activities—it's a kind of acceptance that tries to soften Death's presence. Not the pain, but the shock. One form of Buddhist discipline is to mentally "practice" dying.

Our Western illusion of control over our destinies makes harsh twists of fate, like untimely death, feel all the crueler. This is striking after many years of living in the Muslim world. You can't pass an hour with Muslim friends without the invocation of *Insha'Allah*—God willing—coming to the lips. It's not just an overdose of piety, as most Westerners would assume. You invoke the phrase after any statement of personal *intent* for the future. "I'll be back on the Friday flight, Insha'Allah." Yes, Man may intend, but God determines whether intentions will be fulfilled. We should never mistake mere intentions for absolute certainties. We should be mindful—indeed acknowledge our gratefulness—on each occasion when our plans and expectations do in fact work out as hoped. In an uncertain world they might well not. So you will often hear a Muslim offer soft thanks, for example, after the aircraft wheels touch down, of *al-Hamdu l'illah 'ala-ssalaama*, "Praise God for safety."

You don't even have to have God in the equation, the thought is still there: destiny is fickle, but we made it through OK. Shouldn't we therefore be regularly grateful for each extra passing day in which we skirt hardship or disaster? It's not a pessimistic view at all; it's actually one that is joyous, mindful of another day of life that cannot be routinely taken for granted and for which we are grateful. So in losing Luke as we did, why *not* us? Why *not* him? Or why not at age twenty-one—instead of at age four, fourteen, forty-eight or eighty-four?

And of course other words that come to mind about death from drugs at twenty-one are *meaningless, pointless*—it didn't have to happen. But how can we allow ourselves to think that a death is *meaningless*? We can't … But what then is the meaning we derive?

Friends differed in their responses to our sad news, reflecting different personal and cultural psychologies. Many offered the traditional statements of condolences, expressions of sorrow and loss—exactly as we expected, and appreciated. A number sent back warm letters to us, sharing our sadness and loss in particularly personal terms. A few didn't respond, and even admitted later that they hadn't known what to say. And at work a number of colleagues actually seemed to avoid me for a period, uncertain, embarrassed about how to respond. And maybe for some, the association of Luke's death with the "shameful" issue of illegal drugs perhaps strengthened their wish not to cause us further pain or embarrassment through overt mention.

But it was our Muslim and Jewish friends whose cultures really came through for us, who seemed best equipped to spontaneously share our grief. Take Mamoun, a good Egyptian friend of our family over a five-year period. He'd met Luke at our home many times, they'd smoked cigarettes together and talked on occasion outside on the back deck. Mamoun paid a call on us at home immediately after Luke died, and checked in with us periodically thereafter. Then, during Christmas week, long after Luke's death, the phone rang. It was Mamoun: "I'm thinking about you. I know you're really missing Luke during this Christmas week."

I was astonished. Of course we were missing Luke. Christmas festivities always intensify the sense of a missing family member. But would I ever in a million years have thought of calling up a friend of mine who had suffered a death, many months after the event, to suggest that they must be really missing their lost family member? It would have seemed cruel, thoughtless, an almost gratuitous renewed infliction of pain at a sad time. But after overcoming my initial surprise at Mamoun's Christmas call to me I realized instantly how grateful I felt to him. How wonderful that someone else would acknowledge this pain, now, at this time, still mindful of our loss months after the event. To know that others were still aware of Luke as a person, a lost person, yes, but a person. I realized how this periodic reminder of loss in Muslim culture can be a powerful cultural mechanism for handling grief.

A Turkish ambassador I had known well in the Middle East concluded in his note of condolence: "It is in the case of such a tragedy that we feel how helpless and vulnerable we are before the will of God."

And in the same way so many of our Jewish friends showed the same warm cultural instincts in regularly and explicitly acknowledging Luke's death with us, even many months later. It's all part of a common Semitic tradition of periodic mourning periods, including the all-important forty-day mark, a time-tested moment for revisiting the death of a family member in a new light; the initial terrible shock of the loss has passed, life has returned somewhat to "normal"—but yet it hasn't, the loss is still there, and isn't going away.

Surely cultures and individuals that can celebrate openly these basic rites of human passage lie instinctively closer to the secrets of the human heart.

I took the message aboard. The very next year a friend of ours lost his wife to cancer. Apart from offering all our condolences at the time, I did what I would never have done without my own personal experience. I called him up around Christmas time and uttered the very same words, "Gee, Bill, I know you must be really missing Gail during the holiday." My friend seemed equally astonished, broke down into tears, and said, "You know, you're the first person to tell me that. I miss her terribly. Thank you so much for thinking of me at this time. It's so meaningful that someone else is aware of her."

We've learned that the embrace of death is vastly more rewarding than efforts to cloak it. You don't ever forget the death of someone you love. It warms the heart to have an outsider acknowledge the loss, again and again, forever, to keep the name and the memory alive, on the tongue, and not banished to the nether ranges of the heart and mind.

And so Prue and I early on discovered the kindness and solace of freely talking about Luke openly between ourselves whenever memories rose to mind. For the first few years after he had vanished from our lives, it seemed that those memories cropped up at least once a day, and we gave them regular and comfortable expression. We even took the liberty of mentioning Luke openly and casually in front of good friends; it may have made some of them uncomfortable at first, but I think they rapidly realized that it was part of our own therapy, and effective. We've also ended up observing Luke's birthday each year, frequently celebrating it in a Korean restaurant, sometimes with close friends. Far from morbid, it's a ritual that affords us much warmth and happiness of evocation of the past.

*      *      *

And so we followed up by sending a letter to a number of close friends about our loss. Luke died during the month that Steve Ching was away in Korea. Over lunch with Luke six weeks earlier he had promised to bring him back some Korean object as a souvenir of his birthplace, maybe a flag. I called Kathy to let her know of our sad news a few days after the funeral. But I asked if Steve could still bring back some Korean memento in Luke's memory. Steve wrote to us from the Westin Chosun Hotel in Seoul:

*Dear Prue and Graham,*

*I don't want to intrude during this difficult period. But I wanted to tell you how sad it was to hear about Luke. During our short time together he became the little brother or son I never had. Luke's questionings about cultural identification, his liking for things Latino and his comments about his realization of the consequences of his more immediate problems—as well as what he had to do, and planned to do about them—made me feel all the closer to him.*

*Luke's quest to resolve the dichotomy between his American cultural identity and his physical heritage struck a strong and binding tie with me. I looked forward to bringing him back something that would help him appreciate his ancestral Koreanness and his present US identity and future. He will, unfortunately, not be able to personally appreciate this remembrance, but I promise that I will bring it back for him and you all.*

*Sincerely, Steve*

Steve returned a week after Luke's death and came over to present us with a miniature of a great Korean temple bell, about a foot high wrought in black iron, with swinging log-like clapper. The bell found an important niche in our living room. I found myself often launching the log to strike the bell as a daily invocation of Luke. What could be more fitting than a bell? I strike it, it resonates loudly and clearly, a temple bell brightly heralding life. It then strikes more softly a second time, and a third, until it can only issue a echoing resonance, ever diminishing, ever less perceptible, sinking below the range of audibility—to fade away into silence.

*        *        *

Resonances. Late one afternoon a month or so after Luke's death, Prue and I are walking in the woods with Barney along one of our well-trodden paths. Suddenly Barney spies a good ways off what looks like a teenager, wearing a similar dark hooded jacket that Luke used to wear. He races away from us across a hundred yard open field and towards the boy, only to fall away after approaching closely. No, it is not his master.

What does Barney make of Luke's disappearance? It was Barney who was lone witness to Luke's final, irrevocable minutes of mortal struggle. He watched and heard as Luke's heart ultimately gave out under the crack-driven acceleration and now out-of-control rhythms that ultimately exhausted the heart, caused it to spin down into a flutter and collapse. It was Barney who sat a scant few inches away from Luke's last agonies, hearing a final sharp intake of breath, followed by a final exhalation, a stillness, a cooling and gradually stiffening of a now unresponsive body. Barney's animal instincts must have understood. Barney actually growled at me—extraordinary behavior—as I opened Luke's door the next morning and approached the body. He knew something was not right. Barney's knowledge of the event was far more intimate than mine. So one month later, when Barney spotted the boy in the dark hooded jacket across the field, was it blind, gracious hope that transcended his certain awareness of that final night with Luke, after which Luke had disappeared from his life? Or had he simply forgotten? Yet I found myself sometimes falling into Barney's same sense of illusion. I suddenly catch sight of an Asian boy somewhere whom I could have possibly mistaken for Luke at first casual glance. And then, as I look more closely, the resemblance fades. I'm searching too.

*        *        *

David Ransom is an old family friend with whom I studied Arabic together in Beirut, and we served together in the Middle East. Our daughters are of the same ages and know each other well.

*Dear Graham and Prue and Samantha and Melissa,*

*Marjorie and I were horrified to learn of Luke's death. We have read and re-read your letter of 20 November—with its terse and moving statement of Luke's failings and successes, and your family's effort to deal with them, and with his death.*

*I know how long and how valiantly you all tried to help him, and deal with your own feelings of love, despair, hope and anger about the drugs which he used. To find him "one bright morning" laying lifeless in his bed must have compressed all those conflicting ideas into one searing moment ... I grieve with you—and for Luke.*

*What else could you have done? You did so much. Your extraordinary patience, your search for good counsel, for you and him, your generous funding of schools, treatment, trips and living expenses, your strength as a family—all seem to me to represent a magnificent effort to help. I know from talks with Graham and Samantha that the effort did not produce righteous indignation in you so much as humility and compassion. That may have been a magnificent gift from Luke to you.*

*Luke is the prodigal who returned, again and again, to his family and father; that there were fissures on how to receive him, I am not surprised. But what strikes me is that he died at home, not alone, reviled, uncared for in some distant place. Perhaps the real test which God sets for us is not understanding and correcting the fault, but forgiving it. I believe you met that test.*

*You have all my heart-felt condolences. I urge you to commit to writing your experience and thoughts. There is a lapidary clarity to your letter, but it only begins to tell the story—which may be the real memorial service which Luke deserves.*

And in an even more intensely Middle Eastern mode, I receive a telephone call from another Egyptian friend, Moneim Fadali, a leading thoracic surgeon in Los Angeles—also a Sufi mystic, a writer, and broadcaster on life issues on a local FM station. He calls me from LA, coincidentally on the very afternoon of the day of Luke's death, to ask me to do an interview on his program the next day on the Middle East. I tell Moneim what has befallen us, and beg off. Perceptive of human emotions, Moneim insists that I go on the air by phone the next day—no longer to talk about the Middle East but specifically to share our loss and ponder how to think about these events in human life.

And so the next day I do a fifteen-minute interview and Moneim announces Luke's death to all of Los Angeles, his struggle with drugs and its

229

ravages on a basically kind-hearted and talented kid. He asks Los Angeles to pray for Luke's soul. I think Luke would have been pleased at his moment of commemoration across the vast metropolis where he had once lived.

And I unearth other loose ends in the Luke saga. The week after the funeral I stop in at Dunkin' Donuts where Luke had worked for a number of months, one of the longer stints of employment in the revolving door of his professional life *manqué*. Actually Dunkin' Donuts was his last job with any pretense of seriousness or future—and then Luke one day had told us he had gotten "bored" and moved on to Radio Shack. I was puzzled by the Dunkin' Donuts story. Luke had seemed to like the job, was cheery in recounting to us how he was learning the ropes. He actually had to get up at five am several days a week to open the shop early to make up the new batch of donuts. He learned how to man the counter for sales to the public, and how to finish up and close down at night.

The tempting aroma of sweet frying dough assails me as I step in the door to find the manager. "Hi Jerry, you don't know me, I'm Luke's father—you remember Luke, who used to work here?" I tell him I'm sorry to have to pass along the sad news of what happened to Luke. Jerry's a good guy, he looks shocked and pained at my news, comes out from behind the counter, wipes his hands on his apron and embraces me. "Gee, I'm terribly sorry, Mr. Fuller, what can I say? I really liked Luke, I thought he was a great kid. It was a great disappointment to me that it didn't work out."

"How come it didn't, Jerry?"

"You know, I thought Luke had what it takes to learn to run this small place, in a year or two maybe become one of my managers. He was warm, had a nice personality, was great with customers, always a smile, a joke. He was smart, grasped the business fast. But then one morning I came in after Luke had closed down the place the previous evening, I see where the cash deposit to the bank was a hundred-and-twenty dollars short of the money rung up on the register during the day. So I put it to Luke, where's the missing money? Luke was embarrassed, but then fessed up. He told me he'd needed the money that night to pay a debt. He said he'd pay us back soon out of his salary. He didn't try to hide it … But you know what, Mr. Fuller? I just can't have that. If he's to be in a position of trust, he can't go pulling something like that—even once. I had no choice, I had to let him go, with real regret. I had hopes for him. It's a damn shame, nice kid like that."

\*                    \*                    \*

It's Christmas, a little over a month after Luke's death; Samantha, Melissa and Jim are with us. It is of course a sober holiday, but we are trying to get on with our lives, with the new reality. We all talk a lot about Luke, and I'm still tracking down leads of people to contact who had been close to him, scattered pieces of a puzzle that may never even fit together into one coherent whole. It's more like partial pieces from several different puzzles. And it's kind of therapeutic.

What do we find in the mailbox? A paycheck arrives for Luke from Radio Shack, his wages from his last two weeks there. Prue and I take the money and go out and buy a new stereo set for Samantha to replace the one Luke had stolen and hocked. We put it under the tree marked, "To Samantha from Luke." It is indeed from Luke, we're just the agents. It was his money, and his intention had been to try to make good on the theft. Samantha is deeply conflicted for a moment … then, "Thank you, Luke," she says simply.

*     *     *

"How many children do you have?"—a common enough question from casual acquaintances. What do we say? We can't bring ourselves to say "two." That would be to deny Luke's existence, to expunge him from the family record. So, depending on circumstances we'll often say "three," and let it go at that. If pressed for more detail about them, we'll talk about our daughters. If further pressed about the third we mention that we had a son who died. Or we'll just say that we have three children, two living. But we cannot deny Luke in death. Sometimes this may be more than some people want to know. Maybe we're imposing our own emotional tale upon unsuspecting casual questioners. But it's our life, our children, our son, our experience.

Yet often this mention of a dead son pries open doors in others—complete strangers—who pour forth stories of their own loss of a child. It paves the way to unanticipated but rich encounters, another form of blessing in these human exchanges.

*     *     *

Full circle. A few years on, Barney is reaching the end of his natural days—an adopted foundling, just like Luke, and adopted by Luke. He is at least fifteen now and over the past two days he has stopped eating—and then drinking. The vet says his liver is deteriorating rapidly, but there are no signs of pain. We are loath to put Barney down immediately—always a painful decision. But during the night he simply drops dead in the living room after we have gone to bed. We are moved at his passing, this dog who lived fifteen years out of Luke's twenty one, who took with him the memory of Luke's last minutes and seconds as he lay next to him in Luke's death bed.

Still, the search for Luke does not wind down here.

# CHAPTER TWENTY-ONE

# IN SEARCH OF LUKE

The swirl of ongoing daily life shrouds the grand picture. Only when his life is over do its multiple pieces begin to fall into place. One by one Luke's good friends come around to see us. I'm hungry for their perspective. They are the observant friends who hung out with Luke for days, months, years on his adventures and misadventures, things we rarely could witness from our side of the moon. In searching for Luke I see one narrative, but his own generation sees another.

For them he was just a good buddy—no assumptions, no inhibiting, fierce parental optics. They hadn't had to sign on with Luke for the duration, through thick and thin. They possessed the luxury of no-responsibility: just friends, neutral observers, good-time partners in the riveting adventure of adolescence—hey dude, it's all good. But for us now they bring comforting reminders that Luke still exists out there—in other people's memories out in the broader world. I want to track down some of these friends, to pass along the sad news, to ask them to stop by sometime, to help me grasp this kid, even after he is gone.

And we quickly discover some different faces of Luke. Lisa sends us a surprising letter, a girl whose photo Luke held in his wallet from age fourteen on and often talked about.

*Dear Mr. and Mrs. Fuller,*

*This is what I wrote in my journal when I found out that Luke had died.*

*24 December 1995*

*I just found out my friend Luke died … I'm in shock. I always believed that I would see him again. He's one of those people … Luke was a good friend. He was the type of person that could read people very well. He was modest and down to earth. He had a manner that was both relaxed and sophisticated at the same time. Even though Luke could impress a person with his insight, he would laugh a little and then let you know that he had his own flaws.*

*Luke had a certain philosophy about the world that I adopted quite a bit. He once said to me that it doesn't matter what kind of work a person does, a guy could be a garbage man and still be the happiest person. What matters is that a person is happy doing whatever they are doing. He seemed to believe that the truly important thing was to enjoy life and pursue happiness, not money.*

*Luke also said that he felt that kids who grow up having a lot of money don't value its worth; whereas the kids that have to earn money have better understanding.*

*Luke's beliefs about the world influenced me in a good way. I can still see his face and hear his words. I think of him often and wish I could see him again. He was a great person. I will miss him very much ...*

*With love,*

*Lisa*

Some reactions are harsher. I call Mark in California. His uncle had a horse-farm where he and Luke sometimes went for wild rides. He'd been in our house a good bit, always comfortable in our presence. He was a welcome change from Luke's *malos amigos* who always reverted to sullen avoidance of us, wrapping themselves in a teenage oath of silence, *omertá*, in the presence of anyone's parents. Yeah, Mark had been one of Luke's pot-buddies as well, but basically a nice kid traversing the same rocky years, and who gradually managed to get his shit together.

But I'm struck: even at age twenty-one the idea of the death of a contemporary is about as expected as a meteor hurtling in from outer space, or a lone sniper-shot shattering the peace of a respectable neighborhood. Death is something on TV, or vicariously dished out on a handheld video game, or, if you must, a specter that haunts those over forty. The young are wrapped in a mantle of invulnerability, protected by the certain talisman of youth.

So when I tell Mark what has happened he is audibly shocked, pained, emotional at the loss of his friend. More, Mark is angry. As I recount the circumstances of Luke's last weeks and days, he breaks into tears, he loses it, he addresses him directly: "Goddamn you Luke, you asshole, we always talked about never doing anything harder than weed. You stupid son-of-a-bitch, what in hell were you doing! What were you thinking!" The whisper of the wings of death have passed over Mark in close proximity and he has heard them.

Dan, two years older than Luke and working towards an eventual law degree, had encountered Luke through friends and they had hung out together periodically. He is quite shaken by Luke's death. He was one of those who occasionally came over for Luke's cook-outs and experiments in do-it-yourself Asian concoctions. But Dan also watched Luke decline over the last six months he had known him; Luke once asked Dan to pull over as he pulled out a pipe for a quick crack fix in Dan's car, much to Dan's dismay. He also recalls Luke high on coke and quite paranoid once while cooking dinner for his friends. He remembers too, how Luke in his last year of life also stole money from the purse of the mother of a friend whose house he was visiting.

And Dan offers the same striking contradictions: "Luke was also a good friend, interesting to know, had a pile of fascinating stories, was entertaining and filled with insights into life beyond his years. He was open and honest about himself, warts and all. He didn't hide the fact that he had stolen a stereo from Chris' house and how ashamed he felt about it … He could be quite wise in many ways—even in talking about drugs with other people—even when he couldn't get his own life together. The time I spent with him was like a breath of fresh air between the office job I worked that summer and the LSAT prep courses I was taking … You wouldn't expect it, but he often had good advice for his friends; people always wanted to come to talk to him; he was funny …" *Wise, insightful?* Lisa had said something similar. Perhaps Luke always had a sense that his own path was not the right one, and while he couldn't change course himself he could still warn off others from it.

And actually, isn't this a well-known phenomenon? Don't many teachers, leaders, even spiritual mentors who offer inspiration, deeply touch others, often maintain lifestyles that seem to violate their own principles? We came to recognize that Luke often did have insights into other people and their predicaments that constituted a kind of wisdom, even if quite unavailing to himself.

This was all part of what Luke's friends helped me to compile: this conglomerate montage, this posthumous composite, even as we could only build it in death. Yes, there were many *malos amigos*, but the *buenos* came forward in surprising numbers to provide the fascinating and often appealing details that help make up the portrait.

High on my list for recontact is John, Luke's old classmate in Maryland. John was the one who had thrown the brick through the Gardiners' window with Luke's name on it a month after we had moved to California. I find John's old number and reach his father. He tells me that John is doing very well and is going on to college. He'll pass along my message. John comes over the very next afternoon after work, visibly upset. He is smitten with shock, sorrow, and anger. "Luke was one of the best friends I ever had," he says, "he was funny, you could rely on him as a friend. He was always caring … I remember how he was fond of an older guy who was janitor at our elementary school, a nice guy, Afro-American. Luke and I used to visit him every so often to find out how he was doing, even after we had left elementary school."

"But … how could Luke be so stupid!" and he breaks into tears. He remembers sitting up on the roof of our house once in Luke's last year while

Luke smoked some crack and stared off into the empty sky. He invited John to join him but John didn't feel comfortable with it. He says he hadn't realized how far down the drug road Luke had progressed. "As always, Luke was walking along his independent road."

I remind John about the brick incident, the first time we've ever talked about it together, and he smiles. "God, I'll never forget that night. Luke had called me that day and we talked about the idea of throwing a brick through the Gardiners' window, especially since Luke had the perfect alibi being in California. I was totally into it. I got a brick and found a yellow grease marker to personalize my weapon of choice and wrote 'A present from Luke' on it. I changed into dark clothing and biked over in the dark and hid behind their house until the lights went out, around ten-thirty. My heart was throbbing as I waited another half hour, and then I moved forward, lobbed the brick with all my might right through the bay window. What a sound! What a rush! I then grabbed my bike and took off back down the hill onto the dark bike path, on home and onto the telephone. 'The eagle has landed,' I told Luke."

"You know, John," I say, clapping him on the back, "I hate to admit it, but I'm still glad you did it. You did it for Luke."

Yet, as I write this book, sorting through old letters of condolence from lots of people, I feel a slight sense of shame as I come across the short note from the Gardiners themselves that they sent to us via a neighbor at the time. They were living in another town some distance away at the time of Luke's death. The Gardiners write gently that they can hardly imagine the sense of loss we are experiencing. In what may have been one of the last redoubts of still-embastioned—no, cherished—anger in my heart, I feel a melting; I must, I will think more kindly of the Gardiners. Indeed, part of my anger at the time reflected my own sense of helplessness at my situation and my awareness that their interventions were, infuriatingly, on the right side of the law.

Then Chris: he had suffered the double whammy of being a good friend of Luke, then becoming the victim of Luke's burglary of his home, and his subsequent avoidance of Luke thereafter. He recalls meeting one of Luke's Asian friends of acquaintances at our house one night when we were out. I believe this must have been his Korean friend, Cho, who got shot in a drug transaction in Luke's presence. "The guy looked like someone you wouldn't want to mess with. Dan remarked to me that he thought the guy was perhaps a gangster or something and expressed concern that perhaps Luke might be getting involved with a dangerous organization. He told me once that Luke had mentioned something about an opportunity he had to join some sort of criminal organization, but had thought better of it." Luke as budding Yakuza?

Yet he says, "Luke's death hit me hard. I remember crying and lying on the floor of my parents' house ... at some point I felt like I was literally paralyzed; I was unable to physically move even if my brain told my limbs to do so. I had already lost two of my grandparents at that point, but I had never before experienced the impact of a death that had such a blunt impact on both my emotional and physical state."

Another close friend, Morgan, had spent a lot of time in our house but had moved away to the West less than a year before Luke died. Luke had told us of Morgan's frustrations with his rigid parenting. Morgan only got word about Luke's death some ten years later. Out of the blue I get an email:

*I am terribly saddened by the news of Luke's passing. It was his influence that helped me gain the strength to be myself, regardless. I think about him often and with the truest of admiration.*

*Prior to meeting Luke in 4th grade, I was my father's child. Shirt buttoned to the top, pants uncomfortably high, and constantly nervous about making him angry. I'd play at home alone with Legos and listen to top-forty hits with Casey Kasem. Within a year of befriending Luke I was listening to Ozzy on Black Sabbath, sneaking out at night, and grounded every other week. Despite sounding bad, it was my bar mitzvah and Luke was both rabbi and best friend. It was about new horizons.*

Morgan claims Luke virtually saved his life when Morgan fell through the ice in a deep portion of a local creek; Luke laughed in sympathy and overcame Morgan's panic, helped him climb out and, as Morgan stood scared and freezing in the cold air, shared some of his clothes and helped Morgan get home—a powerful memory. He writes, *Fear of getting into trouble was always my first concern. For Luke it wasn't. He'd do things, fun things, and worry about consequences later if they ever came. This wasn't rebellion. Rebellion is to act out against something. He simply acted without letting consideration of consequences dominate. This was quite contagious and ended up becoming the seed of my confidence. Experience triumphed over fear of reprisal.*

His cousin Laurel echoed these same thoughts many years later: "Luke was curious about boundaries beyond most kids' curiosity. He seemed easily bored, and he was into danger. But I always felt Luke had a sense of mischief, drama and curiosity—attributes that *could* have seen him into a fun and productive life. But in the end they didn't."

And where Morgan had the maturity to channel his newfound freedom and confidence to become himself in positive and constructive directions, Luke didn't. I can now look back and see the early signs of the *attraction* to Luke to test or overstep boundaries. It wasn't clear then, but it was indeed a sign of what was to come. Some of this greater clarity comes late, from these close friends and cousins who, astonishingly, are themselves now approaching forty.

*        *        *

As I wander through all his meager collection of possessions, talk to his friends, the question grows stronger in my mind: who did Luke think he was? His self-image poses another mystery, one of conflicting faces.

Luke always had an interest in fantasy: creating characters in Dungeons and Dragons, Japanese transformer warrior toys, shape-shifters, and the wily Coyote. Even more, he had a real touch of the poseur to him; this is why people were so often impressed with this artful composite. He wasn't lying, he was just spontaneously and skillfully weaving together a persona from multiple sources of his unusual life, presenting an image of the worldly, the traveled, the knowledgeable and the sophisticated, the possessor of myriad contacts and a wealth of incidental knowledge on a lot of subjects gleaned from all over everywhere.

His organizer offers fascinating clues: it's a thick faux leather thing with all kinds of tabs and pockets, but the huge clear-plastic calling card section where he can handily display all his contacts tells it all. He's squirreled away a pile of calling cards of dozens of seemingly important, unique or impressive individuals, including a few cards lifted from my professional stash that he corralled. Look at them: a card from a US Senate Foreign Relations Committee Staffer, one from the US Ambassador to Azerbaijan, a US Information Agency official, an Economic Councilor to the US Embassy in Tunis, a Minister Councilor at the Pakistani Embassy in DC—but then also cards he acquired on his own: a Psychic Advisor in Thousand Oaks, a representative of Pacific Coast Properties, a United Airlines flight attendant, the Piano Pub in Madrid, a Tae Kwon Do Master in Thousand Oaks, the Scuba Shack in Hawaii, a USAIR manager in Houston, the Foundation for Affordable Housing, the Joyería (Jewelers) in Costa Rica, a specialist in Scientific Handwriting Analysis, a Marine Corps Recruiter, a Vancouver Japanese Restaurant, a shop for Cutlery and Fine Arts in Louisiana, a Master Piercer in New Orleans, a Reiki Master in Thousand Oaks, a Licensed Psychologist in Chevy Chase, a GMAC Mortgage rep in Portsmouth NH— on and on. Nearly all were people Luke had encountered on his own. He also had a photograph of himself meeting the Director of Central Intelligence (along with the rest of the family) at an awards ceremony for me.

I'm sure that he was able to spin out a tale with each card to new acquaintances—I mean, who wouldn't be impressed by the US Ambassador to bloody Azerbaijan? I can hear it now: "Well, the Ambassador was interested in my experiences in Mexico in tourism and told me that they could use an experienced tour guide to help out with Americans visiting Azerbaijan." Or, "Yeah, I have this psychic advisor in California who helps me on a lot of my decisions." Or, "When I'm in Madrid you can always catch me at the Piano Pub there." Or, "If you're ever in Vancouver, check out the Kirin restaurant and tell them I sent you." One of Luke's many constructed personas. The key to his success in playing Three Truths and a Lie.

There's this contradiction. "He needs to define himself as somehow *different* from his immediate world," my niece Laurel notes. "Yet at the same time your memoirs of him show how often he feels *vulnerable* in being different than others." I remember how he would get annoyed when I would point out discreetly from a distance other families with an obviously adopted child of a different ethnicity. He was angered at being called *Chinito* or *Indio* in Mexico. He gratuitously reminded Chinese that he wasn't Chinese. He was annoyed at being a "banana" to his Korean friends. Americans often congratulated him on his English. And he knew that temperamentally he wasn't really a Fuller either.

"It's clear to me now," Laurel continues, "that Luke doesn't really know who he is, so he has romantic ideas of who he might be—Bruce Lee-cool, part of an elite criminal gang, world traveler, well connected—but it all springs from insecurity. He seems very scared underneath it all; his stress response is to flee, never to fight. Luke is an escapist—but what is he escaping from? What does he not want to face?" Was this what he was avoiding on his very last night of life? Someone who really fits in nowhere? His inability to function over the longer run in school or jobs? Luke telling me in the darkness of the car at the time of his tentative diagnosis of ADHD: "I'm not like other people ..."

*      *      *

Luke is often not far from our minds and I find myself seeking on occasion to ritualize it. When Prue and I are in Mexico we often visit historic cathedrals and churches that preserve treasures of Spanish-Mexican art and architecture. To push open the heavy wooden doors and step into the musty stone interior of a church in Mexico is to travel back in time, to an age of absolute faith in which the treasure of the community was lavished upon a gilded altar and its radiating silver-plated monstrances and other Eucharistic regalia for celebration of Mass. I am drawn to the racks of dozens of offertory candles recessed back into the dark naves, lit in prayer, thanksgiving, or in supplication for some intensely important moment in the personal lives of anonymous visitors or for succor of the troubled, dying or dead. What does the flickering flame on the candle third from the right on the second row stand for? For what private torment, sadness, grief—or joy and thankfulness? Or the last candle on the upper row left? Who put it there and with what story? The candles are mute, do not speak individually, but collectively offer a powerful sense of spiritual yearning.

In beholding this luminescent display of hopes, fears, griefs, and thanksgivings, we too are drawn in to blend with the culture, to join the process, even if we are not Catholic; our personal theologies long ago drifted well outside of the orbit of traditional Christianity. But we appreciate the symbolism, the gesture, the ritual; we have taken to regularly dropping a few coins in through the worn wooden slot of the medieval alms box that clink to the bottom to pay for our purchase of a little candle in its red glass cup to offer in memory of Luke, to place it in the rack along with other anonymously-kindled lights. We use one of the lighting sticks to transfer a living flame from someone else's candle over to light our own. Who knows what connection or link we have inadvertently created between the unknown, inadvertent donor of the flame we have borrowed—surely they would not object—to provide the flame for Luke's newly lit candle. Might they now be linked in death and memory? Or thanksgiving for a life? We can do both.

Even in the twenty-first century a lit candle does not lose its quality of mystery; its ruby glow adds an imperceptible few extra lumens to the racked collective of wavering flames that dispel only a few of the shadows in the recess of the nave. The walls are ancient, the smell of the wax earthy, the uncertain flickering light more mysteriously powerful than unwavering electric light; we feel something alive at work, an ebb and flow of spirit. We'll often find ourselves checking back on our way out of the church minutes later, just to be sure that our little flame is surviving and working, for a few days anyway, whatever magic and balm it can bestow upon us, or Luke, or anyone else.

*     *     *

And so it is that we happen to take a second trip to Mexico, this time with some close friends, the spring after Luke's death. We cross over the border once again into that Mexican universe so sharply demarcated from the powerful American "reality" on this side. Mexico struggles for its own identity distinct from America. It's divided between its rich indigenous

Mayan/Aztecan/*Indio* heritage, and those more light-skinned Mexicans who like to persuade themselves that they are of strictly Spanish origin. In Mexico Luke was an *Indio* to some, a *Chinito* to others. Never a white *gringo*. I'm the gringo.

We drive up into the Chiapas highlands once again in the darkness from the Tuxtla's airport. We negotiate numerous police barriers, gruff interrogations to our taxi driver; flashlights swung into our faces through the back window, peremptory searches of the trunk in back. We are back in the land of the semi-siege, the ongoing Zapatista rebellion.

San Cristóbal had captivated our hearts the first time when Melissa took us there—the crisp mountain air, the small cobble stone streets, the secretive courtyards, the classic colonial town, hillsides set with its typical houses run riot in acrylic colors, masking the poverty that marks Chiapas, the poorer, Mayan part of Mexico. Now back, I feel particularly impelled to return to the Instituto de Idiomas in search of traces of Luke, to re-experience those emotional links of a person to a time and a place. Perhaps this might bring some specific additional detail, color and texture to help fill out the portrait of his posthumous biography.

For some reason I feel strongly drawn towards meeting again with the director of the school, Dr. Carlos Guzmán who had known Luke. Might he have some memories that would both bring warmth, some additional independent insight into Luke as an autonomous person living in his own independent world?

We enter the gardens of the Instituto, pass into the *recepción,* and ask to see Dr. Guzmán. The director is busy, could we state our business? Not wanting to pass along such personal news except in person, we mention only that our son had been a student at the Instituto several years earlier. Finally we gain admission. Dr. Guzmán has aged somewhat, seems mildly distracted. With his best Latin courtesy he professes to remember who we are, but it seems vague. When I mention *el Chinito* he suddenly brightens, "Ah yes! Lucas!" We tell him we are grateful to him for what the Instituto did for Luke—Lucas. But the tale ends sadly, I say, Luke died some six months ago, of drugs. Dr. Guzmán perceptibly blanches. He asks a few questions then sits straight up.

"Señor Fuller, I am truly sorry for your loss, but, pardon my asking, why have you come to tell me this?"

I mumble something about the fact that we find comfort in retracing some of Luke's old footsteps and haunts and felt an obligation to let a few of those who knew him of his sad end. And we wanted to thank the Instituto for having shepherded Luke throughout a happy year in his life.

Dr. Guzmán looks at his watch.

"Señor, I have a busy schedule this afternoon, but if you like I can meet you for a few minutes early this evening in the cafe down the street, we can talk about it."

Late in the afternoon, even as the setting sun over the hills drench the colorful hillside structures with gold, we note angry clouds of a classic late afternoon thunder shower hovering not far off. San Cristóbal is rarely just tourist-pretty, it can be a highly striking location with its arid mountains still dotted with animist churches, old Mayan ways of life, hard-scrabble life in the nearby mountains, and dramatic shifts in weather.

At a sidewalk table we order two bottles of *Dos Equis Oscuro* while waiting for Dr. Guzmán to arrive. Freshly home-fried tortilla chips, hot from the fat, are set down in front of us with the beer on the checkered tablecloth, mocking my efforts to avoid such lard-drenched delights. Fatal perhaps over time, but not as certain and swift as crack.

Half an hour, still no Guzmán. Is this just Mexican time, or simply a polite avoidance of an unrewarding discussion of the saddened memories of two gringo parents trying to fill in the gaps of the loss of their son? In Chiapas death by drugs can scarcely be noteworthy in such an oppressed region still engaged in theatrical guerrilla war and a border porous to drug runners up from Guatemala.

Dr. Guzmán finally arrives, looking tired. He apologizes—busy afternoon, unexpected meetings. After a few moments of polite indulgence to my Spanish, Guzmán interrupts in English.

"Pardon me, Señor Fuller, again I am sorry about your loss. I wonder if you do not mind, I would like to hear about what exactly happened to Lucas."

I sketch in the brief account of Luke's last two years after returning home, his downward descent into loss of control, inability to keep a job, and eventual death.

"But again, I would like to know, why did you feel you wanted to come to tell me this about your son?"

I repeat our vague wish to bring some closure to our son's life and death, in part by offering farewells to those that knew him.

Dr. Guzmán listens attentively then speaks with some animation.

"Señor Fuller, I am very moved. But I still do not know why you have come all the way to San Cristóbal to tell me this ... I must say, this message of yours is very special to me. Of course I knew Lucas when he was a student here, and we sometimes went to bars together after school." He smiles wryly. "For him the café was a better classroom than our school, I'm afraid. But I enjoyed his company, he was funny, he had seen the world, we had many laughs. But I had no idea what happened to Lucas after he returned to the United States."

Guzmán draws himself up closer and lowers his voice. "I have not mentioned this to anyone, Señor. But I will tell you something. I myself have struggled with alcohol and drugs for a number of years now. Many people know I enjoy drinking with my students, but not many know about the drugs I have also been taking for many years. I want very much to stop. They are preventing me from working well, from living a proper life. They threaten my position, they will injure my family. I am trying to stop. That is why your story has shocked me. Frankly between us, Señor Fuller, your news has frightened me. You have opened a door … that shows me death."

And, to our astonishment, the polished Director del Instituto, proceeds to tell us in great frankness about his own struggles, his missed hours at work, his concealment of the problem except from his doctor, his fears for the impact on his public position, his family life and his own health. "I tell you frankly I have been tormented by dreams of my own death."

And, in this country of highly refined linguistic formality, Dr. Guzmán who scarcely knows me, abruptly breaks into the intimate *tú* form of the verb in referring to me in his occasional use of Spanish. "Please call me Carlos. I will call you Graham … You have brought me a sign from God. Your message is clearly a warning to me, that I must stop or I will die too. Yes, I believe that God has sent you to me to tell me this story about Lucas. Surely this was not a coincidence. I am very grateful to you that you came all the way to tell me this."

And before I can take it all in, Carlos soon takes his leave, emotionally thanking us for our visit. He requests that we preserve the confidentiality of all that he imparted to us (and his identity heavily disguised in this account.) Then he is gone.

Prue and I look at each other across the table, speechless, unable to process quite what we have just heard, as we sit on the darkening street of the cafe. Indeed, why exactly are we here? For us? Or for Dr. Guzmán? In what strange way had Luke forged this connection?

Overwhelmed at this intersection of lives, even through death, we wander back to our small hotel with its colonial courtyard and bubbling fountain. All around the evening lights are coming up across the town. They cast an entirely different aura over the hillsides, the gardens, the cactuses, the old stone … Linkages abound.

# CHAPTER TWENTY-TWO

# WRITING LUKE

It's been twelve years. His death ages ago, a minute ago. Time eases sadness, yes, but does not erase. Events remain in the mind, but they do not remain static: they are marinated, filtered and modulated by time, through aging and perspective.

And now here I am writing this book. Our lives have gone forward meaningfully and positively, but Luke has not fully let go of me, nor I him. I am still haunted by what this experience means, and what might have been.

I am "writing Luke." We're beyond biographical records and events here and into the realm of meaning.

I am attempting to impose a framework of unity on these events—of a life arbitrarily begun and arbitrarily ended. Luke sears like a comet into my life and then out of it. I can trace it. I can frame his life within the dimensions of my own life—he cannot. I can subjectively draw meaning out of his life for me—he cannot. Even to write this chronicle is to select among a huge sea of facts; a tale woven by me might be woven differently by you. Maybe what I choose says as much about me as about Luke.

I painfully go through file after file that Prue had kept. She kept these records at the time, not out of sentiment, but because Luke's life was in constant legal and procedural turmoil. She was serving as a law clerk, without remuneration, and taxed with a high emotional price. We needed the records of what he had done and what he had left undone. And once his life had flickered out, we had no immediate heart to chuck his files on the spot like so many old bank statements.

So much of this documented trip saddens me: his paper trail lies out there like some sort of trail of crumbs in the wilderness for a voracious legal predator. Even to sort out all these events takes me months. I seek to impose a flow and clarity to them. Clarity? Give me a break—I'm not sure anything is clearer.

I tell friends of my writing project, they tell me, "Oh, that must be cathartic." But it isn't. I tell myself that if I can put it down in black and white, measure it out by days, years, events, places and people, paragraphs and chapters, it will fall into perspective, make sense. But these details don't fully speak to me yet. I see only multiple tableaux, separate plays, various dramas, diverse scenes and acts taking place, moral tales, comedies, farces, tragedies, but all on different stages, different audiences, different times, playing simultaneously without forming any coherent whole. Parts of a potential quilt whose pieces don't fit together except through artistry.

The story is supposed to be about Luke's life. But one day I tell Prue, "You know what? It's clearer to me now, at the end of all this writing, that my efforts over those years to force Luke to develop, in the end really rather forced *me* to develop." In all of this I find I have inadvertently chronicled myself more than I have him—Luke, the mirror.

Now I'm seized with a deeper question: not just who *was* Luke, but who *is* Luke? What does he signify? What does this life—this death—still mean? How has it changed me—or others? Prue captures it: "If Luke were still alive, his life might have much less grand meaning for you than his death does."

I am reminded of Béla Bartók's opera *Bluebeard's Castle*. Instead of taking his new wife back to his castle as one more of his many wives previously killed as in the folk tale, in the opera he takes his most recent wife on a tour of his castle. There are seven doors with great locks; she insists that he open each one to her in turn. Inside she finds scenes that represent the psychological state of mind, the neuroses or pathologies of mind that helped cripple Bluebeard emotionally, that destroyed his relationship with his previous wives. She flings open the doors, bringing in light, airing out these states of mind, releasing them. She is recovering the whole person in Bluebeard, attempting to save him from the desolations of each of the rooms. I feel like I am flinging open doors in myself in this process of search; this is no longer even about Luke, but rather what Luke has come to represent for me, in the search to find myself in my own prisons.

One of my opaque chambers is the ability to hide behind a mask of verbal articulation—the ability to talk, expound, chatter—to artfully conceal my limits on expressing emotion. Yes, facility with words can help communicate—but they can also obfuscate openness and directness, they can throw up transparent walls. I can spin words around uncomfortable emotional situations, they can be an intellectualized substitute for the spontaneous emotions of the hug, or the touch in silence that speak more than words. I'm crippled by words, trapped behind words, corralled by words, hiding behind words, my emotional spontaneity sapped by words.

I think back on Prue's words many years ago: "Luke loves you, but he is sometimes intimidated by you. He loves you, but he is more comfortable with me ..."

\*                          \*                          \*

So who *is* Luke now to me? During the twenty-year life journey with him, how much have I projected my own hopes, values, philosophy, gut feelings about the world, my own rebellious impulses, upon him? Was Luke a free spirit as I liked to imagine, an image that romantically appealed to me? A free spirit whom I could release like a dove into the sky flying against the norms of routinized conventional society? Or maybe he was more likely a trapped and confused bird struggling to stay aloft, figuring out how to survive the assault of the elements. Not a free, but a lost spirit.

Luke was unconventional and stimulating company—all his friends testify to that. His friend Chris—a victim of Luke's burglary, yet overwhelmed by the news of Luke's death—tells me: "When I lost touch with Luke, my social life all of a sudden became somewhat boring: fewer adventures with Luke or hearing about his previous ones, less exposure to exotic cuisine, less mischief, less stimulating conversations, less fun." For them this daring was part of his appeal. And, accordingly, I tried to treat his problems through unconventional means. But maybe what I took as unconventionalities in him were really weaknesses, efforts to improvise and adapt, that I chose to interpret as anarchistic or rebellious strains that appealed to me. Did I have a greater tolerance for his swerving from the path because I can readily see why people do swerve from the conventional paths in life? Swerving may be OK, but it had better be grounded in some reality if you do it; Luke lacked that grounding. He seemed to be awash among greater forces.

\*                          \*                          \*

This relentless search for Luke sometimes moves into the surreal. Take, for example, Luke, Maryland. Never heard of it? Not surprising, it's at the end of the western panhandle of the state of Maryland—a tiny town in Allegheny County. We wouldn't even know about it if Prue and I hadn't happened to pass by along the interstate in western Maryland one time on a return trip from the West. I catch sight of the name on a local exit sign. On impulse I twist the steering wheel onto the exit. But what in God's name can turning off into a tiny town called Luke do for me? Curiosity at the unusual name? Emotional hunger? Some deeper impulse?

Indeed, what's in a name? I can't deny its impact: an inexplicable comforting warmth in catching sight of these four familiar, simple letters, here given official, enduring status on the town's green signboard. Our Luke's span was fleeting—two decades out of the seven in my own life—but surely Luke, Maryland possesses greater permanency. Yet, not quite so: in a grander cycle of life played out over multiple generations, even a town's life can be threatened. We learn that Luke, Maryland is in parlous shape. The settlement took the name after William Luke who spearheaded the town's substantial forest industry. But even this colonial village called Luke is losing its grasp on permanency: it's faded, any semblance of real town life has given way to a huge papermill industry that has devoured the old social community. The town is now little more than a commercial designation of convenience for the factory. Yet hundreds of loyal natives come back each year for the Annual Homecoming in Luke, in quest, in celebration of their community that once was, that is no longer.

My photo shows a large green sign, "Welcome to Luke, MD," population now 80; Barney sits beneath the sign, likely unaware of why he is posing there in this passing moment of imagination loosely linked to his former master. Now that our Luke and his Barney are both gone, only the green sign remains out here, its years too probably numbered and on its way into history.

In a strange way I too have inadvertently come back, turning off the highway to momentarily celebrate what no longer is, come to share in meaning of the name of the town. For me the town's name holds a personal poignancy that is unknown and irrelevant to the others at their Homecoming. But would they begrudge me my alternative evocation—a more personal form of homecoming?

And time plays tricks, too. The future can change the *past*. Each event as we lived it with Luke was of course his story only up to that moment in time; at any given moment multiple paths remained open to the future. The first day of the rest of his life as they say. But now, with the hindsight of death, earlier events take on a quite different character. Now I can see how options were closing down here, shutting off there, turning points forcing us to shuffle into an ever-narrower series of cattle pens in a stockyard that inexorably culminates in a single chute leading only to the end of the line.

Nor am I the same person I was then, nor are Prue, Samantha and Melissa. We each continue to process the past in new and different ways as we mature and undergo new experiences. Our present state of mind seeps backwards in time, coloring it, creating new readings of the past. Melissa tells me on reading this manuscript that she starts to view these events with somewhat different eyes. She is older, now a mother herself. She reads our parental anguish in a different light now than before, when the cooler rationality of a young adult and sibling observed Luke's follies with reproach.

\*　　　　　　\*　　　　　　\*

I can't help imagine what might have been. Try this tale. It's Christmas 2012. Luke arrives home to spend some days with us. At thirty-eight, he's bronzed, sporting just a touch of gray here and there in his hair that's short once again; he's casual, slightly gangly. He tells us about his work as an eco-tour guide in the back woods of Chile, Peru, Bolivia and Argentina, taking more adventuresome visitors on camping trips on horseback to see the high plains, glaciers, with llamas carrying up the rear. It's not great money, but he's happy. He been at this job about eight years now, earns reasonable money due to his outdoor skills, good Spanish, his knowledge of the areas, his natural skills with the local people who see him a bit more as one of their own than the usual gringo guide down there. Everyone likes *el Chinito*'s comfortable way with people, his wealth of stories regularly recounted to the urgings of outsiders that we could never quite induce him to do within the family. "Ba, you should come down some time, you'd like it," he says. Yes, I would, Luke, I say, I know I would.

Or how about this one: It's September 2010, Prue and I drive into Vancouver, British Columbia, for the day. We don't want to be late for our lunch with Luke at The Golden Wok. He's going to cook up a few special dishes for us that day that aren't on their regular menu. He comes out of the kitchen to hug us, grinning, his chef's hat tipped rakishly back, slight swagger of confidence and success in his own world. He's now one of the better-known chefs for neo-Asian cuisine in the city. He moved up to Vancouver a few years after we did to check it out. He'd been cooking around in the East Coast gaining experience after his graduation from the other CIA, the Culinary Institute of America, but that wasn't his scene. He took right away to Vancouver's laid-back character, its large Asian population. He's got a serious Japanese girlfriend Yukiko whom he introduces to us; she's working on green urban development. After a great lunch we agree to all meet up in the evening together at the local Steamworks brewpub and hear about Luke's hopes to eventually establish his own little restaurant. We swap reminiscences of eating out in Hong Kong, how he was way ahead of us in his adventuresomeness in new foods. "Hey Ba, you should check out my new dog I got, a wire-haired retriever, his name is Barnaby." "For real? Not Barney?" "Nope, Barnaby."

Or: It's July 2010 and we drive up to northern Maine in the interval between the Outward Bound programs to visit Luke who's a councilor. He's planned a leisurely hike for us around the area, to point out some of the local scene. Luke has three sessions of kids this summer, keeping him busy. It's hard to think that this was the course that he himself took twenty years ago, for "troubled kids." The kids all like him, and he's one of the best councilors, he knows just how to spell out to them what it was like to be strung out on crack, barely coming out of some really bad shit one time that he wouldn't have survived if we hadn't rushed him to the hospital. Luke speaks with real authenticity to these kids, many of whom are out of the ghetto, who may be on the same downward path that he took, who still think of drugs as cool, a good way to escape, but Luke's story shakes them up. Luke is thinking about maybe taking some night classes at Boston University on sociology and the drug culture, but isn't sure he can manage the concentration of having to hit the textbooks night after night. But Outward Bound encourages him to do it; they think one day he could help train a lot more councilors on how best to handle druggie kids. Later we sit over some beers—he won't touch anything stronger—and talk about the bad old days; Luke shakes his head, acknowledges what a long trip it's been. "Sorry I'm going to miss the family reunion this year," he says, "but, you know, three days is a bit too intense for me with all of you guys under one roof. I'll catch Aunt Meredith and maybe Uncle David myself this winter when I'll have some time on my hands between the fall and spring sessions." "No sweat Luke, come see us anytime, whenever is good. We'll take you up into our mountains in BC. Samantha may be up here to see you in the spring too; she's never seen your Maine set-up here." "Yeah, that's great, she sent me a message about coming." I slow-slug him in the belly as we head out.

All alternative fantasies—all might-have-beens that warm my heart. But there is also another, darker, alternative.

It's July 2011 and Prue and I turn off Interstate 95 in Jarratt, Virginia, toward the Greensville Correctional Center. It sits on the hillside in a series of four pod-style buildings arranged in a semi-circle on what looks disturbingly like a campus, masking its nature as a medium security penitentiary. Luke has been here for eight years now, seven more to go on if he's on good behavior. Three different counts of robbery, the last one armed in which Luke's partner ending up killing a night watchman. Same old story—all aimed at feeding his habit. He'd left off stealing our stuff—a certain relief—and moved on to less emotional and more lucrative targets. When the police finally caught up to him his health was terrible: he'd turned to heroin and was diagnosed with HIV picked up from needles. We could only imagine his life after he had dropped out of sight. He had been too ashamed to even come and see us—just a few brief periodic phone calls once in a while from unknown locations, asking how we were. "Everything's OK, Ba, I'm alright." "What's going on, Luke," we'd ask, "where are you?" "Don't worry, I'm alright, I'll come by to see you some time. Things are complicated, but I'm still trying to work things out."

At his trial he had looked like hell, I caught a glimpse of track marks on his inner arms. He was pale, thin, wan, his smile gone, an impassive, sometimes angry, expression on his face. Even after years supposedly off drugs in prison, we hear that it is still possible to get ahold of them there. His health is bad, his liver's shot, and he's on a lot of medication to manage the HIV. The doctors admit frankly he may not survive to his release time. And what kind of care and support could we manage if he does survive until his release? Any pleasure Luke might have in seeing us seems heavily crowded with shame. As we look at him through the glass, he's aged at least ten years over the past few. His features are coarser, less mobile. His spirit is gone. "Thanks for coming, you guys, but you really should just forget about me. I'm done, I'm not going anywhere, I'm just a drag on you. I appreciate what you tried to do, but I'm just fucked up, always will be. Just don't worry about me anymore." I tear over, but what can I say? We pass along news of ourselves, of Samantha and Melissa and other family members. "Say hello to all of them for me", he says. "If they can write that would be cool." We bring him a few books, he tells us briefly about his work as a cook in the prison, and his artwork. He reads. But there's not a lot of life in his eyes anymore. "We're still here for you, Luke, whenever you want to talk or see us, just call, we'll come." We wave goodbye, the glass denying us even the minimal soul-regenerating human touch, and are ushered out through the multiple steel gates to the outside. What do Prue and I say to each other during the sad, silent drive home?

It didn't happen that way either. As events turned out, at least I remember Luke as eternally young, the promise still intact. He is not aging, stumbling, coarsening in front of my eyes as a mature adult. His early death perhaps spared him—and us—something less dramatically compelling than a youthful death, something darker, dirtier, lengthier, uglier, tawdrier, seedier, utterly stripped of hope.

*      *      *

As I work on this book, the material takes on its own life. It's now part of the raw material of my own view of life around me, the loam for future growth. The Tibetan teacher Chögyam Trungpa Rinpoche once commented that what's shit for some is manure for others; it all depends on how you think about it.

I can go back and interrogate pieces of paper in the file for answers to my faulty reconstruction of the past. But can you ever have a full perspective of events when they come at you head-on in a maelstrom? Can the kayaker running white water have a simultaneous strong conscious awareness of the sky, the trees along the riverbank, the way the light strikes forest, water and rock in a particular way, the smell of the mist from the falls, a full recall of the world at the time? Or does he just recall the vital, immediate, pressing, life-threatening elements of rocks, swells, whirlpools and the urgent second-by-second decisions for survival?

With each happening there was no leisure for the long view. A court document thrusts into my face the hard facts of the moment; I've got to respond to a county prosecutor or a pending jail sentence. Calling for an ambulance is not a time for reflection or the long view. A philosophy is not an action plan. We ended up ad-hocking it all the way every day as events spun out of control.

Maybe the "full story" is revealed only in the slow settling of the lees in our particular home brew. Maybe clarity comes only with the passage of time, serenity, composure, peace and acceptance.

*     *     *

I think back on the thoughts flitting through my mind at the time of Luke's arrival at JFK: the person who would shortly get the brand-new name, Luke Byungbae Fuller. The person whom I will mold, shape, for whom I believe I will create a new identity. But does this new name conceal who the "real" Luke had first been? Very likely the real Luke with his true Korean name, growing up in Daegu, would have had a very different life: left in a circle of Korean drug addicts or alcoholics, uncaring parents or no parents, maybe starting out as a street urchin, a petty chiseler, moving into the drug trade himself, and ultimately ending up on a slab in the morgue. Same slab, different morgue, different country.

Still, I idly note that in this world of seven billion people Luke is almost surely the only person in history ever to be called Luke Byungbae Fuller. That is a strange kind of uniqueness—for what it's worth.

And in a crazy moment in the spirit of our cyber-age, I google Luke Fuller, omitting for the moment the more complicating and unique Byungbae. I feel sure that only if Google's informational maw had chewed its way into Luke's legal file would I get a hit on his unique full name. What in hell do I really expect to find here anyway in a compulsive google shot?

Well, in fact, it turns out there was a fairly well-known Luke Fuller, known to millions of people, roughly contemporaneous with our Luke. Only he wasn't real. He was a minor character in the American TV series *Dynasty*, a

251

show I have never seen. The Luke Fuller on that show in 1985—when Luke Byungbae Fuller was very much alive in Rockville, Maryland—was the gay lover of a major character on the show and attracted a lot of attention in the role. It seems there was an episode at the end of one season where the major character went to Moldova for a wedding, bringing along with him his boyfriend, Luke Fuller. And at the wedding episode, some armed dissidents barged in with machine guns and started firing. Luke Fuller caught a bullet in the head and died. A lot of people wrote in to say they liked the character, but others hated him. Incredible, here is a Luke Fuller who was a construct of some screenwriter's mind—like mine?—who obviously touched a lot of people. And he was killed off young for the convenience of the screenwriters. This is weird—stumbling across a semi-biography of a famous but non-existent Luke Fuller—where am I going here?

*       *       *

Luke was the black hole in the constellation of our family—the powerful invisible force that somehow drew everything into its vortex, demanding our constant focus, our vigilant resistance against its destructive aspects. It influenced everything, directly or indirectly. It robbed our daughters of a fairer share of my time and attention that they deserved. It put painful strain on my wife and on our own relationship together. And we could never adequately fill the black hole's emptiness either, as it sucked constant resources—time, emotion, money, attention, fear, anxiety and energy into itself irresistibly. Luke did not want that, or seek that, or perhaps even quite fully realize that, but that was what increasingly became his transcendental role for us.

Look, I'm an intelligence officer, a CIA officer trained to sense realities, observe, report and analyze, later heading up long-range strategic forecasting. Where were all my professional instincts through all of this? Whatever political and cultural powers of insight I might have had in my professional life were stunted and worthless against this challenge. No strategic forecast here. I blew the call.

So where might have been the tipping point of events? Looking back, where is the moment that decisively foreclosed further good options, when suddenly there was no way back, only a slope so precipitous that even a seasoned mountain goat could no longer negotiate it? The events were legion, take your pick, starting from a possibly alcoholic conception.

In the end I see only one major unexplored option that might have changed things. "Maybe you and the girls were right," I tell Prue, "maybe we should have let things take their natural course, via the 'prison solution.'

Maybe that was the only real radical alternative, a kind of real world alternative. Maybe I shouldn't have sought to fend it off. Total laissez-faire policy, just let the Law do its thing. *No defense, no bail, no council, no parental vouchings and intercessions, no alternative programs—just let Luke rot in juvy, or in prison for five, seven, ten—whatever it takes to reflect.* At the least he would have gained some incremental maturity—after all, even insurance companies put young male drivers firmly into the high risk premium bracket until age twenty-six or so. Would a chastened twenty-six- or thirty-year-old Luke emerging from prison, presumably clean of drug usage over several years, have then been ready to start a new life?

OK, we might have bought time that way. But that way we would likely have only seen Luke from behind plexiglass for many long years. And he would have come out a convicted felon. On top of that, what about the ADHD and the limitations *that* places on many people from holding regular jobs? Luke might have found some niche, perhaps in some "alternative style" job that could have given him a shot at a normal life span. I can't know.

By hindsight I clearly missed the indicators of the depths into which Luke had sunk over his head early on in his first brushes with drugs, flailing, gasping for breath, going under again and again—as surely as if he had fifty-pound weights tied to his legs and it was just a calculable matter of time before the arms grow ever more exhausted, resistance to the weights no longer possible, until even the fear of death is no longer able to overcome the exhaustion of the limbs, when death suddenly becomes thinkable, even acceptable in the face of discouragement, failure, loss of will, sheer exhaustion. Prue sensed all this far earlier on than I did. But she was always deeply uncomfortable with that thought, and reluctant to impose it on me.

"So face the hard question," my alter ego demands, "if you had known how the movie comes out, if you had it to do all over again, would you have done anything really differently?" I cringe at the question. Did I decisively fail him by not taking him to the hospital that last afternoon? Otherwise I wonder what else I really would have done differently. I would be subject to the same hopes, errors, braveries, arrogancies, creative steps, self-deceptions, magnificent struggles and foolishnesses against losing odds. I would love to change Luke's fate, my fate, but I do not think I can.

*So are you telling me that if you had possessed total clairvoyance, knew where all this was heading, you still would have taken the same route?* "Yes," I reply, "if I had truly known where all this was inevitably headed, what incentive would I have had to try to mount a magnificent resistance? True clairvoyance would only have led me to abandon the fight early on."

Because, in the end, as we struggled, what else did we have to support us other than hope? Isn't hope—and action—better than resignation? Here, maybe, is one of the points of this tale. We do what we can, we do what we must, and we will make mistakes, and maybe some things are never meant to be. But we must do what we can when we can.

But I know one thing for sure. I still would have adopted him. Whatever mistakes I made, that was not one of them. This has been a powerful milestone in my existence and personal vision and a profound personal experience for all of us.

I talk with Samantha, who is now a businesswoman in Scotland, about my thoughts on these matters. "You need to get beyond all this, Baba," she says. "It's time to end it. You need to bury Luke." She's more right than she knows. Because that box of ashes from the funeral home in Maryland remained with us in a back closet in British Columbia for many years. It's not that we wanted to keep them around. It's more that we didn't know where to bury them. We had known we were ultimately clearing out from life in the Washington DC area, we didn't feel there was much point in burying him in a place that has no connection with anyone in the family. And we have ended up settling in British Columbia, a place we have long loved, in the small town of Squamish, at the end of a fjord about one hour north of Vancouver. This is where Luke's ashes have finally been buried, in a cemetery at the foot of high snowcapped peaks. His stone reads "I will be in the wind that blows by you," a quotation from Emerson. Where we'll be one day.

*   *   *

It took a trip deep into the heart of the Third World much later to visit Melissa for her to really put it to me. I'm sometimes slow to catch onto reality in the things of the heart. In the real world it's December 2007 and Prue and I really are on our way to Addis Ababa, Ethiopia to spend Christmas with Melissa and her family. And it's kind of where I hit psychological rock bottom in grappling with all my chronicling.

It's a long haul, all the way to Addis. Melissa is a senior political officer in the embassy there. She meets us at the airport in the early hours towards dawn—the hour when flights from Europe to the Third World all seem to touch down. The pre-dawn cocoon of darkness conceals a world psychologically remote from the West just outside the airport gates.

Prue's bags make it, mine don't. I file a claim with the sleepy airline official as a pretend gesture of faith that he and I actually believe the bags will eventually show up. We then head into town in her dusty Land Rover. I don't need much more daylight than the emerging pink–purple glow on the horizon, intensified at an eight-thousand-feet altitude, to know where I am. This is generic Third World—it's almost in my genes, even if I'm a bit out of training for it now. The dust-swept streets, the yawning potholes that punctuate even many of the main boulevards. Hunched figures whose dawn identities are wrapped in earth-colored blankets meander across the road in front of us, never quite seeming to accurately gauge the speed of an oncoming car. I note the generic piebald street dogs that stray out into the road with no fear. Street signs, originally designed to offer orientation, instead loll twisted on their sides, making it unclear whether Debre Zeit Road is really to the right or straight ahead, but you should know anyway and if you don't know you shouldn't be here. The anonymous high-walled compounds conceal from the prying eyes of destitute passersby the degree of relative luxury hidden back inside; goats and shiftless lounger-arounders lean back against the walls that will later provide hours of shade from the brilliant equatorial sun.

It all comes back. This is just a new iteration of the places we dragged our kids to for years; their personalities long ago lost the innocence of protected American childhood. They still vividly remember the harsh violent coup in Kabul. They too have become infected with the dust of ambient poverty, the color and pull of intense and distinct foreign cultures; life isn't quite real for them without it. Does opening an American child's awareness to the back door of the rest of the world constitute a favor? Because you can't ever go back home again in innocence of the rest of the world. And here now are our three granddaughters, two, four and six, to whom these exotic settings are not exotic at all either, just the norm, daily reality, home.

"Roll up your windows," Melissa warns as we approach her neighborhood. "We're passing by the Bone Yard here, the city slaughter house." And certainly its malevolent odors suggest the animal horrors that transpire inside. Indeed, a few days later as we drive by again Ethiopian figures in tan-colored robes and sandals are beating a bunch of cattle with sticks, trying to drive them into the huge Bone Yard compound; the animals know what this place is, they smell the blood and the feces and the fear and the death and they keep trying to twist away and flee the gaping gate until they are finally forced inside by brandished sticks to meet their destiny.

For me it's a quick refresher course in the precepts of vegetarianism. Flocks of vultures circle and soar over the huge compound with its fetid charnel house waiting for the daily offerings of red bones and offal to be chucked out onto the bone pile that covers half a hillside. I note my hypocritical Western fastidiousness here, reviling this source of honest proteins of vital daily sustenance to the natives in a country where daily sustenance is never assured. Ethiopia is big on meat.

"You know what's really bad," Melissa says, "sometimes vultures clutch some hunk of something from the Bone Yard and fly over and perch on our roof to gnaw on it. And they shit on the roof." A few months ago, at the first welcome drops that herald the rainy season, she tells me her daughters went out to dance in the downfall, and opened their mouths under the spouting roof to imbibe the first offerings of the rains, only to consume the dark vulture water, a potion of evil. They quickly succumbed to terrible retching sickness, spewing forth liquid from both ends for twenty-four hours until their bodies were utterly purged of the vultures' evil.

I'm relieved to leave the Bone Yard behind. We turn onto a dirt road to the left and bounce and jolt over deep holes and twisting turns around unrecognizably identical walled corners and byways, a maze I could never renegotiate. And then a high, wide metal gate—indistinguishable from their neighbors'—swings open and admits us into a pleasant compound, small yard and a comfortable white stucco house of colonial mode.

Melissa shows us our room, to leave us to take a long nap to take the first nick out of an eleven-hour change of time zones. "So, Baba, I've finished reading your draft of the Luke book. I was very moved and also found a great deal of it painful to read. It brought back a lot of memories—things in there I had forgotten, or never knew about, or saw them in a different context of events when I was younger. So let's talk about it tonight."

That evening Jim stirs up a great dinner, a variety of Italian veggie dishes. I have a good-nite song for the girls that I play for them on the guitar—actually a song I once wrote for Luke, *Here comes Luke with his jammies on*—melody stolen from Woody Guthrie's *Poor Howard*. It's now been recycled for my granddaughters, each one gets a stanza with her own name. Now they're off to bed. And after some talk of what life is like in Addis Ababa, we quickly get around to the "Luke book."

I want their frank take on the manuscript. But this is no discussion of literary technique; we're talking family lives here, their lives, my life, Luke's life, difficult and painful memories filtered through each of our distinct and particular lenses. Melissa indeed has frank takes and offers them. The book has dredged up a lot from the past, things perhaps not addressed among ourselves in any systematic way. It is a kind of necessary purgative to revisit some old issues, or sloughed-off issues, that never were properly processed in the family at the time.

Nuggets of comments, revelations from them whiz by me, register in my consciousness and I try to take some notes. I have talked in the past about the project as a book about our family. "Baba, you know, this is not a story of our family. It's really about you—dealing with Luke. The rest of us don't figure much in the story. That's OK. It would be almost artificial to put us into it in any serious way. It's really about you. You need to face that. Don't pretend you're writing it for all the rest of us." She isn't accusatory, but she is looking at me hard, determined that I not dodge the weight of her words.

"But that's not what I want," I protest, "I don't want to exclude anyone. Inclusion is what I seek. I do want it to be about the family, our common struggle, even our disagreements over how to handle Luke. I had tried to do that."

"OK, but that's not what it really is. It isn't even a father-son story. In fact, it's a father's story. This is your story, your struggle, your effort to make this work. It's *your project*. You still haven't fully come to terms with what has happened, what this has been all about." Elements of pain lie within her words, not as something new, but as something newly articulated, perhaps clarified by the manuscript. My project ...

"You are still obsessed with Luke in trying to understand him, to understand what happened, to reach out to him, grasp him, justify your project, even ten years later. That's what the book is about. I mean, look at yourself, you're looking to *Dynasty* reruns, and Luke Maryland to try to understand what he was about. You're trying to grasp some tiny piece of Luke in places where you know bloody well he's not even there. You can't google him back. You've exhausted every bloody avenue to reach him, you can't make it. You can't discover anything more. Face it. It's over. Take it for what it has been."

It's true, just look at the manuscript, what I'm doing here with it. I'm combing Enya, rock lyrics, films, friends, family, letters, contacts, counselors, websites, googles, and everything else as intermediaries to help me reach him, to communicate even if indirectly, to understand. This is no mere literary project, or a simple memoir. It is an obsession of a kind, perhaps fading, but no less obsessive in character.

That night I remember that the novels I'd packed to read on the trip are all off in my lost luggage. So I scan Melissa and Jim's bookshelf for something to read. What do I unconsciously settle on? Melville. *Moby Dick*. What in hell does that tell me, as I think back on it later? A fruitless quest for a white whale.

Prue and I eventually retreat to our room, still time-zonked. But I'm hopped up by our conversations, and the eleven-hour time zone won't let me go; I wake up at four in the morning, unable to sleep, still mulling over what this book has become, what it says about me. Despite our talk with Melissa and Jim after dinner, this is not closure at all, even after ten years. It's still an exposed, charged live wire flopping around on the ground, that I must keep on dancing around, not quite daring to fully grasp it.

I grope around for the bedside light in the darkness, haul out my laptop. But I'm foiled again: I can't even plug in to the European-style wall socket. A European plug stands between me and my urgent night-writing mission. I cannibalize one from another appliance in the dark house, turn on my laptop as I sit up in bed.

I'm overwhelmed with the setting, at that predawn moment when nothing is real, when fears are magnified by the primal dark that our consciousness never learns to overcome. It rushes out at me in a surge of feelings, I've got to get the sense of this all down; it's like a dream, I'm driven. The sheer place and circumstances overwhelm my consciousness. I'm in a frightening, lonely and desolate void. The symbolism is all around me. I'm ten-thousand miles from home, still searching, still writing down, still taking notes. Melissa and Jim have just delivered the real unvarnished message to me of my saga with Luke, made it clear that I'm not liberated from the material at all; the same dynamic of Luke's first arrival off the 707 from Seoul is still at work here. It's my project and it's still not finished.

I feel depressed, beaten down, my bearings lost. A cool dawn is breaking again in Addis, mottled sky against distant hills. What kind of a city is this—a cock is scratching, noisily crowing in the dirt compound of the shacks and corrugated iron roofs across the way—crowing for the dawn of what, in this impoverished city? I hear in the distance the echo of a call to dawn prayer in Arabic—"prayer is worthier than sleep"—intones the muezzin, words I've heard over decades in my travels, now comfortingly familiar. Another message I should heed? Is this Muslim world closer to my identity?

And I consider the meanings, the over-the-top symbols all around me. I'm near the Bone Yard, where bones of past animals and slaughters lie open, exposed to the elements. We want to shut the car windows against its stench of reality, but we can't. The bones are there, the past is there, they're not buried away, vultures can still circle. They can still deliver their vulture water. The white bones abide.

And me, I'm naked and sleepless in my dawn bed, far from home, with no bags, no extra clothes, exposed to myself and the reality of what I am. The crowing cock still keeps sleep at bay. I—the experienced, worldly, sophisticated, knowledgable, adventurous intelligence officer and international traveler—I now wish I were home, just home and at peace with the material.

I want to hear that everyone is alright with the way things happened. In a way, the real catharsis is not in writing but in sharing this manuscript. Look, it says, here it is, this is what it was, this is what *I* was, this is what happened, this is what I am. This is my version of this family story. This is who Luke was, who Luke still is, what he represents, what pivotal role he had in my life through his spiral into death that I could not control, and my efforts to understand reality. *This* is what I had sought, but *that* is what really ended up happening. This is partly what I have imposed on all of you. This is me with all my failings, now maybe joined in greater frankness and honesty with the family I love. In this human story I acknowledge the elements of folly, the unknowability of what really happened, the mystery of all of this, the failure, the arrogance of believing myself in control of my environment, the obsession of the quest into which I dragged my whole family along, like a Captain Ahab who still hasn't found his white whale.

But I guess it's a kind of a belated recognition, an acknowledgment of things that are. A sort of fretful but acceptable peace with the course of events and time.

*      *      *

And I do know that Luke's death has not left an "emptiness" or a "hole" in my heart—a phrase I often hear others use about loss from death. My heart has not hardened, nor has it withdrawn or atrophied through the experience. On the contrary, I feel more as if I have grown a second heart. In fact I have now become a more emotional person. I often find tears in my eyes when I read about death, especially of a young person, in the newspaper. But more than that: I become more emotional in every respect: seeing films, hearing music can now bring out deeper emotions. Happy events too, now cause me to tear up more readily. I'm more open, more vulnerable to the world, more sensitive to its emotional elements. That is an unexpected blessing for someone who took routine refuge in an analytical mind.

Luke's life made it clear, even while he was alive, that we would never be able to go around talking about "my son, the doctor." That was never our style anyway. Besides, we are immensely proud of our daughters, their spirit, talents and accomplishments—and their exhilarating company. But instead, as we trudged down the long gray corridors of legal institutions, courthouses, lawyers' offices and probation officers, what I was dealing with was very clearly about "my son—the druggie, my son—the felon." It's not what we would have preferred for ourselves, or for Luke. But that was our reality. And it implanted some degree of humility into our hearts. We can't sit in courtrooms alongside other saddened parents and their teenagers—all wounded and afoul of the Law, all waiting for the magistrate to come in to judge their lives—without feeling some sense of solidarity, common predicament, common suffering, common compassion, common humanity.

And such was the journey for me. Through this struggle I am forced to acknowledge things in myself, shortcomings, overreachings, insensitivities. Ultimately Melissa was absolutely right: this has been my story. I have been lucky enough to negotiate this emotional and spiritual arc, to have the years for it all to percolate more deeply into my sensibilities. It could not be the story of Luke, because his life was emotionally and intellectually failing until he flew into the flame; it was cut short before he could ever begin to seriously grapple with the same emotional, moral and spiritual questions. His life never came to fruition. All he could do was to struggle to survive. But he could leave me with the gift of helping my life come to greater fruition through that same struggle.

In our sojourn on this Earth we course through specific time and specific space; these intersections of lives with other lives—spiritual and physical—are what change us. But like all spiritual experiences, the moments and events are what we make of them. Are we open to perceiving the deeper rhythms and subterranean flows that are there? Or do we remain insensitive to them? My niece Laurel suggests that this awareness of gaining a second heart is where Luke's gift for me lies—it's what gave meaning to Luke's life—not for him, but for me. It was my part of the "bargain" in the unspoken contract between myself and Luke in a sense; I was ultimately forced to discern my lessons for my life, even if Luke wasn't able to learn his. Luke served as a catalyst for my growth to the degree that I could let it. "My guess is that something in you desperately wanted that opening, which is why you felt so obsessively compelled by your relationship with him—but it took his dying to truly open that in you, or to reveal that to you, for you to find that part of yourself."

I note the words of Luke's friend Morgan many years later: "Luke was almost single-handedly the biggest reason I am who I am today. Luke was my guide into the world of the free spirit. A torch I still carry. Luke's influence helped me gain the strength to be myself, regardless." My eyes tear up. A "loser" kid has touched someone else's life too, in a positive and permanent way. Like Dr. Guzmán.

Luke seemed to represent some kind of independent blithe spirit to others—even to me at times—and even romanticized a bit. Romantic can also mean foolish, even tragic in its consequences. We romanticize—but do not wish to emulate—the downward plunge of "bad boys" like the poets Rimbaud or Byron, or in our times James Dean, Jim Morrison, Janis Joplin, Jimi Hendrix, or River Phoenix. They cannot represent our ultimate ideals in life, but their rebellion may help keep alive some flame of feisty individualism in us—even as we are entangled in the demands of more conventionally productive lives. That is what so many of Luke's friends found in him. We are all deriving meaning out of those painful events—the specific meanings relevant to each of us.

That may not have been the particular gift Luke sought to give us. He may never even have been really aware of bearing a gift. He surely was aware of the pain that he brought to us in his final years. And that pain was not what he wanted to leave either. It remains a gift nonetheless: it sparks deep personal growth and affords a spiritual access to a greater self-knowledge, a deeper opening to the world.

I feel blessed.

# ACKNOWLEDGMENTS

My first thanks go to all the members of my family who lived through the events, contributed their memories and recollections to this tale and made comments on the manuscript, especially Prue, Meredith, Faith, Melissa, Jim, Grayson and Laurel.

My special thanks go to Luke's own close friends and contemporaries: Chris, Dan, John, and Morgan; and to my many friends who provided rare glimpses into Luke at one time or another.

To Laisha Rosnau who first encouraged me to turn these events into a book at a writers' workshop in Whistler, and then valuably critiqued the first draft;

And to all those who read the manuscript and provided specific thoughtful feedback and valuable suggestions: particularly Steve and Hala Buck, Larry and Kay Thompson, Misha Tsypkin;

My special thanks to George Fowler who has been a constant source of encouragement, support, ideas, and valuable criticism over the years on this project—in broad terms as well as specific detail;

To Jim McKean for his estimable course on memoir writing and his sympathetic and supportive approach at the Tinker Mountain Writers' Workshop;

To David Ransom (in memoriam) and Marjorie Ransom for their friendship and support over the years with Luke and first encouragement to write a book;

To Junie Dahn at Little, Brown who read the manuscript sympathetically and suggested changes;

To those members of the Squamish Writers Group who offered thoughtful comments;

And to Margreet Dietz for helping me prepare the manuscript, layout and art for publication, and to Jude Goodwin for developing a website for the book.

## ABOUT THE AUTHOR

Graham E. Fuller received his BA and MA at Harvard University in Russian and Middle Eastern studies. He served 20 years as an operations officer in the CIA, working in Germany, Turkey, Lebanon, Saudi Arabia, North Yemen, Afghanistan, and Hong Kong. In 1982 he was appointed the National Intelligence Officer for Near East and South Asia at CIA, and in 1986 Vice-Chairman of the National Intelligence Council at CIA, with overall responsibility for national level strategic forecasting.

In 1988 Mr. Fuller left government and joined the RAND Corporation where he was a senior political scientist for 12 years. His research focused primarily on the Middle East, Central Asia, South and Southeast Asia, and the politics of ethnicity and religion. He is a well-known Middle East specialist and author of dozens of articles and books on Muslim world politics and Islamic fundamentalism; he is now finishing a first novel, on Pakistan.

Mr. Fuller is currently an independent writer and Adjunct Professor of History at Simon Fraser University in Vancouver. He lives with his wife in Squamish, British Columbia, where, apart from writing, he devotes much of his spare time to eagles, salmon and bears and riding his mountain bike.